D0982748

F.el Allmeye.

Systemic Earthquake and the Struggle for World Order

Using the analogy of a devastating series of earthquakes, Davutoğlu provides a new theoretical approach, conceptualization, and methodology for understanding crisis in the post-Cold War era.

In order to grasp the scale and scope of the ongoing crises we are experiencing today, Davutoğlu conceptualizes them as "aftershocks," following in the wake of the four great "quakes" that have shaken the world in recent times – namely, the geopolitical earthquake triggered by dissolution of the Soviet Union, 1991; the security earthquake, post-9/11, 2001; the economic earthquake associated with the global economic crisis, 2008; and the structural earthquake of the Arab Spring, 2011. By contextualizing international order as being impacted by a number of intertwined processes, the book then looks to the possible futures ahead. Following his analysis of the ongoing systemic crisis, Davutoğlu forges a vision for a new order of global democracy, built from the rubble of the systemic earthquake.

Professor Ahmet Davutoğlu served as the Prime Minister of the 62nd, 63rd, and 64th governments of the Republic of Turkey. Prior to this, he was Chief Foreign Policy Advisor to the Prime Minister, and Minister of Foreign Affairs. In his academic career, he has held the position of professor at Marmara and Beykent Universities, Turkey, and the International Islamic University of Malaysia. He is author of many books including *Alternative Paradigms, Civilizational Transformation and the Muslim World*, and *Stratejik Derinlik: Türkiye'nin Uluslararası Konumu*. He has received several awards, including the Woodrow Wilson Award for Public Service in 2010. He was named as one of the Top 100 Global Thinkers by *Foreign Policy* magazine in 2010, 2011, and 2012, and as one of the 100 Most Influential People in the World by *Time* magazine in 2012.

Systemic Earthquake and the Struggle for World Order

Exclusive Populism versus Inclusive Democracy

Ahmet Davutoğlu
Former Prime Minister of Turkey
Professor of Political Science and International Relations

English translation by Andrew Boord
Foreword by Richard Falk

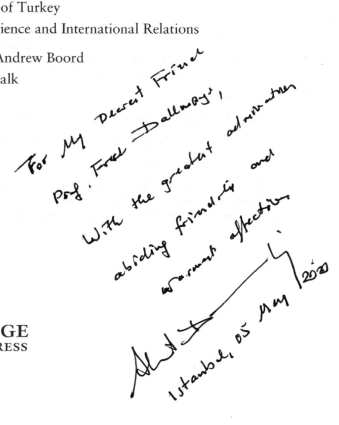

For My Dearest Friend
Prof. Fred Dallmay',
With the greatest admiration
abiding friendship and
warmest affections

Istanbul, 05 May 2020

🔶 CAMBRIDGE
UNIVERSITY PRESS

CAMBRIDGE
UNIVERSITY PRESS

University Printing House, Cambridge CB2 8BS, United Kingdom

One Liberty Plaza, 20th Floor, New York, NY 10006, USA

477 Williamstown Road, Port Melbourne, VIC 3207, Australia

314–321, 3rd Floor, Plot 3, Splendor Forum, Jasola District Centre, New Delhi – 110025, India

79 Anson Road, #06–04/06, Singapore 079906

Cambridge University Press is part of the University of Cambridge.

It furthers the University's mission by disseminating knowledge in the pursuit of education, learning, and research at the highest international levels of excellence.

www.cambridge.org
Information on this title: www.cambridge.org/9781108485517
DOI: 10.1017/9781108751643

© Ahmet Davutoğlu 2020

First published 2020

Printed in the United Kingdom by TJ International Ltd, Padstow Cornwall

A catalogue record for this publication is available from the British Library.

ISBN 978-1-108-48551-7 Hardback

To victims of World (Dis)Order
in every corner of the Earth

CONTENTS

FOREWORD

By Richard Falk

Ahmet Davutoğlu is not only one of the most accomplished among recent political leaders, he is also one of the world's foremost public intellectuals and creative scholars currently at work. This combination of government experience at the highest levels in an important country and academic eminence is rare. In searching for contemporary comparisons only Henry Kissinger and Zbigniew Brzezinski come to mind, although their public roles were more in rendering high-level service to leaders rather than leading themselves or charting new directions and commitments for US foreign policy. As academicians, in contrast to Davutoğlu, their contributions were not of durable scholarly contribution but rather policy assessments arousing intense public interest for the moment, lacking any lasting impact.

In this regard it is important to recognize Davutoğlu as a principal architect of the still unfolding post-Ottoman republican phase of Turkish history. Beyond this, Davutoğlu exhibits his familiarity with a vast spectrum of scholarly materials, spanning history, philosophy, culture, as well as world politics. This rich body of knowledge lends authority to his imaginative interpretations of the struggles for humane world order, which he has done his best to enact in both theory and practice underpinned by an impressive fusion of realist and ethical perspectives. It is to be understood that not all of Davutoğlu's initiatives worked out as he would have wished. The Middle East as a region entered a period of severe turmoil, further aggravated by the miscalculations and mistakes of political actors. In this regard some hold Davutoğlu responsible for misjudging the unfolding situation in Syria, but before criticisms are made it should be appreciated that none of the intervening governments, including the United States, got Syria right.

While serving as Turkey's Foreign Minister in a period filled with challenges and unexpected developments (2009–2014), Davutoğlu displayed energy and creativity in addressing a wide range of regional instabilities and tensions. He played a leading role in securing for Turkey a coveted seat at the UN Security Council. He took many foreign policy initiatives that raised Turkey's regional and global profile. These important initiatives had the notable side-effect of making Istanbul a favorite venue for innovative diplomacy, especially for UN activities and civil society. Among the more influential of these were the Alliance of Civilizations and Friends of Mediation. Additionally, Davutoğlu displayed impressive energy by undertaking several challenging peace and mediation efforts: presiding over so-called indirect talks between Israel and Syria (2008); overcoming tensions between Serbia and Bosnia through the work of a trilateral mechanism; finalizing normalization arrangements with Armenia; collaborating with the Brazilian Foreign Minister to reach what could (and should) have been a breakthrough compromise on Iran's nuclear program if not blocked by geopolitics; humanely handling the largest refugee flow that ever faced a country; increasing Turkey's humanitarian assistance program to the point that it became the world's largest donor as measured by share of GDP.

Beyond this feverish diplomatic activity, Davutoğlu engaged in extensive personal diplomacy. He made high-profile visits of support to the deeply distressed Rohingya region of Myanmar and to Somalia at the time of its deepest national crisis. He was also active in greatly increasing Turkish diplomatic participation in an expanded number of foreign countries and international institutions. Davutoğlu's impact was recognized by *Foreign Policy Magazine,* listing him as the eighth most influential thinker on international relations in the entire world.

Aside from these concrete achievements, Davutoğlu will be long associated with two innovative ideas relevant to the exemplary practice of statecraft: (1) "strategic depth" as the recommended foundation of diplomacy and statecraft, an original approach combining a sophisticated historical and geographic understanding with an awareness of civilizational values, ethical responsibilities, and national interests; (2) "zero problems with neighbors," a win/win approach to foreign policy that stresses the mutual benefits of peaceful relations, economic trade and investment, and cultural exchange as applied to interactions with surrounding countries, and indeed with the region and the world as we are all neighbors, whether or not geographically proximate, given the dynamics of globalization in the digital age.

Critics of Turkey and Davutoğlu, of which there are many, take pleasure in deriding "zero problems" as a misguided Turkish foreign policy doctrine. It was alleged to be overwhelmed by Middle Eastern developments that seemed overnight to change the positive turn toward friendly relations with neighbors into combat zones and relations of heightened tension. There is no doubt that the "zero problems" approach proved inapplicable in the period following the eruptions within the Arab world of 2011, familiarly known as "the Arab Spring." Yet more dispassionately considered, "zero problems" is a benevolent exploration of the normative potential for a win/win foreign policy in a given regional and international context. It should never have been understood as a mindless and ahistorical assurance that the desirable goal of friendly relations between neighboring governments can be achieved under all circumstances, a limitation Davutoğlu well understood despite commentators tending to give the doctrine an absolute, and misleading spin.

Two sets of developments precluded the sunshine agenda that Davutoğlu followed with such impressive results between 2002 and 2011, initially as principal foreign policy advisor to the top Turkish leaders, and then as Foreign Minister. His early successes in smoothing relations with neighbors were overwhelmed by the quite unexpected fury and mendacity of Arab counterrevolutionary reversals of the hopeful expectations earlier associated with the Arab Spring, and perhaps even more so by the Western indifference, or worse. These strivings by the Arab multitudes for a new political order based on democracy, human dignity, and social and economic justice that seemed so promising in 2012 were not then adequately welcomed and supported by the supposed champions of liberal democracy in the West. Did the West negligently miss this opportunity to incubate the birth of a more humane and stable regional order or was this another disheartening confirmation that the geopolitics of oil and "special relationships" with Israel and Saudi Arabia reflected the true priorities of Washington and its European allies, taking precedence over democratizing movements of reform?

These disappointments were accentuated by the orchestrated anti-Turkish international campaign mounted in the aftermath of a series of confrontations with Israel. This hostility to Turkey seemed to originate after an official meeting with Hamas leaders that the Turkish government arranged after Hamas won 2006 democratic elections in Gaza. It should be remembered that Washington had encouraged Hamas to participate in the elections, and then repudiated the results after Hamas unexpectedly won. The Turkish initiative actually deserved support as it was seeking to encourage Hamas to maintain its tactical shift to "a political track," which necessarily involved abandoning an armed struggle strategy. Unfortunately, Israel, backed by the United States, found it more politically opportune to keep Hamas locked into "a terrorist box" so that their demonization could continue, and the claim made that Israel could not be expected to negotiate a peace agreement while terrorists governed Gaza. The Turkish/Israeli confrontation reached its climax in the aftermath of the Mavi Marmara incident of 2010 when Israeli commandos killed nine Turkish nationals on international waters while halting a voyage of a Turkish commercial vessel carrying humanitarian supplies to the blockaded people of Gaza. This broader international anti-Turkish campaign was intensified and expanded by the forces behind the failed military coup of mid-2016.

It is also true that internal political developments in Turkey after 2011 lent a measure of credibility to the rising chorus of international criticisms, but the venomous tone of the attacks along with the failure to offer comparable criticism of the autocratic practices of such other major countries in the region as Egypt and Saudi Arabia lends credibility to suspicions that the real motives of these critics is to erode the legitimacy of Turkey as a sovereign state and NATO partner. In effect, the "zero problems" approach should be qualified, but not discredited, because unanticipated events spoiled what was initially an innovative and impressive application of the doctrine. In my view, this doctrinal innovation remains the most constructive approach for Turkish foreign policy under normal circumstances, and indeed possesses relevance for the foreign policy of any country, although the present regional turmoil and sectarian tensions currently constrain its potential for actualization in the Middle East.

It is against this background that we must welcome the publication of *Systemic Earthquake*, a masterful diagnosis of the disorders afflicting our planet at the present time together with a detailed prescriptive vision of how to establish a framework of inquiry for world order that is responsive to the various dimensions of political life under the complex and varied conditions of rapidly evolving globalization. The book achieves coherence by reliance on the earthquake metaphor. Davutoğlu explains his reliance on the metaphor. As with a strong earthquake the political developments that he analyzes amount to a severe shaking of the principal foundations of world order, including its geopolitical, security, economic, technological, and structural dimensions. Davutoğlu explicates each dimension in a perceptive and illuminating manner while being mindful of seeking coherent explanations of the distinctive set of circumstances confronting humanity at this time.

What Davutoğlu brings to this most ambitious undertaking is a deep historical understanding of how state-centric world order emerged in the West, became globalized at first via European colonialism, and then reached its present critical threshold: in Davutoğlu's view these manifold forms of globalization must either be transformed for the wellbeing, indeed for the sake of civilizational sustainability and even species survival, or chaos and disaster are virtually certain to ensue. At the same time Davutoğlu is well aware of the postcolonial global setting, which demands that if an orderly transition is to be achieved it must be accompanied by the de-Westernization of the ideas and structures of governance now embedded in world order. Among many other considerations, a great effort must be made to end the era of violent geopolitics, or at least greatly to restrict its impact on diplomacy and international institutions. Such a transformation of world politics requires a major upgrading of the role of international law, international institutions, and especially the United Nations as arbiters of the behavior of the strong as well as the weak.

A salient insight of this illuminating overview of the global problematique is the recognition of the diplomatic and conceptual failures of the West, especially of the United States, to make necessary, possible, and desirable adjustments after the end of the Cold War. In effect, Davutoğlu is convinced that with the collapse of the Soviet Union, an end-point had been reached with respect to balance of power geopolitics that had been the hard-power basis of world order for the several centuries following the Peace of Westphalia (1648). This emphasis is informed by the extremely important historical observation that past major ruptures in world politics that resulted in major wars were always followed by a peace diplomacy that attempted to address the revealed weaknesses of balance of power mechanisms. This dynamic culminated in Woodrow Wilson's realization in the course of the First World War that state-centrism needed to be transcended, both by limiting recourse to war through an acceptance of the discipline of international law and by a degree of institutionalization of authority on a global scale, taking the form of the League of Nations. As we know, Wilson's visionary aspirations were greatly weakened by the cynical impact of European colonial ambitions to reap the geopolitical spoils of the war.

This recognition of postwar fluidity was repeated after the Second World War in a somewhat more ambitious framework, taking some account of the failures of the League as well as the economic challenges of avoiding a second Great Depression. This latter concern led to the establishment of the Bretton Woods institutions and induced the Marshall Plan for the reconstruction of the devastated European economies, which was so non-punitive as to include Germany. It also overcame the lack of great-power participation in the League by fashioning the United Nations in ways that accommodated geopolitical actors as well as normal states. Perhaps unrealistically, the UN Charter also committed itself to making war prevention the central aim of the Organization as proclaimed in the Preamble. From the outset, influential political realists dissented from these lofty expectations being associated with the UN, believing that national interests and a stable world order depended more than ever in the nuclear age on intelligent applications of balance of power geopolitics.

Davutoğlu is on firm ground in asserting that the Cold War ended without any relevant political realization that state-centric world order must take steps to accommodate the scale of globality and the accelerated velocity of technological change. George H. W. Bush famously dismissed the world-order challenge and opportunity of the early 1990s when asked about his hopes for world order after the Cold War: "Oh, you mean the vision thing." In effect, as Davutoğlu points out, this disappointing response by the American President was complemented by two dominant views of the global setting after the Cold War, both of which evaded the structural and normative challenges and opportunities that were latent in the international situation facing the world in 1945. These disabling metanarratives were articulated not by the political leaders of the victor, but by two prominent academic observers situated on the sidelines of diplomacy.

In this regard, Davutoğlu singles out for attention Francis Fukuyama's *End of History* and Samuel Huntington's *Clash of Civilizations*, which he believes were, at best, distractions and, at worst, reinforcements of the power of negative thinking. Fukuyama's view is that the historical clash of ideas that shapes political and economic behavior through the ages effectively ended with the collapse of the Soviet Union, and the ideological triumph of Western constitutional and liberal capitalism. Fukuyama's interpretation of the post-Cold War world is rejected by Davutoğlu as a shallow, yet impressively theorized instance of "triumphalism." By Davutoğlu's reading, Fukuyama completely misses the decisive characteristic of the human condition, that historical change and challenge are integral to its dynamic reality, and hence, struggles over ideas and beliefs not only will persist, but these struggles were being greatly magnified in scale, velocity, and variety on many levels by dominant global trends present at the end of the Cold War.

Davutoğlu is equally critical of Huntington whom he believes confuses traditional statist conflicts with intercivilizational strife, and by doing so fails to give any attention to the *real* and truly unprecedented challenges and opportunities present at the end of the Cold War. It was a time when creative diplomacy, especially if emanating from Washington, could have taken the lead in strengthening the United Nations to uphold global and human interests, to achieve phased nuclear disarmament to safeguard the world against risks of unprecedented catastrophe in a future war, and, later on, produce a roadmap for sustainable development that addressed climate change in a manner responsive to scientific evidence and sensitive to considerations of climate justice in the face of global inequality.

It is Davutoğlu's extensively reasoned view that lacking a proper diagnosis and corrective responses, the circumstances of world order will tumble from crisis to crisis, while raising risks of catastrophe to unmanageable heights and leaving unattended the main challenges and threats confronting humanity. Davutoğlu articulates this failure of perception and response by reference to the rise of what he labels as "exclusionary populism," which relies on extremism, escapism, chauvinism, scapegoating, and demagoguery. Such features of this global populist surge mislead people about the nature of the challenges and misconceives the nature of reconstructive responses that are required. This menacing dynamic is epitomized by the presidency of Donald Trump who self-consciously withdraws the United States from the constructive engagements associated with its global-leadership role exercised ever since 1945. Trump gave concrete meaning to his demagogic exhortations by intense frontal attacks on such positive elements of global politics as world trading arrangements, the UN, and climate-change multilateralism, and even human rights. Trump reinforces these destructive swipes at a more enlightened approach to a globalizing world with a scary militarist bravado, threatening the use of nuclear weapons to intimidate and, if necessary, to impose policies on countries portrayed as pariah states such as North Korea and Iran.

Davutoğlu also is distressed by the moral impoverishment of global problem-solving and atrocity prevention. He regards the failures to address the symbolic and substantive challenges of Palestinian rights or the spectacle of the Srebrenica massacre and the Rohingya genocide as symptomatic of a systemic inability of existing world-order mechanisms to address the most minimal expectations of justice, legality, and order. Such events as reported by a globalized media in actual time has shaken the confidence of ordinary people in the ethical foundations and functional problem-solving capacities of world order, inducing moods of despair and denialism, and creating this disturbing collective receptivity to demagogues and scapegoating.

In prescriptive chapters Davutoğlu outlines what needs to be done to restore public confidence in the system of governance affecting our individual and collective lives. There has been an essential failure to adapt to changes in the underlying reality of living together peaceably on a planet where the globalizing scale and accelerating velocity of key sectors of human activity is occurring at an unprecedented rate due primarily to impacts deriving from technological innovations. These underlying developments have drastically altered political conditions in ways that make state structures dangerously anachronistic, incapable of effective transnational problem-solving and proper ethical behavior. These tendencies are accentuated by an unwillingness to acknowledge the failings of current global arrangements due to what Davutoğlu suggestively calls "learned helplessness" (that is, patterns translating behaviorally into denialism, passivity, and hedonistic escapism, acting as if the old ways still work). To overcome these shortcomings requires nothing less than a shift of individual and collective mentality, greatly augmenting national consciousness by thinking, feeling, and acting on the basis of species consciousness and shared destiny.

Davutoğlu recalls speaking to a group of foreign ministers at an international meeting, reminding them that they are not only national officials of a sovereign state, but necessarily representing the world by being pressed into service as "Interior Ministers of Humankind." I can imagine that such officials would welcome Davutoğlu's rhetorical appeal in such an international setting, yet embarrassed to mention his speech when reporting to their political leaders and opinion leaders back home. There is a kind of political correctness that affirms progressive internationalism when abroad, regressive nationalism when operating within a domestic setting. The result is that conventional wisdom, no matter how dysfunctional, remains entrenched, even reinforced.

An aspect of Davutoğlu's distinctive approach is his illuminating way of weaving into the narrative two types of personal recollections: memorable moments where his ideas about how the world works were tested in the course of his own diplomatic encounters and clarifying references to his own earlier academic writings that anticipated developments in the lifeworld of global politics. Such a personalization of the narrative adds qualities of concreteness to his use of history and civilizational identities to interpret the relevance of political antecedents of the past to the challenges of the present. On these solid foundations Davutoğlu puts forward his remedies for the ills that afflict and threaten humanity, creating a coherent unity of past, present, and future.

The end result is a vital book for engaged citizens inhabiting any part of the planet who seek to understand what has gone wrong and what might yet be done to create a sustainable and equitable future for the peoples of the world. In this regard, Davutoğlu's outlook reflects the reality of his native Turkey, a crossroads of civilizations, neither entirely East nor West, nor wholly North nor South, yet partaking of all planetary pespectives. The overall presentation is powerfully vindicated and enriched by Davutoğlu's ecumenical consciousness that affirms and encompasses democracy, pluralism, dialogue, human rights, ecological responsibility, and global justice.

ACKNOWLEDGMENTS

While the act of writing is of its nature a solitary one, this book is no exception to others of its kind in being the end-product of a process of exchanges and investigations on intellectual, discursive, even conversational, spiritual, and emotional levels. So many people have played a role in this process that it would be quite impossible to acknowledge all of them here.

I would like first to express my thanks for the unstinting encouragement and ever insightful comments of my dear friend Richard Falk, who has been involved in the genesis of this book from its nucleic publication as an article in *global-e* entitled "The Future of National and Global (Dis)Order: Exclusive Populism versus Inclusive Global Governance" (*global-e* 10, 22 (30 March 2017), www.21global.ucsb .edu/global-e), right through to publication in its current form; to my old friend the former Foreign Minister of Brazil Celso Amorim; to Louis René Beres, Joseph A. Camilleri, and Robert C. Johansen whose criticism and comments on that article were instrumental in the process of turning it into a book; and to Victor Faessel and his team at global-e; to John Berger for his encouragement and editorial contributions to this project, and to John Haslem, Chris Harrison, Laura Blake and Jem Langworthy for their most efficient work and friendly manner throughout the publication process, to my friends, Feridun Sinirlioğlu, Ali Sarıkaya, Hilal Elver, Mustafa Özel, Taha Özhan, İbrahim Turhan, Ahmet Okumuş, Osman Sert, Hatem Ete, Tuba Kor, Galip Dalay, and Harun Tan for sharing their views and comments; to those at Küre Publishing House who simultaneously prepared the Turkish version;

to Andrew Boord for his meticulous and graceful English translation; to Mustafa Demiray for his invaluable efforts and critical editorial support including indexing; and to my valued academic assistant Sevinç Alkan Özcan for her work in monitoring and coordinating every step of the process with her customary diligence and perception.

Words cannot express my feelings of gratitude to my wife Sare and my family, who have made all manner of sacrifices throughout my academic and political life, from which journey this book has emerged. And finally, I must offer my eternal thanks to my parents, for whose upbringing I owe everything.

ABBREVIATIONS

AK Party   Justice and Development Party
APEC   Asia-Pacific Economic Cooperation
ASEAN   Association of Southeast Asian Nations
BRF   Belt and Road Forum
BTC   Baku–Tbilisi–Ceyhan
BTK   Baku–Tbilisi–Kars
CFSP   Common Foreign and Security Policy
CSCE   Commission on Security and Cooperation in Europe
CWC   Chemical Weapons Convention
DHKP-C   Revolutionary People's Liberation Party (*Devrimci Halk Kurtuluş Partisi-Cephesi*)
EC   European Community
ECO   Economic Cooperation Organization
ECOWAS   Economic Community of West African States
ECSC   European Coal and Steel Community
EEC   European Economic Community
EU   European Union
FSA   Free Syrian Army
FSB   Financial Stability Board
GCC   Gulf Cooperation Council
GDP   gross domestic product
IAEA   International Atomic Energy Agency
IMF   International Monetary Fund
LDCs   least developed countries
LIDCs   low income and developing countries

MENA	Middle East and North Africa
NAFTA	North American Free Trade Agreement
NATO	North Atlantic Treaty Organization
NPT	Non-Proliferation Treaty
OIC	Organization of Islamic Cooperation
OSCE	Organization for Security and Co-operation in Europe
P5 (+1)	UN Security Council's five permanent members – China, France, Russia, the United Kingdom, and the United States (plus Germany)
PKK	Kurdistan Workers' Party (*Partiya Karkerên Kurdistanê*)
PYD	Democratic Union Party (*Partiya Yekîtiya Demokrat*)
TANAP	Trans-Anatolian Natural Gas Pipeline
UN	United Nations
UNAOC	United Nations Alliance of Civilizations
UNESCO	United Nations Educational, Scientific and Cultural Organization
UNHCR	United Nations High Commissioner for Refugees
UNICEF	United Nations Children's Fund
UNRWA	United Nations Relief and Works Agency for Palestine Refugees in the Near East
UNSC	United Nations Security Council
USSR	Union of Soviet Socialist Republics
WASP	White Anglo-Saxon Protestant
YPG	People's Protection Units (*Yekîneyên Parastina Gel*)

INTRODUCTION: CONCEPTUAL AND METHODOLOGICAL FRAMEWORK

From Utopic Optimism to Nihilistic Pessimism: A Psycho-Methodological Dilemma

The discussions and debate we had around the "Toward a Greater Eurasia: How to Build a Common Future" in the fourth Astana Club Meeting (12–13 November 2018), held while I was working on *Systemic Earthquake*, contained significant clues with respect to understanding the psychology of the international environment and bringing out the main focus of this book's methodological approach. The prevailing intellectual currents among participants emerged right from the opening session of this wide-ranging roundtable gathering hosted by the President of Kazakhstan, Nursultan Nazarbayev, and attended by a number of former presidents, prime ministers, and ministers together with a host of academics distinguished for their work on the issue of international order.

One group had a relatively optimistic vision of the future in spite of the crises we were going through, while another argued that humanity was on the threshold of a major debacle from which it would be very hard to emerge. Advocates of the first approach provided comparative historical references to emphasize the fact that in terms of the losses relative to the population of mankind incurred in these ongoing crises we were in a far more favorable position than previous centuries, while those arguing for the second approach did not limit themselves to depicting the current spiral of crises in anticipating an extremely gloomy future.

I argued that it was this very swing between "utopic optimism" and "nihilistic pessimism" in the psychological background to post-Cold War turbulence that constituted the underlying differentiating factor between these two tendencies, criticizing both approaches as I stressed that the psychologies on which they were based were effectively preventing the development of an accurate perception of reality and a common vision of the future. When the moderator Nik Gowing asked what my proposed method was, I bore the methodological and theoretical framework I was working to develop with regard to *Systemic Earthquake* in mind when I replied "realistic optimism."

I believe that a little more elucidation of these three approaches will contribute to a greater understanding of this work's objective, and the method it adopts. Generally speaking, *utopic optimism* is a psychology that occurs in the founding phases of a new era in the wake of a great victory. This psychology stems from a belief that a new order is going to be established that will resolve all elements of tension through the rest of the era. Inspired by Toynbee's term *egocentric illusion*,[1] we might call this the *victors' illusion*. The end of the Cold War bore the theoretical and practical marks of just such a phenomenon. While the *End of History* hypothesis,[2] which declared that humanity's grand quest had concluded with the victory of liberalism ensured by the end of the Cold War, provided the theoretical basis for this utopic optimism, the mission set out for the United Nations (UN) in the new era by US President George H. W. Bush defined the practical hub of this new utopia: "This is a new and different world. Not since 1945 have we seen the real possibility of using the United Nations as it was designed: as a center for international collective security ... The U.N. is now fulfilling its promise as the world's parliament of peace."[3]

Today I recall the immensely optimistic predictions for the future that were presented at the International Studies Association's annual congress held between 20 and 23 March 1991 in the prevailing atmosphere in the immediate wake of the Gulf War during which US-led coalition forces drove Saddam Hussein's army out of Kuwait. And I remember how the main thrust of the "Civilizational Transformation and Political Consequences" paper I presented to the congress – namely, that contrary to the central claims of the *End of History* hypothesis the ongoing process was not the end of history but a comprehensive civilizational transformation; that the foundations of conventional modern philosophy were being shaken by new elements brought by globalization; that the Eurocentric understanding of order would change as a result of the revival under way in traditional civilizational basins and that as a consequence of the political outcomes of this process of transformation tensions stemming from the reawakening of historical factors would initially emerge before the transition from a unipolar world to a balance of power system; and that humankind would ultimately go through the pangs of a civilizational axial shift to enter a new era – ran contrary to the overwhelmingly optimistic atmosphere of those days.

Yet history does not operate on auto-pilot; the end of one period does not automatically mean the beginning of a new order. The establishment of a new order depends on how the victors perform in drawing the old order to an end as well as their ability to demonstrate the vision and the will to establish a new order. Indeed, the failure to manifest the will and vision required by the inherent momentum of history led first to the loss of the utopia of that utopic optimism and then the dissolution of the broader psychology of optimism upon which it was based.

In subsequent stages, the failure to resolve successive crises and the loss of the existing order's elements of effectiveness and endurance led to the progressive replacement of a psychology of optimism with one of pessimism, while accumulating pessimism led to the spread of a mentality that envisioned a nihilistic future. Although a striking theoretical framework resembling that of the utopic optimism-fueled *End of History* hypothesis has yet to emerge for nihilistic pessimism, it is clear that this approach has seriously insinuated itself into the international environment over the past few years and created a bleak psychological climate.

Every disappointment arising from the failure to meet utopic optimism's expectations and predictions has helped to pave the way for the nihilistic pessimism from which the current climate is formed. In other words, the psychology of surrender to the spiral of crises generated by nihilistic pessimism has been the product of the disappointments and frustrations engendered by utopic optimism. However, just as history does not run on auto-pilot, nor is it just the aggregate total of free-flowing processes running independently of human will. The thing that will detach humankind from this spiral of pessimism will be its ability to create its own will and vision.

In the context of these debates, we face two fundamental issues, one concerning the nature of the flow of history, the other the method employed in trying to understand this flow. In a sense, the conception of order envisioned by the *End of History* hypothesis, the theoretical formulation of utopic optimism, is the declaration of the end of the dialectic of history arising from the contradictions that accelerate its flow. Such a conception of order as the conclusive realization of the quest of human history is no different from the assumptions of a religious utopia based on God's kingdom on earth eradicating the elements of tension arising from human nature through merging divinity and humanity, or those of a Marxist utopia achieving absolute equality by eradicating class contradictions.

The nihilistic pessimism engendered by intensive ongoing tensions and contradictions is the result of the loss of any belief that an order will arise from these contradictions and tensions. In the first, it is claimed that a utopia has been reached following the end of the dialectic of history, while in the second a psychology of abandonment and surrender to the flow of history is evinced by absolutizing its dialectic. The first emphasizes an absolute order forged by human will, the other the vision of a chaotic future that disregards human will.

An Alternative Approach: Realistic Optimism

This is precisely the point where we can clarify our proposed approach, realistic optimism. When we take a realistic look at the overall flow of human history and critical transformation thresholds, we see that every conflict or tension contains the seeds of the subsequent order, and every order contains the seeds of the next conflict or tension. Long-term orders can extend their lifespans as long as they are able to manage their inherent seeds of tension. Likewise, the earlier the elements of order that harbor widespread wars and tensions are uncovered, the greater the degree to which the impacts of these wars and tensions can be contained. Adopting a utopic optimism that ignores elements of tension at the threshold of a new order makes it impossible to see potential obstacles to efforts to form a new order and take measures to overcome them. On the other hand, reacting incident-by-incident within the air of panic that takes over in periods of intensive tension and chaos only serves to intensify the chaos while also psychologically obstructing the emergence of the vision to make the transition from chaos to a new order.

The methodology to get out of the vicious circle formed by this dual clamp is to show realistic optimism in determining and analyzing elements of tension in the international order, and visionary optimism in conceptualizing the future. The chief common feature between excessively optimistic and pessimistic approaches is their reliance on a conjunctural snapshot analysis. Analyses that rely on conjunctural pictures of a single moment or period are based on power parameters that add their own color to these images. While the utopic optimism that held sway in the final years of the Cold War was based on the conjunctural picture between 1989 and 1991, the nihilistic pessimism underlying the currently prevalent psychology is based on conjunctural images reflecting recent years' crises. Conjunctural snapshot analyses carried out in the later years of the Cold War prevented people from seeing the tensions that were to emerge in the following years and led to the detachment of efforts to establish a new order from reality. And today's pessimistic snapshot analyses, which reflect areas of tension proliferating throughout the world, make it difficult to confront reality and evince a new vision.

The required method is not static snapshot analysis but dynamic process analysis. And the *sine qua non* of being able to conduct enduring strategic analysis and develop a long term vision based on this analysis is not to be influenced by the deceptive appearances of conjuncture-dependent static images. Absolutizing the colors, lines, and perspectives of static images based on an instant depiction of cases and phenomena makes it hard to be able to develop frameworks for accurate description, explanation, and understanding. And without a proper basis of description, explanation, and understanding, it is not possible to develop a fresh vision posited in a consistent interpretative framework.

Avoiding this methodological pitfall means resisting the ease of one-dimensional description in favor of multidimensional process analysis. Process is to international relations and strategic analysis what the law of motion is to physics. And physics becomes meaningless in depictions of a static world where dynamism has been invalidated. In such depictions, for example, power formulae cannot be rendered operable. Likewise, international relations analyses that pay no heed to the flow, and the process, of history make it very hard to foresee strategic shifts and waves emanating from deep beneath the surface.[4]

While the *realist* aspect of realistic optimism endeavors to expose ongoing spirals of crisis and disorder in a framework of process analysis, its *optimism* aspect breaks free of this spiral of crises as it aims to define the visionary characteristics of its transformation into an order. The earthquake analogy that forms the work's theoretical framework aims to bring out a multidimensional process analysis of the spiral of crises and quest for order at issue.

The Earthquake Analogy: A Conceptualization of (Dis)Order

Today, more than twenty-five years after the end of the Cold War, the failure to establish a new order confronts us with an intensifying spiral of crises and a condition of disorder. A conceptual framework based on an earthquake analogy may present a suitable platform from which to define this spiral of crises and disorder, expose the existential significance of the situation we now face, and determine what process-management action to take.

First of all, the earthquake begins with seismic waves emanating from an energy within the bowels of the earth, which triggers a dynamic process that leads to the rupturing of a state of static equilibrium. The release of this energy leads to seismic waves; seismic waves to the shaking, shifting, and rupturing of the earth's crust. The preliminary signs of this dynamic process at its epicenter maintain a continuous impact in the areas to which it spreads through its aftershocks.

In fact, this seismic activity has always been there, but we only feel it when it is of sufficient force to shake the earth's crust. The severity of an earthquake is not the only factor that determines its destructive consequences. Two other factors play a more determinant role: the geological features of the earthquake zone and the static characteristics of the buildings above it. The geological structure of a region struck by even low-intensity quakes may be such that it is felt with great intensity and force. This effect, known to seismologists as amplification, in one sense shows the inadequacy of the natural structure's ability to withstand the seismic wave. The static characteristics of structures built on the surface of the earth also determine the quake's destructive force. It follows that every earthquake may have a different degree of impact on every region and every building.

This process brings with it a state of uncertainty and disorder right from the moment it first strikes. Structures that were developed according to the previous static state of order face a test of resistance. Fragile structures unable to resist shocks collapse, while surviving structures show the need for serious rehabilitation. Depending on the scale of the earthquake, cities, entire countries, or regions need to be rebuilt. Risks and uncertainties continue until the creation of a new order as tectonic shifts yield to a new equilibrium and rehabilitation is achieved.

In using the earthquake analogy for the analysis of international disorder, I am of course aware of the difference between a physical change and human social changes. My aim with this analogy is to try to clarify the processes of crisis management and the formation of a new order by comparing the psychological and structural features of these two states of disorder.

Analysis of the Order–Change Dialectic

The international system's order–change dialectic may also be meaningfully framed within a similar process analysis. Even in the best functioning international order, there is always a systemic dynamism, comparable to seismic movement. This movement is one of the most important principles of the flow of history, just as it is of the universe. The critical point is how it impacts the stability of the order, and the manner in which the consequences of this impact are evaluated and managed. If the functioning of the international system has the capacity to absorb and manage systemic movement and dynamism, each movement will serve to consolidate the order envisioned by the system. However, if the tension engendered by this movement is deeper and more wide-ranging than the resistance afforded by the inner workings of the system, the state of order begins to turn into a state of disorder at every twist in the tension. The emergence of such tension in such a way that it catches the system unawares, at an unexpected moment and with a high degree of severity, gives rise to consequences similar to the effects of earthquakes on the surface of the earth.

Sometimes, the transition from a state of order to one of disorder occurs in a manner that gradually escalates from tensions to crises, from crises to wars. Tensions, crises, and wars also give rise to outcomes that similarly shake and reshape the international order. Minor tensions begin to shake a static and predictable state of order, crises turn these tremors into medium-scale earthquakes, and wars trigger far more permanent ruptures on the fault line. Following these ruptures, there is either a transition to a new static order, or a wholesale transformation in the international order via global-scale world wars associated with larger-scale and more expansive ruptures.

The Cold War order was based on a static bipolar state of equilibrium. From the smallest-scale tensions to the largest-scale conflicts of interest, every potential crisis was subject to negotiation between the lead actors of each pole, following which a new state of equilibrium was established according to both sides' conjunctural positions and projections of power. These quests for balance within the Cold War's global rivalry led to the division of countries such as Germany, Korea, Vietnam, and Yemen through unnatural geographical definitions while also causing the deaths of millions of people, especially in Korea, Vietnam, and Yemen, in wars that were rooted in these divisions. In such a state of equilibrium, the existence even of unnaturally divided states such as East and West Germany, North and South Korea, and North and South Yemen could be perpetuated throughout the Cold War; inherently fragile structures can gain sustainability through the predominance of ideologically based balances.

In the early post-Cold War period, a new order based on the conceptualization of a "New World Order" was envisaged centered on the United States, which was seen as the absolute victor of the Cold War. However, as a result of the inability to reconstruct a post-Cold War world order in line with dynamic new conditions, four severe earthquakes struck, which lead the international order to evolve ever more rapidly towards a state of disorder: the *geopolitical* earthquake (1989–1991); the *security* earthquake (2001); the *economic* earthquake (2008); and the *structural* earthquake (2011). Their aftershocks and fracturings of world order have exposed the fact that we are now facing a far more systematic and profound set of problems with respect to the world order.

The fact that these earthquakes – some centered on regions (Eurasia and the Middle East/North Africa), others sectoral (security and economic) – have evolved without resolving their underlying problems, tensions, and crises has caused a far more widespread state of disorder and uncertainty. The shocks created by successive earthquakes have convulsed nation-states with fragile structures, devastated regional-balance mechanisms, and led to key players in international organizations becoming dysfunctional. Today, the system's structural components are being rocked.

The prevalence and depth of the crises and destruction caused by these earthquakes, whether they are sectoral or regional, have now gained global scale. This is what we mean when we talk of a *systemic* earthquake, because at issue is a spiral of crises that has transmogrified into a vicious circle and a state of dynamic uncertainty and instability involving the entire international system. In such a dynamic uncertainty, "experts" on these earthquakes are no more able to predict future earthquakes than are geological specialists able to predict shifts in tectonic plates.

In order to understand the nature of this systemic crisis and the severity of the state of paralysis it has caused, we may once again refer to two concepts analogous to earthquakes: aftershocks and earthquake swarms. Aftershocks are the natural consequence and the ongoing tremblings of an earthquake. Earthquake swarms constitute a succession of separate earthquakes. When these two seismic processes coincide, aftershocks and new quakes come in quick succession before the ravages of the previous earthquake have been put right. People and structures still in the throes of the initial shock of the first main earthquake are then repeatedly shaken by fresh seismic waves while they are still trying to deal with the aftershocks of the initial quake. The conglomeration of the aftershocks of different earthquakes and the transformation of a seismic state and psychology from the exception to the rule thus creates an ongoing "new normal." The order systematics on the earth's crust are ruptured and take the form of systemic seismic activity that becomes the source of disorder and anarchy.

The systemic earthquake we are facing in the international arena today is the product of seismic activity of this kind in the international structure. The 2001 (9/11) security earthquake began while the aftershocks of the 1989–1991 geopolitical earthquake were still rumbling; the aftershocks of both earthquakes combined to amplify the devastating effects of these seismic shocks. The 2008 economic earthquake, which struck while the interaction of both these earthquakes' aftershocks was still under way, amplified the destructive nature of these effects and expanded their scope. The 2011 structural earthquake that took place in the midst of all these chaotic processes then served to shake the nation-state structures that constitute the very foundation stones of the international system.

To borrow a concept borrowed once again from our earthquake analogy, the amplification of these earthquakes, which depends on the characteristics of their regional bedrock, naturally differed. Certain regions whose natural bedrock was not earthquake-resistant, and certain countries whose static/institutional structures were similarly earthquake-prone, were more profoundly affected by this systemic earthquake than others.

Like a double-edged sword, the technological revolution that took place within this dynamic process hugely amplified both the potential to establish order, and the destructive effects of successive seismic shocks. The technological revolution, which has such a positive impact when efforts to establish order are intensified, can be transformed into a destructive weapon in moments of crisis, when such efforts are replaced by a state of affairs in which each actor thinks only of their own survival.

Earthquake Psychology Reflections

There are signs that the transformation of a series of shocks that combined the main earthquakes with all their aftershocks into a systemic crisis is working as a vicious circle. The first of these is the fact that pessimism has become ever more widespread and begun to take hold not only of the general mass of people but policy-makers as well. The fact that these crises have come one after the other and stimulated a cumulative impact serves to strengthen this pessimistic psychology's basis in fact. The destructive impact of these earthquakes has become so normalized that people have begun to become inured even to the most egregious events. The fact that the conscience of humanity was susceptible to activation (albeit late and with difficulty) during the ethnic slaughter in Bosnia, which constituted an element of the aftershocks to the geopolitical earthquake, whereas it has proven impossible to do so in the case of the war crimes and ethnic slaughters in Syria, which constitute one of the epicenters of the international mechanisms' structural earthquake and have gone on for longer and even more destructively, is a reflection of such a psychology.

Secondly, the virus-like spread of this psychology means that urgent preparations for pessimistic scenarios start to gain priority over any enduring and visionary steps to construct a new order. This psychology causes actors to adopt a reflexive approach that drives them to defensive measures and reactive responses. Such an approach induces them to defend their own positions and interests by means of short-term micro-policies rather than pursuing actions based on a vision of the whole picture. Principles give way to seemingly pragmatic opportunism, strategic outlooks to tactical maneuvers. This approach leads to a situation in which the very actors who threaten world order are regarded as somehow tolerable. Just as a situation in which people living in two adjoining buildings fall into a state of egocentric survival during the period of aftershocks rather than working together to make their buildings able to withstand a new seismic wave causes both buildings to collapse when the next wave hits, so it is that in spirals of international crisis, short-term efforts for egocentric survival that digress from a consciousness of shared destiny bring with them only shared annihilation.

Thirdly, the inability to solve limited individual crises let alone deep wide-ranging ones leads first to their banalization, then their normalization, and finally to their incorporation as an integral feature of the system. While "learned helplessness" against crises encourages those who wish to provoke them, it completely destroys any belief the victims of these crises might have in the system. Today, the audacity fostered by this learned helplessness underlies the brazen stance of the Syrian regime in killing thousands of innocent civilians with all types of weapons of mass destruction, including chemical weapons, in UN-recognized atrocities, as well as the insouciance of the leadership of Myanmar taking refuge behind its Nobel Peace Prize as it remains silent in the face of the genocide perpetrated against the Rohingya Muslims. Moreover, the ambivalent attitudes of international actors, especially the United States, towards weapons of mass destruction make it difficult to resolve these problems within a framework of objective criteria.

Fourthly, this state of crisis is no longer seen as a factor susceptible to external intervention; the very actors and institutions expected to solve these crises have been taken captive by them. When the spiral of crisis reaches such a state that the various components of the system lose any crisis-resolution capacity, history's direction of flow begins to be defined not by international actors but only by the nature of the spiral of crisis. The inability to build a new post-Cold War order in any philosophical/intellectual, institutional, or operational sense has made it impossible to bring a succession of comprehensive earthquakes under control, and opened the way to the development of this kind of spiral, which not only destroys the existing system but itself takes on a systemic form.

Our application of an earthquake analogy to these wide-ranging crises may also serve an enlightening function in terms of crisis-management parallels. An ability to carry out effective post-earthquake disaster crisis management requires a pre-earthquake strengthening of structures in order to prevent their collapse, emergency intervention using the correct methods during the earthquake, getting the impact of aftershocks under control in its immediate aftermath, and finally the operation of a comprehensive post-earthquake process of restoration and rehabilitation.

The structural nature of the international order necessitates similar processes in emergent crises. The international system can renew and sustain itself by consolidating the principal elements of order in the system before a crisis breaks out, by taking measures to prevent the domino-effect spread of crisis aftershocks, and by carrying out a process of restoration and rehabilitation to enable the construction of an order that will form a "new normal" using post-crisis damage control to determine the situation. Neglecting this kind of process management only turns the accumulated damage into a primer for more comprehensive and destructive crises at every stage. Eventually the world order slowly surrenders, first to disruption, then to fracture, and finally to chaos; rather than a new state of order, a state of disorder in which every actor might carry out all manner of deeds becomes "normal"-ized. In this way, fresh elements of disorder progressively turn the system into a field of ever-intensifying conflict. When we look at the conditions that prevailed at the outbreak of the great wars in history, we can easily spot the traces of cycles of crisis of this kind.

The failure to operate a proper process of earthquake crisis management has left us to confront a currently ongoing fifth earthquake that may be defined as a "systemic crisis." Thus, the international system's operating platform has shifted and belief in the system's capacity to find resolution has largely evaporated. Finding reflection on regional and international planes, this state of crisis has taken on a systemic form.

The next chapters of this book aim to apply our proposed realistic optimism with a view to understanding this systemic crisis and eliciting a new order from it. With this end in mind the work is divided into two main parts, each comprising four chapters. Part I contains a realistic analysis of the ongoing systemic crisis while Part II attempts to forge a vision for a new order from the rubble of the systemic earthquake.

In this context, a background to the historical course of world order is provided (Chapter 1), following which the geopolitical, security, economic, and structural earthquakes that have generated a spiral of crises in the post-Cold War period that have laid the ground for the chaotic environment of today are taken into consideration (Chapter 2). The next chapter examines the effects of the systemic earthquake that has emerged from within this accumulated legacy on national, regional, and global structures (Chapter 3), following which we analyze the characteristics of the multiple powers system shaped by the response of global powers to these earthquakes (Chapter 4).

In Part II, after initially establishing the principles of a vision for a new order (Chapter 5), the challenges facing the formation of national (Chapter 6), regional (Chapter 7), global (Chapter 8) orders, and the principal elements of a vision for a possible new order are discussed.

Part I

SYSTEMIC EARTHQUAKE: ANALYSIS AND CONSEQUENCES OF WORLD (DIS)ORDER

1 TRADITIONAL, MODERN, AND GLOBAL "WORLD ORDERS"
A Historical Perspective

The idea of creating a sustainable social order is as old as the history of mankind and has come to be perceived by all civilizations as their ultimate goal. These quests to establish order have sometimes remained at a city-state level, while at other times they have transcended geographical limits to transform into comprehensive and inclusive political orders. When it encompassed a number of civilizational basins, this comprehensive nature ultimately embraced the assertion of establishing a world order.

Cities where the law constitutes the basis of social order, where a specific market culture is formed, and where the political structure's mechanical means is its bureaucracy, have been the focal centers of order.[1] States reflect how these orders become more deep-rooted in integrated geographical regions at the cultural, economic, and political levels. In this sense, the concept of world order points to the most comprehensive realization of order in terms of historical continuity, geographic expansion, and endogenous social consistency.

The history of civilizations shows us how major philosophical and intellectual transformations have paved the way for social, economic, and political transformations centuries down the road, and constituted the intellectual basis for new world orders. In other words, the kinetic dynamism of thought that accompanies intellectual renewal lays the ground for a certain socioeconomic and sociopolitical idea of "order" as a conventional and institutional structure.

The fact that the intellectual revival and renewal observed in all the traditional civilizational basins in the sixth and fifth centuries BC led to the formation of new orders in these basins, the transformative impact of Islamic *Tawhid* monotheistic belief from North Africa to China on orders in local civilizational basins from the seventh to the seventeenth century, and the influence of the intellectual upheavals from the Reformation and Renaissance to the Newtonian scientific revolution and Enlightenment philosophy on the birth of the modern concept of "order" from the fifteenth to the eighteenth centuries, reflect the interaction between the idea, and the actuality, of order. The intellectual dynamism that gained such extraordinary momentum through globalism inevitably became the cradle of new understandings of order. The coming decades – perhaps even centuries – are set to witness the processes that add momentum to this kinesis.

While their basic creeds, ideologies, and tools may differ, these endeavors can be classified in terms of method and type of approach into three eras: antiquity/traditional, modernity, and globality. An understanding of these eras' intrinsically shared features as well as the elements of continuity between them is a prerequisite to being able to shed light on the problematics we face today with respect to the world order.

The Traditional World Order

The ancient world's concept of order involved the deployment of a central authority in an effort to create a trans-territorial sphere of security and domination, to control trade routes, and to accommodate the accumulated legacies of different civilizations. This objective was a common ground between almost all the great imperial traditions, regardless of their differences of thought and belief. Intellectual awakenings provided the philosophical/spiritual content of this common ground, while the control of trade routes determined the sources of economic power, military might specified areas of expansion, and urban structures shaped the plurality of cultural lifestyles.

In this context, the struggle to establish orders that emerged from the intellectual/philosophical/spiritual awakening in the "axial age"[2] in the middle of the first millennium BC in different parts of the world is of particular note.[3] The post-Zarathustra Persian order of the Achaemenid Empire as "the earliest and largest of the known 'world empires'"[4] based in Persepolis, the Han order established in China after the Confucian and Taoist reinterpretation of Chinese wisdom,[5] the post-Buddha Mauryan order of Ashoka that established a subcontinental order in South Asia based on the policy of *dhamma* as a civic ethic intended to hold together a multicultural empire and transform Buddhism into a world religion,[6] and finally the post-Platonic/ Aristotelian Alexandrian order extending from the Balkans to Egypt and India, represent historic experiences of the earliest, limited form of globalization. Portrayals of delegations from all around Caucasus as far as Egypt in the reliefs of ancient Persepolis were keen to depict the existence of a center of world order. Alexandrian cities built along a geocultural line served as hegemonic staging-posts for the control of trade routes, as well as bringing together different civilizational legacies.[7]

In fact, three elements of the world order established by *Pax Romana*, seen as a source of continuity directly linking the traditions of the ancient order to modernity, constitute the pillars of any order: law implemented throughout the empire; roads and routes leading to the capital from every corner of the empire; and military power commensurate to the task of protecting these routes and enforcing the law. It is also worth mentioning that another equally important success of the Roman order was the unification of Mediterranean monetary systems. The Roman silver denarius was a unit of monetary value that would stand for centuries.

In this respect, the Roman order was a source of inspiration to those who sought to establish trans-territorial states of order from the primeval era to modernity.[8] The Holy Roman imperial order along the Charlemagne–Charles V continuum throughout the medieval period from the eighth to the sixteenth centuries and modernity's Eurocentric, ideology-based concept of order – as exemplified by Napoleon, Mussolini, and Hitler – strove to maintain the ideal of new Rome. For example, Frederick Barbarossa "asserted the indestructible rights of Rome" and his letter to Saladin "bids the Soldan to withdraw at once from the dominions of Rome, else will she, with her new Teutonic defenders, of whom a pompous list follows, drive him from them with all her ancient might."[9] Rulers' Caesarian titles in the following centuries from the medieval to the modern era in different traditions – Russia's *Tsar*, Germany's *Kaiser*, and the Ottomans' *Kayzer-i Rūm* – were symbolic manifestations of their claim to be the founders of an order that referred back to Rome. The rivalry between Charles V as the *Holy Roman Emperor* and Süleyman the Magnificent as the *Kayzer-i Rūm* for the domination in Europe was based on the mutual claim of being heir to the legacy of the Roman order, although they also used the same title for different faiths: "Defender of the Faith."[10]

The rise of Islamic civilization, which, with its *Weltanschauung* in the unmediated and absolute equality of mankind before God (*Tawhid*),[11] soon demonstrated an expansionary trend and took command of the Egypt, Mesopotamia, Levant, and Iran basins within thirty years of its emergence onto the stage of history during the Caliphate of 'Umar bin al-Khattāb, also took place on the back of this ancient legacy. As Marshall Hodgson strikingly emphasizes, "in a 'history of mankind' Islamic civilization should be studied not only in several regions where it flourished, but also as a historical whole, as a major element in forming the destiny of all mankind."[12] Amira K. Bennison's observation that "one of the most striking examples of an earlier world system with impressive reach is the Islamic ecumene which, like the global society emerging today, exhibited the subsistence, interaction and engagement of the local and universal in the economic, political and cultural spheres"[13] reflects such an approach. As a center of order, Hārūn al-Rashīd's Baghdad bore the features and characteristics of Caesar's Rome. Not only the roads, but knowledge, flowed to Baghdad.[14]

The "lost enlightenment," as it has been called by S. Frederick Starr,[15] in Central Asia between the years 800 and 1200 was a result of this new civilizational revival essentially reflected in four phenomena: trade and economic development along the Silk Road; sophisticated urban life in cities as the cultural centers; political order connecting different ancient civilizations; and advancement of knowledge and arts. The same civilizational revival created similar achievements in Andalucia, on the western fringe of Eurasia.

This world order, which was shaken by the Crusades and then lost its symbolic capital upon the Mongol destruction of Baghdad, was then rebuilt as the Istanbul-centered *Pax Ottomana* order[16] on the same pillars and on the intellectual foundations of an Islamic order set out along the line where the Alexandrian and Roman orders intersected.[17] In a desire to manifest this continuity, Ottoman sultans took care to use titles that symbolized the leaders of ancient orders: Caliph (Islam), Pādishāh (Iran), Khān/Khākān (Tūrān), and Kayzer-i Rūm (Rome). This cultural/civilizational inclusivity[18] and institutional/administrative

flexibility in economic[19] and political life[20] are the basic factors underlying the longevity of the Ottoman order.[21]

This might be seen as the continuation of the tradition of
Alexander the Great who "used the Achaemenid signet while dealing
with Asian questions and Macedonian royal ring when it came
to European affairs."[22] The two terms that the Ottomans used to
describe the purpose and nature of their state reflected a common quest
for the orders of the ancient world: World Order (*Niẓām-i ʿĀlem*) and
Eternal State (*Dawlat-i abad-muddat*). As Arnold Toynbee underlines,
the Ottoman order "occupied the focal area of the Old World where
the backwaters of the Indian and Atlantic Oceans approaches closest
to each other" and "in which three Old World continents meet."
"The Empire bestrode the portages from the Persian Gulf and the Red
Sea to the Mediterranean and it commanded the Straits linking the
Mediterranean with the Black Sea and Sea of Azov" in this strategic
geography, "a zone through which nearly all the round-the-world air
routes pass" in the contemporary world.[23]

Looked at from another perspective, the famous "All Roads
Lead to Rome" motto attributed to Pax Romana, the Ottoman conceptualization of *Niẓām-i ʿĀlem* (World Order) to define *Pax Ottomana*,
and *Pax Britannica*'s use of the motto "the empire on which the sun
never sets" were reflections of claims of absolute hegemony and may
also be seen as their own "end of history" claims. Rome's time- and
space-transcending hegemony was recognized not as a mere objective,
but as an established historical fact, and found expression in various
different ways. While in 56 BC the great statesman and intellectual of
the Republican era Cicero stated "it has now finally come about that the
limits of our empire and of the earth are one and the same," "the poet
Virgil had Jupiter sanctify the empire in the *Aeneid*: 'For these (Romans)
I place neither physical bounds nor temporal limits; I have given empire
without end.'"[24] The titles of two books, the first referring to the
European colonial empires and the second to the Ottoman State, reflect
this Roman legacy as well as the claim to be the founders of the time-
and space-transcending world order: *Lords of All the World: Ideologies
of Empires in Spain, Britain and France (1500–1800)*[25] and *Lords of
Horizons: A History of the Ottoman Empire*.[26]

All of these definitions of world order from different political
traditions claimed that their established order would go on forever and
that they had brought the flow of history to an end by halting the

internal dialectic of history. However, history continued to flow by sweeping aside these "egocentric illusions." As Robert Cox emphasizes, the approach of Ibn Khaldūn, who theorized about political realities at a time when political orders were being shaken, may have something to contribute in terms of understanding of post-hegemonic periods.[27] As in his quote from Ibn Khaldūn, every process of change brings with it its own dynamics and psychology: "When there is a general change of conditions, it is as if the entire creation had changed and the whole world been altered, as if it were a new and repeated creation, a world brought into existence anew."[28]

The Modern World Order

Modernity's concept of order emerged and developed as a result of a comprehensive civilizational transformation with philosophical/intellectual, economic, and political dimensions. The first signs of this transformation can be glimpsed between the twelfth and fifteenth centuries, while its fundamental characteristics came into sharper focus between the sixteenth and eighteenth centuries. It came to full maturity during the nineteenth and twentieth centuries; within a dynamic process, it caused a paradigm shift in the traditional concept of order.

The transformation from scholastic thought to the Reformation–Renaissance period, and from there to a Newtonian understanding of a natural order and Enlightenment philosophy-based modern ideologies, created changes in the main philosophical/intellectual axis of this paradigm shift. In the economic field, the transition from a static feudal order to dynamic mercantilism and from there to new production technologies and market concepts via the industrial revolution radically changed traditional understandings of economic order. Paradigmatic philosophical/intellectual and economic shifts created the substructure for political transitions from the traditional Holy Roman order to the centralized Westphalian nation-state order, and from there to modern political structures buttressed by the values of the French Revolution and colonial imperial world orders. Initially occurring within Europe itself, in time this transformative paradigm shift spread to other civilizational basins as the European powers' spheres of domination expanded, forcing change on the traditional fabric of each basin through different historic periods.

When viewed from the perspective of the modern era's efforts to establish an international order, there is a direct relationship between wars that shake the old order and create disorder, and periods marked by the intensification of efforts to form a new world order. The treaties, congresses, and new international institutions that take shape in the wake of large-scale wars also serve to set out the principles of the new order. In the context of this transformational paradigm shift, the perception of world order associated with modernity developed in four phases.

The Thirty Years War and the Westphalian Order: The Emergence of the "Nation-State" System

The first phase in the wake of the Thirty Years War was limited to Europe. This war resulted in the disintegration of the Holy Roman Empire, which represented the medieval order, while the subsequent Peace of Westphalia (1648) laid the ground for a new world order based on the nation-state unit. The Peace of Westphalia, a series of treaties signed in the immediate wake of the Thirty Years War (1618–1648) that caused the collapse of the centuries-old Holy Roman-German imperial order, paved the way for a new order; the Peace had a far wider impact than just ending the war; it enabled the emergence of the new order that bore its name (the Westphalian Order), which operated according to new rules and procedures.[29]

The definition of states' reciprocal areas of sovereignty and the inclusion of religious identity within these definitions ushered a new unit of world order onto the stage of history: the nation-state. This new political unit was fed by two significant and comprehensive processes of change, one intellectual, the other economic. The Reformation that constituted the fundamental basis of the intellectual transformation brought with it bloody and prolonged religious wars to such an extent that it was also accompanied by the replacement of the idea of order based on the medieval era's Vatican-centered concept of a Christian Commonwealth with one based on secular identities. The economic transformation gained momentum through the mercantilism that gained prominence in national economic units. The conceptual and factual formation of the nation-state thus developed in conjunction with the secular national identity brought by the Reformation, and the national economic legs lent by mercantilism.

In the intellectual background to this new concept of world order lay a climate of thought informed by the physics-centered naturalistic cosmological understanding of order of Galileo (who died in 1642, six years before the Peace of Westphalia); the mechanistic understanding of the natural order of Newton (who was born in 1642, the year Galileo died and six years before the Peace of Westphalia); and the concept of order based on an absolutist state authority drawing legitimacy from natural law set out in Hobbes's *Leviathan* with its exposition of a *scienza nuova* (published in 1651, three years after the Peace of Westphalia). This intellectual background later found its political basis in the French Revolution, its economic basis in the Industrial Revolution.

From that day to the present, all attempts to construct orders' legal foundations have been made on the basis of this nation-state unit. Its definition as the principal unit of order brought with it the concept of an international order for territorial and transboundary orders, together with institutionalized diplomacy as the basic instrument of establishing international order.

However, one can hardly claim that the Peace of Westphalia forged a lasting order.[30] The new elements of rivalry brought about by the transition from mercantilism to the industrial revolution, together with intra-European rivalries spreading to a wider field of transcontinental colonial rivalry and the struggles for supremacy and socioeconomic elements of order arising from the nature of new concepts of the absolutist state, fostered a process of change which led to the emergence of fresh tensions, conflicts, and wars.

The Napoleonic Wars and the Congress of Vienna: The Emergence of the "Balance of Power"

The second phase began with Napoleon's quest to replicate the Holy Roman tradition in modern guise with a new empire founded on the intellectual and normative impetus that accompanied the French Revolution. The Napoleonic Wars instigated with the aim of establishing a new Franco-centric order in Europe under the leadership of Napoleon presented Europe with a bi-optional projection of historical flow; a new imperial order constructed with modern tools, or a new Westphalian order structured on a balance between the powers. The Battle of Waterloo in 1815 removed the first option from the stage of history while the Congress of Vienna was held in the same year to define the second option's actors and rules.[31]

The Congress of Vienna promulgated a dynamic concept of order by a process of balancing various power centers rather than a hegemonic order dominated by a single power center.[32] The "Balance of Power" system which operated in line with rules agreed at the Congress of Vienna lasted almost a century.[33] It also reflected the institutionalization of "dynastic legitimacy" and monarchy. It shaped an international environment in which alliances may change at any moment, but in which order is maintained by means of new balances.

This phenomenon brought with it two developments, one on a European scale, the other more global. The European-scale development drew the curtain on a focus of power on the continent of Europe that had been defined in terms of a Franco-German power dialectic within the Holy Roman imperial tradition and paved the way for non-continental Britain to gain prominence as the actor of equilibrium in this balance of powers. The actuality of the "empire upon which the sun never set" opened up a space for itself as a sea power within these balances.[34] There is a natural parallel between this rise of Britain as "the only great commercial and industrial state at the end of Napoleonic wars" and the expansion of world trade based on ocean commerce in the nineteenth century: "the total value of the world's import and export trade in 1800 amounted in round numbers to 1.5 billion dollars, in 1850 to 4 billion dollars and in 1900 to nearly 24 billion. In other words, during a period in which the population of the world was no more than tripled, its international exchange of commodities was increased 16-fold."[35] In reaction to this Germany and Italy, who considered themselves as having been weakened and outperformed in the race for colonies, established national unions after periods of significant challenge and turmoil.

The global-scale development consisted of a global rivalry between the colonial empires of the intra-European balances of power to such a degree that it paved the way for the concurrent penetration of institutions, technological tools, and mindset factors associated with modernity into other civilizational basins, and their consequent transformation. In this framework the remnants of imperial/traditional cosmopolitan orders in Asia were liquidated by the colonial empires. As McNeill rightly underlines, "four events clustering near the midyear of the nineteenth century aptly symbolize the irremediable collapse of the traditional order of each of the major Asian civilizations":[36] the Taiping rebellion in China in 1850, which transformed the social fabric of Chinese civilization; the beginning of the drastic top-down revolution in Japan in 1854 leading to the end of the traditional military order of the Tokugawa shogunate; the mutiny in India in 1857–1858 that dissolved the traditional Moghul Empire founded by the Timurid Prince Babur more than three centuries before; and the Crimean war (1853–1856) that transformed the institutions of the Ottoman traditional order and created sizeable public debt owed to European investors.[37]

This process was in fact the dissolution of the traditional cosmopolitan orders and their replacement by the hegemonic cosmopolitan order of the modern colonial system. The final such dissolution took place with the departure of the Ottoman State from the stage of history after the First World War, which was a consequence of the rivalry of colonial powers to control a strategic geographic zone stretching from "Africa and the Eastern Mediterranean across Central Asia and the Indian Ocean to the Pacific."[38] As strikingly stressed by Arnold Toynbee, this dissolution of the last traditional cosmopolitan order did not however bring a sustainable order during the colonial era and afterwards: "This survey of the experiences of a number of ex-Ottoman peoples, since the dates at which they ceased to be under Ottoman rule shows that under Ottoman rule, like Habsburg rule, has been unjustly maligned. Even in its last phase, which was not its best phase, this imperial regime was a happier dispensation for its subjects than their subsequent tribulations."[39]

In Europe, the order that was provided by the balance of power umbrella relied on unilateral impositions and domination sharpened by colonial structures beyond Europe. The ensuing struggle, which encompassed the entire global map of the colonial empires, gained theoretical depth and practical expansion as each actor with a claim to the global order developed their own geopolitical perspective.

It is certainly no coincidence that the theoretical framework of classical geopolitics was born during this period.[40] The modern colonial order, which treated the world as a single entity and whose spheres of rivalry were delineated by their priorities within these geopolitical domains, brought two discontinuities and ruptures – one between the center and the periphery, the other of a regional nature.

Contrary to traditional concepts of order, global-scale colonial rivalry was based on the geographic discontinuity of center-periphery relations. The traditional Persian, Alexandrian, Mongol, Roman, and Ottoman orders relied on the perpetuation of a geographically continuous order through political/military power. There was an uninterrupted link in political dominance between the order's center and its periphery. On the other hand, modern colonial empires were based on a geographic discontinuity that differentiated the fate of the center from that of the periphery and evaluated every peripheral area simply in terms of its economic contribution. In this context, and quite contrary to the Roman or Ottoman domination of Egypt or the Balkans, the political and economic ties between Britain and India, France and West Africa, or the Netherlands and Indonesia did not reflect a concept of order based on geographical continuity. The French in particular were intent on imposing cultural hegemony while engaging in economic exploitation, a policy that was quite distinct from British colonialism, which focused on economic dimensions and maintained a "color bar" that facilitated subsequent exits. The main focus of domination was aimed at maintaining the continuity of resource flows rather than maintaining lasting geographic continuity.

We see the reflection of this new geopolitics on areas beyond the colonial centers in the rupturing of traditional cultural and economic basins one from the other. For example, the colonization of Malaysia and Indonesia, which had been seen as extensions of one another for centuries, by the two transcontinental colonial systems of Britain and Holland respectively, caused ruptures in the traditional order and geographic continuity that had existed in these regions. The fact that the Iraq–Syria–Lebanon line that comprises the most critical crisis belt of recent times became a part of the British and French colonial systems also led to a similar rupturing effect and the disintegration of a centuries-old network of traditional economic and cultural relations.[41]

Colonial empires developed by forming security zones whose *political* foundations rested on military control; whose *economic* foundations rested on economic production-consumption networks linked to the colonial power's center; and whose *cultural* foundations rested on the propagation of the cultural mindset that would nourish this new world order. The similarities between the proliferation of colonial transit cities around the Eurasian continent (Aden, Karachi, Bombay, Calcutta, Singapore, Malacca, Kuala Lumpur, Hong Kong) and the role played by cities in the ancient world order of the Alexandrian period, represent good examples of the status of cities as staging posts of the orders of different historic periods.[42]

In fact, the origins of many of the international problems we face today may be found in the elements that were discarded in this balance of power order. It is extremely hard for powers that change global geopolitics and the economic–political axis to understand and find solutions to problems in today's international order without understanding the dynamics of that balance of power era.

The competitive environment nurtured by the internal contradictions of this balance of power system, which took on a more dynamic form as colonial rivalries developed, generated outcomes that set the stage for an even larger-scale conflict. This rivalry led to a polarization between the balancing actors of the balance of power system such as the Triple Entente (France, Russia, and Britain) and the Triple Alliance (Germany, Austria-Hungary, and Italy). Although conflict was triggered by intra-European rivalries, its appearance in the world's major prewar centers signaled the advent of a global-scale interaction.[43] This rivalry and interaction paved the way for the onset of "the war that ended peace"[44] – the First World War, as well as the "Age of Extremes" that covered two global-scale hot wars and one cold war.[45]

The First World War and the League of Nations: The Interwar Era as a Historical Experience of "Systemic Earthquake"

In the third phase, beginning with the League of Nations, the international order matured towards the UN system by means of international law and international organizations. While this period is an important phase of human history in terms of the development of an international order, an analysis of the intervening one hundred years is vitally important in being able to overcome the systemic crisis we currently face.

The final of the *Fourteen Points* enumerated by that era's harbinger of principles US President Woodrow Wilson, on 8 January 1918, was a call for "a general association of nations formed under specific covenants for the purpose of affording mutual guarantees of political independence and territorial integrity to great and small states alike."[46] The bringing to life of this enterprise, which had been the dream of so many thinkers throughout history from East to West, from al-Fārābī[47] to Kant,[48] was indeed a truly historic step.

This time, and as a result of the lessons drawn from the most widespread and devastating war history had yet seen, a guiding will was developed in which the new order would be forged not by means of a treaty or congress, but a permanent international institution bringing all the actors together. Nonetheless, the first-time realization of this dream with the founding of the League of Nations on 10 January 1920 became a doomed enterprise from various points of view. First and foremost, the inability to overcome domestic isolationist opposition in spite of the best efforts of Woodrow Wilson,[49] recognized as the mastermind behind the League, precluded US membership just when the United States had risen to the status of a global power. Secondly, its membership structure was stubbornly unstable. The Union of Soviet Socialist Republics (USSR), which became a member fourteen years after the League's establishment in 1934, resigned its membership in 1939; Germany remained a member only from 1926 to 1933. Permanent member Japan, which had played an instrumental role in the founding of the League, left in 1933; Italy in 1937. Founding member Brazil left the organization early on, in 1926. Thirdly, the organization's institutional structure remained dysfunctional as *realpolitik* continued to be the colonial powers' driving force within their own balance of power nature, given their own balance of power orientation.

When this new experiment, based on a Kantian philosophical background and Wilsonian principles, proved insufficient in the face of a post-First World War ideological psychology coupled with the impact of power balances and global economic crisis, it lacked any capacity to prevent another massive conflict; it remained an effort to establish a fruitless, short-term order. This abortive experiment was able neither to establish an enduring international order, nor prevent the emergence of the Second World War.

In the period between the two World Wars we underwent a systemic crisis initiated by geopolitical disintegration, intensified by economic crisis, rendered irresolvable by the dysfunction of international structures, and finally ignited by exclusionist racist ideologies' metamorphosis into autocratic regimes. E. H. Carr's observation that "the characteristic feature of the crisis of the twenty years between 1919 and 1939 was the abrupt descent from the visionary hopes of the first decade to the grim despair of the second, from a utopia which took little account of the reality to a reality from which every element of utopia was rigorously excluded"[50] is a striking historical experience of the shift from *utopic optimism* to *nihilistic pessimism* we are facing today mentioned in the introductory chapter.

An accurate interpretation of the systemic earthquake through which we are now passing requires us to take on board both the instructive and the cautionary elements of this historic experience because "the relation of totalitarianism to the crisis was clearly one not of cause, but of effect": "Totalitarianism was not the disease, but one of the symptoms. Wherever the crisis raged, traces of this symptom could be found."[51] Looking from this perspective of psychopolitical shift, we are facing today a thirty-year crisis (1989–2019) in the post-Cold War era similar to the *twenty-year crisis* (1919–1939) in the post-First World War era. What will happen in the future will depend on our performance in drawing the correct lessons from historical experiences.

In this case from the past, a severe earthquake first manifested itself in the form of a major geopolitical earthquake in Europe, triggered by the disintegration of traditional imperial structures in the wake of the First World War. This earthquake, a consequence of the dissolution of the German, Austro-Hungarian, Russian, and Ottoman states that had represented the traditional order over centuries, created a large-scale geopolitical vacuum.

While the sphere of influence of Russia, reconstituted as the Soviet Union as a result of an ideological revolution that had itself been thrown up by this earthquake, was maintained largely intact by means of Stalin's harsh methods, including mass deportations and massacres, Germany embarked on an endeavor to regain its former might based on an ideological reorientation to establish dominance over its former imperial Central and Eastern European hinterland. As Austria underwent a diminution of scale to fall under Germany's sway, the rivalry of two imperial forces striving to regroup as autocratic regimes within modern ideological frameworks put pressure on the newly emergent nation-states in the Baltic–Black Sea–Adriatic triangle. The confrontations that broke these new nation-states laid the geopolitical groundwork that led to the Second World War.

The separation of geopolitical, geoeconomic, and geocultural basins that had shared the same living space for centuries by borders redrawn between the French and British colonial empires throughout the strategic area from where the Ottoman State had withdrawn as an upshot of this geopolitical earthquake stretching from the Black Sea to Yemen, Mesopotamia to North Africa, also destroyed the substructure of a possible new regional order.[52] Moreover, the advent of oil as a new strategic commodity radically changed the nature of regional rivalries.

Echoing current predicaments, the League of Nations and Wilsonian principles, which were aimed at furthering interwar quests for a new order, were debased; whereas they had originally represented a platform of shared values for the formation of a new order, they were turned into a mere tactical tool. This was then exploited in line with the needs of the key players in this new environment of geopolitical rivalry, a process that rendered these principles ineffective. Confidence in the system's underlying values was thus weakened and each actor began to prioritize its own short-term interests over the long-term quest for a new order. The impossibility of establishing such an order in areas abandoned by collapsing classical empires was accompanied by a severe security earthquake. The failure of the League of Nations, which lacked adequate tools and institutionalization, to establish an area of security led to the normalization of a state of crisis.

The blow that served to deepen and globalize this environment of crisis was struck by the economic crisis of 1929. The mass of people impoverished by the most comprehensive economic crisis of human history became susceptible to provocation and mobilization by racist and exclusionist ideologies. The psychology of exclusion fomented by these ideologies progressively took national, regional, and finally international form. At the national level, foreigners and "outsiders," especially the Jews, were held responsible for the crisis and the seeds of a global-scale war were sown around the idea of a new world order to be governed by superior races.

These developments also paved the way for a mass migration of peoples seeking exile or fleeing from all kinds of risks. Resistance groups and "inferior races" in Nazi-controlled territories faced persecution and forced migration, while the Soviet regime, founded on claims of a more egalitarian ideology, drove millions of people from their ancestral homelands on the allegation that they were members of exploitative class structures.

These developments initially met a narrow, short-sighted response, following which, in a reaction of "learned helplessness," crises were left to follow their own course right up until Hitler's invasion of Poland. With the crises having reached such a huge scale, there was no other option but war. The most destructive war in human history occurred as a result of the grotesque irresponsibility of being caught unprepared for the earthquake, although its ever-growing seismic waves were perfectly obvious.

The technological revolutions that have taken place during – and partly as a consequence of – this earthquake have led to the technology of war gaining greater sophistication and its destructive capacity growing exponentially, as evidenced by the development of the atomic bomb. With the use of the atom bomb, the destructiveness of battlefield technology, which had previously been limited to the theater of war and the generation who were living through that war, reached the level of being able to destroy the ontological security of subsequent generations.

The lesson we need to draw from this is as follows: unless an international system in a spiral of crises is rehabilitated through correct interventions implemented at the correct time, it will likewise face the collapse of buildings being shaken by the aftershocks of that same earthquake.

The Second World War and the UN System: International Order under the Shadow of the Bipolar Cold War

The fourth phase was unfurled after the Second World War, a conflict triggered by the systemic earthquake of the interwar era. With the devastating impact of this war, which had threatened the entire future of humanity, the most comprehensive effort to establish a new world order guided by the experiences of the past formed the philosophical foundations, legal substructure, and institutional framework of the concept of international order to which that period was heir.

The idea of an international order based on international law was revived within the framework of the UN system after the Second World War, during which process efforts were made to shape an integrated new order to achieve a balance resting on three pillars. First, a number of assemblies were held to develop a set of principal ideals, most significantly the *Universal Declaration of Human Rights* (1948).

Secondly, the institutionalization envisaged in order to protect this set of values adopted the organizational/legal guise of the then-prevailing power structure in such a way that the functioning of the United Nations Security Council (UNSC) was tied to the will of its permanent members (the victors of the Second World War) and internal UNSC negotiation. The shift in China's official representation from

Taiwan to Beijing, recognized by UN Resolution 2758 in 1971, and the permanent members' (known as the P5) power of veto, granted them the privileged status of being able to influence or halt all kinds of international processes. This dialectic between values and the institutionalization of power has over time rendered the values underpinning the international order a passive element in power negotiations between the P5 countries, based on their national interests.

Thirdly, the economic and cultural pillars of the political order were established with international organizations within and beyond the UN system. The rules and operational structures of the international economic order were created through the establishment of the Bretton Woods system, the International Monetary Fund (IMF), and the World Bank. Structures like the United Nations Educational, Scientific and Cultural Organization (UNESCO) and the United Nations Children's Fund (UNICEF) worked to consolidate the new order's cultural landscape.

The idealist essence of the post-Second World War world order was defined by the norms of UN-centered international law, while its realist manifestation was determined by the bipolar balance of power. And while the international order gained stability when the bipolar structure was shaped by compromise and balance through policies such as that of *détente*, chaotic processes came into play when, as occurred in such crises as Korea, Suez, Cuba, and Vietnam, regional rivalry between the two poles turned into high tension and even armed conflict.

Nonetheless, the fact that the Cold War did not become a wholesale Hot War during this period, which lasted for about half a century, was largely due to the clearly defined nature of the parties with superpower status in the ultimate tensions between the two poles and the existence of international platforms able to bring these parties together, albeit in the form of tense disputatiousness. Summits between the two superpowers and negotiations within the UNSC ensured the maintenance of a certain status quo. When one of these poles lost its superpower status, the order based on the relative stability brought by this status quo was radically shaken. And the fact that this shock occurred in conjunction with the phenomenon of globalization has brought with it the most comprehensive problematic of order in history. The psychology of complacency induced by the end of the Cold War coupled with a failure sufficiently to comprehend and evaluate the

extensive challenge of this order problematic, which was further complicated by globalization, led to successive spirals of crisis.

Globalization: The Post-Cold War Era and the Search for a New World Order

The appositely named Cold War that emerged after the Second
World War heralded an era of global tension and conflict between two
poles divided by ideological, political, and economic preferences that
continued by various means for about half a century. Therefore,
together with the most significant visible outcomes of the proclamation
of the end of an era of conflict – namely the fall of the Berlin Wall (1989)
and the dissolution of the Warsaw Pact and the USSR (1991) – the
philosophical/intellectual, institutional, and functional elements of a
new post-Cold War order needed to be restructured while taking into
account the lessons of previous postwar periods. However, the inability
over the past quarter-century to accomplish such an outcome through a
creative mindset and constructive approach has thrust the whole world
into a systemic spiral of crises at national, regional, and global levels.

The concurrent shaking of the bipolar Cold War order by the
phenomenon of globalization has brought with it an overarching challenge. Three features of this new era have influenced both the depth and
the global scale of this challenge: escalation of scale; the technological
communications revolution; and the gathering pace of interaction in
every field.

The most significant impact of globalization has been the extraordinary momentum of its expansion in scale in the cultural, economic,
and political fields. From whichever angle one looks at it, expansions in
scale that used to take centuries have been realized within the space of a
decade in this era. This expansion in scale has had a profound impact on
the course of attempts to establish a new order and the reactions
against them.

A historic example of just such an expansion in scale might
serve to facilitate our understanding of post-Cold War era approaches
and reactions. The psychological, philosophical, and institutional
approaches that accompanied the transition of the city-state order into
an imperial order in the wake of Alexander the Great's conquests and
which stemmed from an expansion in scale that spread to almost every
area of life, may render interesting clues with regard to reactions to the

transition from modernity to globalization. In an article written in the context of a comparative analysis of this kind and in the light of the experiences of the first post-Cold War decade, I defined the expansion in scale undergone during the Alexandrian era as "limited globalization"; I tried to show that the Stoic, Cynic, and Epicurean reactions witnessed during this period of limited globalization could also be discerned in the transition from modernity to globalization.[53]

Indeed, expansions in scale led to reactions that manifested themselves in the aforementioned three philosophical approaches: (i) Stoic approaches that tried to settle expansions in scale within a new framework of order, (ii) attempts to avoid the risks inherent in expansions in scale and to take shelter in smaller scales that were believed to be under their own control, and (iii) attempts to gain the greatest possible personal pleasure from this expansion in scale.

The first reaction, which coincided with the end of the Cold War, manifested itself through a discourse based on the concept of a "New World Order." Employed to define and legitimize the new order emerging from within these processes of great transformation that the rising powers were working to establish, this concept was not of itself new. Having assumed an operational role in efforts to establish postwar orders after the First and Second World Wars, "the NWO has never been more than an ideal type, and this ideal has often been at clear variance with the historical results."[54]

The second reaction found reflection in a postmodernism that sought to take refuge in intraparadigmatic realities in the philosophical sphere, and, in the political sphere, in a return to smaller scales in which the subject felt a greater sense of security. The retreat into smaller-scale ethnic and sectarian identities in the crisis zones of the Middle East and the inward-looking reactions in Europe against refugees who were in fact a natural outcome of globalization may be analyzed in this context.

The reactions of anti-globalization movements against global structures, each of which is becoming more and more leviathan-like, in which people who perceive they are losing their individuality are in a sense withdrawing into spaces where they can express and live their own individualities, have taken on a common characteristic that transcends cultural basins. In a sense, those who are driven to such a reaction are, in the words of Diogenes, saying "Stand out of my light!" to globalization's expansions in scale: "the process (of globalization) must be brought to a halt as soon as possible, and reversed."[55]

The quests of postmodernist approaches have formed the philosophical substructure to this reaction.

The third reaction manifests itself in the form of a consumer culture that is becoming more and more widespread on a global scale and which is rapidly leading to standardized personal-pleasure preferences. The symbolism of the opening of branches of McDonald's and the omnipresence of Coca Cola in the capitals of former socialist countries, meant that this reaction manifested itself against the standardization even of taste and pleasure in The Global Shopping Mall that became known as *McWorldism*.[56] This time, the symbols of victory in capital cities into which tanks had previously rolled after hot wars were the brands of the globalized homogenization of pleasure.

Generating stoic, cynical, and epicurean reactions and fed by the simultaneous impact of global and local tendencies, globalism exposes the multidimensional nature of the process we are currently going through, a process that harbors its own contradictions. Distinctions based on "global" and "local" conceptualizations define two intertwined dynamic processes rather than two mutually contradictory categories. Put starkly, globalization is localizing as localization is globalizing. While a localized trend in one corner of the world rapidly becomes a global phenomenon through social media, a global trend is able to penetrate into every local element in the world at the same speed. This state of affairs is activating new, hard-to-control elements that need to avoid the pitfall of disregarding the vision of, and the struggle to establish, a new order.

This expansion in scale is gathering pace hand in hand with the revolution in communications technology, whose interactive impact exposes even geographically distant societies to identical threats and risks. At the end of the 1980s when the Cold War ended, the most efficient communications tool was the fax machine, which is now more or less archaic. The entry into almost everyone's daily life of the internet in the 1990s, mobile telephones in the 2000s, and social media vehicles such as Twitter in the 2010s has served to boost the pace not only of communications, but the flow of history itself.

Indeed, the speed of this expansion in scale and communications has intensified reciprocal interaction to such an extent that it has left no chance of establishing an example such as Robinson Crusoe, one of the literary symbols of literature in the modern era, even in the imaginary world, because now even the remotest island could not exclude itself from a shared destiny in the sense of being a party to the impact of global climate change. We all recall the psychology of inter-action to which "CNN's war," broadcast live around the world during the 1991 Gulf War, gave rise.[57] In the intervening quarter-century, everyone with a mobile telephone has gained the ability to access all kinds of live broadcast in every corner of the world.

The extraordinary expansion in scale and change associated with globalization necessitated an embracing philosophy, mentality, and structuring for a new order. However, the past quarter-century's predilection for conjunctural and short-term fixes over an embracing endeavor of this kind has made it more difficult to understand and predict an environment which is characterized by an ever-deepening and proliferating spiral of crises.

Fukuyama's *The End of History*[58] and Huntington's *Clash of Civilizations*,[59] two much-discussed theses produced with a view to furnishing the new era with a philosophical/intellectual foundation, undertook the mission to address the prevailing state of affairs and develop a theoretical framework for current political discourse. Yet the first thesis is misleading, the second a series of self-fulfilling prophesies.

Using Toynbee's celebrated definition, we may see the *End of History* thesis as a typical example of the "egocentric illusion" to which hegemonic powers so often fall prey in the euphoria of victory. The premature celebration of the triumph of the US-led West and liberal/democratic values prevented thinkers and political actors from adopting a psychology that would be able to foresee the new era's challenges and provoke consideration of initiatives in line with these challenges. Unilateral proclamations of victory brought unilateral policies and discourse that made it harder to recognize the role of new actors that were coming up from beneath the surface. As I stated at the time, and envisaged and emphasized in subsequent books,[60] history did not end. On the contrary, it continued to flow at an ever-accelerating rate. The "End of History" hypothesis only made it harder to grasp the nature and consequences of this ever-accelerating flow of history,[61] especially for the power centers who laid claim to having brought history to an end.

As for the "Clash of Civilizations" thesis, it put forward a Hobbesian thesis of conflict in opposition to its Hegelian *End of History* counterpart, demoting the concept of Civilization, which up to then had been emblematic of constructive factors, to the status of a mere actor in power conflicts. The "Clash of Civilizations" approach, which indulges in a selective interpretation of historic facts to lay responsibility for the failure of the international system in the Bosnian War on peripheral civilizations rather than its central actors, is accompanied by a series of prejudices that trigger culture-based clashes by virtue of being self-fulfilling prophecies. Under the guise of an academic analysis, this prejudicial approach accommodated two atrocious attempts to mask the true responsibility for an ethnic slaughter that led to the greatest human massacre in post-Second World War Europe. The first deployed the "Clash of Civilizations" thesis to create a false parity between the criminal elements who carried out this ethnic slaughter under Milošević's and Karadzić's leadership, and the Bosniak Muslims who were the victims of the slaughter, as if they were two equal parties. The second involved a cover-up of the failings and responsibilities of the UN and the global powers on the issue of preventing this crime against humanity. In this way the questioning of the operability of the international system that needed to be conducted early on in the post-Cold War era was kicked into the long grass.

So, as Edward Said rightly underlines, "much of the subsequent interest taken in Huntington's essay, ... derives from its timing, rather than exclusively from what it literally says."[62] I was on the teaching faculty of a university in Malaysia, where Malay Muslims, Chinese Buddhists, and Hindu Tamils live side by side, when this hypothesis was published in the form of an article. Seeing the recommendation at the end of the article to Western politicians and policy-makers "to exploit differences and conflicts among Confucian and Islamic states," I was dismayed to observe that this hypothesis was not only wrong in its historical/theoretical selectivity but that it was effectively obstructing the flow of history in such a way as to stymie efforts to establish national, regional, and global order. As a faculty member then lecturing at a Muslim-majority university and living in the Chinese quarter of Kuala Lumpur, and concerned that apart from global fragmentations this hypothesis would lead to tensions in some countries that would spread right down to the level of the street, I wrote an article in those days expressing the view that it was wrong in terms of historical data as well as dangerous as a predictor for the future.[63] It was historically wrong because none of the wars of the modern era, including both World Wars, were actually between civilizations; rather, they had sprung from European-centered intracivilizational tensions and conflicts of interest. The Thirty Years War, the Napoleonic Wars, and both World Wars fundamentally involved not a struggle between two or more civilizations but the impacts of clashing interests and hegemonic ambitions within the same civilization.[64] It was dangerous as a predictor for the future because it sowed the seeds in people's minds for a new confrontational era through its categorizations, which were a hangover from colonial periods:

> The confrontational categorizations based on the provocations of the civilizational differences such as *West vs. Islam, West vs. Rest* can neither contribute anything to global peace and security nor to the process of re-adjustment of the international system. Strategic miscalculations based on these confrontational categorizations will continue to be the main obstacle to global peace. The colonial ambitions and anti-colonial sentiments of the last century may again arise out of this strategic misuse of civilizational differences and ultimately this will be against the interest of the West in general and the US in particular.[65]

In his criticism of this hypothesis as an effort to perpetuate the Cold War era, Edward Said presents an absolutely accurate and cautionary framework:

> So strong and insistent is Huntington's notion that other civilizations necessarily clash with the West, and so relentlessly aggressive and chauvinistic is his prescription for what the West must do to continue winning, we are forced to conclude that he is really most interested in continuing and expanding the cold war by other means rather than advancing ideas about understanding the current world scene or trying to reconcile between cultures.[66]

The philosophical/intellectual inertia and one-dimensional approach that characterized post-Cold War perceptions also manifested itself in institutional structures. Rearguard attempts were made to keep the post-Second World War structures intact in spite of the transformation that taken place in terms of values, technological infrastructure, the nature of economic relations, and political power balances.

Regardless of the fact that the balances of power had changed, the international political and economic architecture was kept unchanged. And despite the context of a progressively intensifying divergence between this structure and the actual economic/political power scale, the hierarchical structure at the heart of the international system's final decision-making process, principally the P5, was preserved intact. The impact of mechanisms such as the G8 and P5+1 that were created over time with a view to closing this gap was restricted to meetings and solving a very small number of international problems. The G20, which was established in order to expand communications and develop common policies vis-à-vis economic crises at the end of the 1990s and was rightly supplemented with annual summits in the wake of the 2008 crisis, has become a highly flexible, rather than effective, platform.

From a functional perspective, the ineffective performance of the structures that constitute the principal elements of the international system in terms of preventing post-Cold War crises has shaken confidence in the system. Just as problems inherited from the Cold War have proved impervious to resolution, attempts have focused on minimizing the damage of freshly emerging issues by just about freezing them. For example, the Oslo Process instigated to resolve the most critical issue inherited by the post-Cold War era from the Cold War period – namely the Palestinian issue – has still not achieved the objective of establishing a Palestinian State after a quarter of a century. We may safely assume that had the Oslo Process achieved the genuine peace that had been anticipated, the fate of the Middle East as well as the nature of international issues would have taken a different course. The prevention right up to the present day of the establishment of a Palestinian State, which was the ultimate goal of the Oslo Process, by Israel and pro-Israel lobbies in the United States has formed the psychological substructure of numerous regional and global-scale crises that have emerged during the past quarter-century and shaken confidence in efforts to establish international order.

In this sense, it was the Srebrenica massacre, carried out in front of well-nigh acquiescing UN forces, that elevated lack of confidence in the international system to such heights. This crisis of confidence was brought to a peak by the massacre not only of thousands of defenseless Muslim Bosniaks, but of all the human values that represented the very basis of international order, in Srebrenica.

Building a process of restoration from the ruins of this systemic crisis will remain beyond the realms of possibility unless and until we finally release ourselves from post-Cold War "End of History" passivity and grab hold of the pulsating flow of history in all its aspects and directions. As I stressed in my criticism of this psychology of "endism" about a quarter-century ago, the flow of history is gaining momentum in all its might and grandeur: "History has not ended. Its configurations are still in gestation and moving towards an ontological equilibrium."[67]

Regrettably, all that has been done from that day to the present is the very opposite of what is needed to achieve such an ontological equilibrium. And today, this flow of history will either find its own ontological equilibrium by means of a fresh initiative, or else the very ontological existence of mankind will come under increasing threat from the impact of the intensifying tensions, clashes, and armed conflicts that accompany systemic crisis.

The experiences undergone from the end of the Cold War to the present day show that the inability to meet on a common platform is associated not with the end of history, but an apocalyptic scenario that could well lead to war. The break from a sense of shared destiny, as the globalization of humankind's living space and the intense interaction brought by the technological revolution become ever more intertwined, constitutes a great danger in store for our future. And without the development of a consciousness of shared destiny relating to humanity's ontological existence, the establishment of a global order sensitive to everyone's identity will remain beyond the bounds of possibility.

Two subjects relating particularly to the ontological existence of humankind risk turning systemic earthquake into systemic doom: nuclear armament, and ecological imbalance. Unless a global consciousness on both these subjects that transcends national interests and power rivalries can be developed, it is impossible to guarantee the ontological security of humankind. It should be remembered that nation-states' individual areas of political security make no sense without such a guarantee. One cannot talk about political security in conditions that lack ontological security.

It might be useful to share an anecdote from my personal experience in this context. The general atmosphere I observed at the Foreign Ministers' meeting held at the UN prior to the 2010 UN Climate Change Conference in Cancún profoundly shook me on this issue. At the meeting, numerous Foreign Ministers took the floor to read prepared texts setting out their national positions on climate change and environmental issues. When it came to my turn, and to draw attention to the fact that a consciousness of shared destiny would be destroyed under the shadow of national interests, I addressed the meeting as follows:

> As Foreign Ministers, our fundamental duty is to convey the views of the states we represent at this platform. The sole exception to this fundamental duty is when it comes to issues that touch on the area of ontological existence that concerns the future of us all. The states we represent are political entities. And let us not forget that there can be no political existence without ontological existence. The issue we are discussing is the ontological existence of humanity itself. On this matter, we should hold our consultations first and foremost not only as the Foreign Ministers of the states we represent, but also as the Interior Ministers of humankind. Otherwise, there will be no states to protect our grandchildren, whose zones of ontological existence will disappear. I propose that from now on we present our official positions to the UN in writing, while having our consultations here in an interactive fashion by listening to each other.

Following this exhortation, a number of speakers expressed their appreciation and affirmation for this approach and the flow of the meeting changed course, yet no changes were made during the technical negotiations. It was then that I realized that these issues of concern to the future of humanity as a whole were being ignored in the merciless field of modern power rivalry.

In short, today we find ourselves poised at a critical historic threshold. We shall either witness a new era of construction in the international order based on a visionary perspective with principle (philosophical/intellectual) and institutional and operational dimensions, or the state of international (dis)order will be normalized, following which we shall find ourselves on the threshold of an utterly devastating global war with the psychology of "learned helplessness" developed during the process of the normalization of disorder.

Yet the emergence of a state in which everyone will try to protect themselves and the country to which they belong will not afford any such protection, because combat technology has now reached such a destructive force that not even the most powerful actor is safe from its impact. In this context, there are no "marginal" powers left in terms of destructive capacity. The acquisition by non-state actors of highly destructive weapons technology may have consequences entirely beyond the system's control capacity. Therefore, the time has come not for tactical steps based on petty interests, but for visionary strategic strides that will first gain control over the state of international (dis)order that represents an increasingly deepening trend, and then bring about a new order.

The Current Systemic Earthquake: Recurrence of History?

The unfortunate fact is that pretty well every element of the historic misfortune in the interwar era between the First and Second World Wars has been evident in the post-Cold War era. It is absolutely no coincidence that the geopolitical earthquakes that took place three-quarters of a century ago activated the same belts in the Afro-Eurasian center stretching from Eastern Europe to Central Asia, the Middle East to the sub-Sahara, North Africa to the Gulf, and as far as the Indian Ocean. And the backbone of a possible new order, as well as the interaction area of potential global-scale tension, lies precisely along this systemic earthquake's central fault line.

The geopolitical earthquake that materialized in the wake of the end of the Cold War has changed boundaries on this central belt, triggering a number of crises. The atmosphere of uncertainty created by this spiral of crises has taken an even more wide-reaching form as a result of the security earthquake, the impact of which has been so evident after 9/11. And the psychology of pessimism arising from the global economic crisis that followed close on its heels has turned into a phenomenon keenly felt by ordinary people. Fed by all this, the earthquake's impact in shaking every political structure in the world's most sensitive strategic regions, especially the Middle East, one by one; the fact that the international institutions and actors that had been expected to produce solutions have acted as onlookers captivated by a psychology of learned helplessness; and the decline of any capacity to intervene as areas of crisis expand day by day, laid the substructure for a systemic earthquake. The level that military technology has reached today brings to mind scenarios not of war, but apocalypse.

The extraordinary speed and momentum of communication capacities compared to the last century are rapidly diffusing this crisis and the state of mind that holds it to be beyond resolution. An even more striking and alarming aspect of the process is the increasingly widespread view of the international system's main players that the only solution to this crisis lies in exclusionist policies. In this context, President Trump's campaign rhetoric and the measures taken by his administration, extreme right-wing trends gaining prominence in Europe as alternative forms of governance, as well as the worldwide rise of autocratic and populist regimes, are making it harder to overcome this systemic crisis as they recall the experiences of the past century.

Just like a physical earthquake, this international systemic earthquake promotes a psychology in which every actor makes individual efforts to safeguard their own existence as they see all kinds of irregular or unlawful behavior to survive as legitimate. Everyone's definition of themselves, their own race, sect, and country as "first" and all other elements as contingent on this priority, is eerily reminiscent of the proliferation of exclusionist racist ideologies in the interwar period. Today, humankind will either rediscover its shared destiny and shared humanity, or we shall stumble over the cliff into an era of far greater destruction than even the Second World War.

The international system will become stable and predictable either by virtue of a certain state of order based on principles adopted by all players, or a state of balance based on different principles adopted between countries or groups of countries. The systemic earthquake scenario remains valid when neither of these two states of affairs applies and the very system expected to deliver order is itself shaken by an earthquake.

This systemic earthquake is the result neither of the rupture of a single fault line, nor a number of ruptures restricted to a single region. On the contrary, it has activated a number of fault lines at every level and on a global scale. In order to be able to grasp the true nature of this systemic crisis and come up with the necessary solutions, we have to comprehend its in-depth features over a widespread area.

This cycle of crises, which we call a systemic earthquake, can be overcome by means of a systemic perspective on an equally large scale. Otherwise, humankind could be left to confront far larger-scale tensions and wars in a state of wanton unpreparedness. We need to envision a systemic perspective of this kind as a formative three-staged process: (i) earthquake and aftershock damage assessment,

(ii) short-term emergency rehabilitation (crisis management), and (iii) a long-term, enduring process of reconstruction (establishment of a sustainable order).

In this framework, the following chapters of Part I of the book shall undertake earthquake damage assessments at national, regional, and global levels, while we shall consider the basic principles of rehabilitation processes and their fields of application in Part II – again, on national, regional, and global levels.

THE ROOTS OF WORLD (DIS)ORDER: GEOPOLITICAL, SECURITY, ECONOMIC, AND STRUCTURAL EARTHQUAKES IN THE POST-COLD WAR ERA

2

In terms of being able to grasp the scale and scope of the systemic earthquake we are experiencing today, it is crucial to gain an understanding of the spiral of ongoing crises and aftershocks in the wake of the geopolitical, security, economic, and structural earthquakes of the post-Cold War era. The international order today is subject to the impact not of a single process, but rather a number of intertwined processes.

Although the starting dates of these periods/processes are chronologically sequential, there is no neat sequence in which one ends and another begins. Rather, the ongoing impact of each maintains its individual effect as well as triggering more complex developments that impact one another. A case-by-case analysis of these periods and processes, and a consideration of their mutual interaction, will serve to lay the groundwork for an attempt to comprehend the uncertainties we face today and expose the *sine qua non* for a prospective new order.

Geopolitical Earthquake (1991)

The Cold War balance, itself a reflection of the internal logic of conventional geopolitics,[1] was based on a bipolar and relatively static equilibrium running along what the political scientist Nicholas

Spykman called the *Rimland* belt[2] – that is, the Eastern European–
Balkan–Black Sea–Caucasian–Caspian–West Asian–Central Asian–
Southeast Asian–East Asian line intersecting the entire length of Eurasia.
The division and boundaries of this belt's Eastern European–Balkan–
Black Sea–Caucasian–Central Asian line were drawn up at the end of
the Second World War; the East Asian line became apparent with the
Korean War in the 1950s, the Southeast Asian line with the Vietnam
and Cambodia wars of the 1960s and 1970s. In the absence of change
in the general bipolar equilibrium which constituted the natural makeup
of its structure, the *Rimland* belt's elucidation led to a conjunctural
stability that was not easily susceptible to change. This conjunctural
stability led to a state of affairs in which tensions between the two poles
on this line remained at the level of Low Intensity Conflict (LIC) without
the parties coming face-to-face in large-scale wars.[3]

    This state of stability continued for as long as the two poles
maintained their capacity to conduct reciprocal strategic moves.
When, as a power whose committed goal was to extend down from
the *Rimland* belt to South Asia and the Indian Ocean, the USSR's
assault on Afghanistan challenged this stability, the keystones in the
static geopolitical equilibrium began to come loose. The mass (and
papal) support gained by the Solidarity movement under Lech Wałesa
in Poland at more or less the same time as the invasion of Afghanistan
represented the first indications of activation on this belt. The USSR's
withdrawal from Afghanistan was not a mere military withdrawal;
it also implied the loss of one pole's ability to act geopolitically against
the other. Moreover, this geopolitical defeat showed the limits of the
Soviet economy's capacity to maintain a geopolitical rivalry. In fact
these developments in Afghanistan and Poland at the beginning of
the 1980s were the first portents of the major geopolitical earthquake
that would strike at the end of that decade and the beginning of the
1990s, the effects of which continue to be felt to this day. The accumulation of seismic energy in the bipolar system began along its fault lines'
most sensitive points, triggering successive earthquakes.

    The foreshocks of the geopolitical earthquake in the Cold War
era's static structure began with the *Glasnost and Perestroika* processes
in the USSR,[4] while dislocation on the fault line gained pace with
the fall of the Berlin Wall in 1989; the *coup de grâce* came with the
dissolution of the Warsaw Pact and the USSR in 1991. Together with
this impact, the rupturing of fault lines along the *Rimland* belt

stretching from the Baltic Sea to Eastern Europe, then over the Black Sea to the Caucasus, Central Asia, and East Asia, which had been viewed as the front line and the line of stability between two poles in the static environment of the Cold War era, began to morph one by one into crises that then turned into armed conflicts. The Moldova/Transdniester, Bosnia, Kosovo, Abkhazia, Ossetia, Chechnya, and Nagorno-Karabakh crises paved the way for large-scale human tragedies as well as causing the development of a severe disparity between international legal boundaries and *realpolitik* spheres of influence. Most recently, the Eastern Ukrainian and Crimean issues present clear evidence that the rupturing of these geopolitical fault lines is continuing.

Faced by these geopolitical shocks, efforts to establish a new order along this belt were carried out by means of four methods: (i) the restoration of Eastern European countries through European Union (EU) expansion and economic assistance, (ii) a security umbrella provided through North Atlantic Treaty Organization (NATO) expansion, (iii) UN security operations, and (iv) diplomatic processes conducted via structures such as the Organization for Security and Co-operation in Europe (OSCE) and the Council of Europe.

At the outset, the structural transformations carried out thanks to EU expansion-linked assistance were effective in restoring Eastern European countries that were undergoing palpable ideological, economic, and strategic change. However, harbingers of future developments were discernible in some Eastern European countries during the economic crisis; these developments would go on to test the durability of this restoration as they gained definition in the refugee crisis.

Although the security umbrella achieved through NATO expansion has thwarted the creation of a geopolitical vacuum in the space vacated by the Warsaw Pact, it has not been able to assume an effective role in resolving present crises. And while the Kosovo intervention may have achieved its immediate goals, the accession process of Kosovo – whose statehood is after all the political outcome of that intervention – to full UN membership has yet to be completed. The failure to achieve coordination between EU and NATO mechanisms during the Ukrainian crisis shows the limits of the 1990s effort to establish an order along an EU (economic resources)–NATO (security umbrella) axis. President Trump's stance on NATO has shaken confidence in the alliance's role as the founder of a new order at a time when NATO constitutes the most powerful multilateral intervention force in the international arena.

The relationship of coordination and complementarity between NATO's security umbrella and the expansion and structural transformation of the EU in the 1990s formed a bridge between economy and strategy.[5] However, the division within the EU caused by the US preference for unilateral intervention in 2003 during the invasion of Iraq and diverging interests in the wake of the 2008 economic crisis weakened this economic-political bridge between the EU and NATO.

The UN's role in crisis prevention and order-establishment was dealt a severe blow in the wake of the Bosnian War and the Srebrenica massacre. The separation of the UNSC permanent members into two blocs (United States, UK, and France vs. China and Russia) reveals the continuation of the Cold War psychology in new forms. The momentum this polarization has gained in various matters now constitutes the most significant impediment to international crisis management, especially on the Syrian issue.

Efforts to achieve a diplomatic resolution to ongoing crises through OSCE and Council of Europe processes have failed to yield a single successful outcome; indeed they have only led to the transformation of escalating tensions from acute to chronic. As the 2008 Georgian crisis showed, the question of which aftershock might reignite frozen crises depends entirely on prevailing conjunctural conditions.

From the perspective of the international order, we confront an alarming conclusion as we reexamine today's situation after a quarter-century of these geopolitical earthquakes. Just as a new world order in the manner promulgated by the first President Bush's ambitious "New World Order" slogan at the beginning of the 1990s has remained beyond reach, even small-scale crises along a geopolitical belt whose fault lines are rupturing continue to defy lasting resolution, because "perturbations that affect geopolitical equilibrium are constant and span the globe."[6]

This quarter-century has thus assumed the features of an "era of prolonged ceasefires" rather than an era of order. Today, Bosnia, Kosovo, Transdniester, Abkhazia, Ossetia, Nagorno-Karabakh, and Crimea are entirely at the mercy of ceasefires that might transmogrify into armed conflicts at any moment according to the concerned parties' day-to-day tactical calculations.

One should remember that ceasefires do not constitute a state of genuine peace and order. A ceasefire is a temporary arrangement made by the concerned parties the moment they see no benefit in continuing hostilities. Its lifespan is as long as the period of time that elapses until one of the parties reckons they can gain an advantage by resuming conflict. It is a period of keeping an eye out for opportunity, biding time, staying alert, and consolidating power. Unless and until this process can be converted into a permanent state of order through a formal peace agreement, it incubates the risk of instantaneous outbreaks of fresh conflict. Complacency and a sense of false security lead to entirely unforeseen wars springing up from protracted ceasefires of this kind. The enduring status of the Korean Peninsula as an area of potential conflict in spite of the passage of more than half a century since the end of active hostilities in the Korean War is the most striking example of this phenomenon. The Russo-Georgian war that blew up with such unexpected velocity in 2008, and the clashes around Nagorno-Karabakh that tend to escalate at regular intervals, demonstrate the fragility of a ceasefire-based geopolitical order. The way in which the ceasefire in Palestine, where peace remains elusive, can morph into conflict with heavy civilian casualties be it in Lebanon or in the Gaza Strip the moment Israel considers such a situation to be in its security interests is another noteworthy case in point.

In summary, even if the ceasefires put into effect to bring the aftershocks of the post-Cold War geopolitical earthquake under control have created a provisionally conflict-free situation, they have not formed the infrastructure of an order with the capacity to prevent the sudden emergence of fresh crises. Without a transformation of this "state of ceasefire" into a lasting state of order, it will be extremely hard to prevent the fragile ceasefires currently papering over the more comprehensive challenges brought by today's systemic earthquake from triggering conflict.

Security Earthquake (2001)

Even before they had got over the aftershocks of the geopolitical earthquake of the early 1990s, another earthquake profoundly shook the international system's key actors and structures' psychology, value/ interest priorities and resolution-finding methods: the security earthquake that emerged in the wake of the 9/11 terror attacks. This security earthquake led to a profound paradigm shift both at the heart of international relations practices and in the rhetoric and theory of international relations. Already existing tensions between power and legitimacy in international relations were further intensified. The rise of the neo-con current, which was attempting theoretically to fulfill the new era's practical requirements, took place in this field of tension in this period.[7]

The post-9/11 security earthquake wrought a psychological trauma in the US administration's political elite and American society as a whole at a time when it was assumed the United States would play the leading role in restructuring the international order thanks to its status as the absolute victor of the Cold War. Feeling secure in a continent which, apart from the possibility of a nuclear attack, remained far from areas of crisis, and having gauged its strategic psychology accordingly, the United States fell prey for the first time to the perception that it might not be secure even in its economic (New York), and political (Washington DC) capitals. This change can be observed in the differences between the political rhetoric of the first and second Presidents Bush. The US administration's psychology in the 1990s, attuned as it was to a vision of reordering the world in its own image, gave way to a psychology that prioritized security risks and threats. The US decision to treat 9/11 attacks as "an act of war" rather than "an act of terror" created a new widespread and comprehensive psychology which radically changed the international atmosphere and the priorities of decision-makers.

The concepts of "preemptive and preventive war" upon which the *National Security Strategy of the United States of America* document announced on 17 September 2002 was based widened the gap between national security interests and international law and led to the unlimited deployment of unilateral intervention.[8] The "we will not hesitate to act alone" expression in this text that summarized unilateral intervention brought about a debate that was absolutely critical to the international order. The strategic tension between these two different approaches was strikingly reflected in the title of Joseph S. Nye's book published the same year: *The Paradox of American Power: Why the World's Only Superpower Can't Go it Alone.*

The intellectual origins of this approach, which came to be defined as the *Bush Doctrine*, lay in the neo-conservative thinking that had arisen in the 1990s.[9] This new approach, which was centered on unilateral national security to which it linked all other international norms, acquired its legitimacy from the psychological atmosphere of security trauma evinced by 9/11. A new psychological wave that separated national security from the international order thus emerged.

This psychology spread to every corner of the world at the speed of a Hollywood movie. Every national and international structure began to adjust its own perspective and strategic posture in line with this new psychology. Thus, everyone fell into precisely the psychological trap desired by the planners of the 9/11 attacks, who aimed to terrorize the psychology of society as a whole by means of these attacks.

This psychology put threats before vision, feelings of vengeance before a comprehensive strategy, and micro-reactive measures before a constructive and enduring order. In terms of values, interests, and methods, the priorities changed completely. Indeed, the 9/11 attacks induced such a powerful shared reaction against terror on a global scale that it formed the basis of a sharply drawn global convention with very well defined priorities within which framework a comprehensive and participatory global strategy could have been developed. Yet instead of this, the new security-focused conjuncture shaped an environment that was appraised differently by each actor in the context of their own interests and perceptions of threat. The emergence of a methodological demarcation in which the concept and phenomenon of "terror," which needed to be seen as a shared threat defined in the context of objective criteria, gained an operational function in which each actor categorized groups that presented a threat to itself as "terrorist" while leaving others in a gray area, served to intensify this earthquake.

This methodology and its associated reactive attitude led to the adoption of an approach based on micro-punishments rather than any notion of establishing a new world order within which a global security system including the struggle against terror could be shaped. It was within this framework that military operations were launched against two countries: Afghanistan and Iraq.

Seventeen years further down the road, we need to make a cold-blooded assessment of the point to which these operations have brought us with respect to the struggle against terror and international security. In spite of the passage of seventeen years since the Afghanistan operation, carried out with broad international legitimacy under the umbrella of NATO, it seems that the internationally recognized government of Afghanistan has yet to gain nationwide control. Moreover, and following an operation that aimed to eradicate Al-Qaeda at its center, the terror organization has gained the capacity to expand its area of activity from within Africa as far as the Pacific islands. The killing of its leader Osama bin Laden in an operation personally directed by US President Obama has not facilitated the complete removal of this threat.

As for the Iraq War, its entire course, from the way it was realized to its implementation and its post-operation restructuring process, has led to outcomes that have shaken international and regional order and security to their core at every stage. Severe doubts have been raised concerning the legitimacy of the operation, which was based on the claim that the Iraqi government possessed weapons of mass destruction, even among those who supported the evidence for this claim at the time. The international legitimacy of the operation, which was not based on any UNSC resolution, has always been debated.

In conjunction with this operation, a process was undergone in which a country's institutions of state were entirely dissolved and a new state and bureaucracy constructed. Errors committed during this process have caused security vacuums, together with ethnic and sectarian clashes that have led to the emergence of a far more wide-ranging security problem on a national, regional, and global scale.[10] Millions of Iraqis have faced death or exile as a result of intense and bloody clashes.

Even more strikingly, the Iraq operation, which was posited on the struggle against Al-Qaeda as the authors of 9/11 gave rise to a power vacuum that lay the ground for the birth of Daesh, another terror organization that implemented far bloodier methods in the same territories. The operational power this organization, achieved from its incubation in prisons under American occupation such as Abu Ghraib and Bucca to its growth through the abuse of a Sunni populace that felt excluded throughout this period in Iraq, could only be fully grasped upon their capture of Mosul. This organization was thus able to reach a level of impact that threatened the entire regional security structure in the vacuum created by the disintegration of the nation-state structures. In turn, the process of disintegration undergone in Iraq had a domino effect, spreading to other countries and facilitating the emergence of non-state actors who recognized none of the norms of international law and the establishment of their own spheres of influence. Daesh's global network gave it the ability to organize large-scale terror attacks in globally central cities such as Istanbul, London, Paris, Brussels, etc.

To summarize, contrary to the development of a new international security structure in the wake of a security earthquake following a geopolitical earthquake which had itself shaken the international order to its core, the methods employed served only to expand and deepen these threats' areas of impact. It is very hard to claim that we are in a better condition today than we were in 2001, be it from the perspective of terror or the international security structure. The fundamental reason for this is the choice of a micro- and tactical punishment method over the construction of a new global strategic architecture in the wake of the security earthquake we have experienced. Engaging only with the mosquitoes has unfortunately failed to drain the swamp; indeed, it has only provoked a more intense swarm of mosquitoes. What is needed is the extermination of the mosquitoes and the establishment of a new security environment to drain the security swamps.

Economic Earthquake (2008)

In 2008 the international order was obliged to confront the shockwaves of history's most widespread global economic crisis without having been able to bring the aftershocks of these geopolitical and security earthquakes under control. A crisis that began with what looked like a sectoral crisis in sub-prime mortgage defaults soon intensified into a crisis of far wider scope and impact. Overconfidence in market self-regulation and reliance on very complex risk management techniques led to excessive lending by banks. Sophisticated financial engineering, which distorted the risk perception of investors, fueled already extravagant financial leveraging. Finally, the financial system, which had been contaminated by bad collateralized debt and derivative products collapsed. The crisis created a domino effect that had a severe impact on all economic structures and, with rising unemployment, on the life of society and individuals, finally intensifying to find its reflection in the political arena. A crisis that started in the United States soon spread to the EU economic basin and the developing world economies. After the banks, the evisceration of countries' abilities to roll over their loans began to ring alarm bells through a domino effect from "too big to save financial institutions" to "too big to save national economies."

The unparalleled scale of this crisis's depth and scope revealed both problems and needs with respect to national, regional, and global economic structures. In this context, we need to consider the intensification of four factors of significance to the structural transformation of the international economic architecture.

The first factor concerns the paradigmatic methodology in approaching the international economic order and related issues. The history of world economics has witnessed different methodologies in this sense. The Alexandrian, Roman, Chinese, and Ottoman imperial traditions strove to protect the economic substructure of their political dominance by keeping trade flows within their area of control within the geographic continuity they had achieved through political order and stability. Colonial empires managed overseas economic production-consumption relations by creating a hegemonic order over the world economy through central planning. The Bretton Woods system that coincided with the post-Second World War dismantlement of the colonial empires and its accompanying economic institutionalization led to an international organizational concept based on the influence of a dominant actor. This is the framework within which the dollarization of international financial flows occurred and the US power of veto in the IMF and the World Bank, which was established to coordinate development and finance structures, was recognized. This general framework was largely maintained throughout the post-Cold War period.

In terms of demonstrating the level of interaction in international economic operations, the global economic earthquake clearly exposes the fact that this centralized method has reached its limits. The speed and interaction of today's international economic relations necessitates an operational approach that includes multistate, international institutions and companies, rather than a single-center administrative paradigm. Yet such an operational change has so far been impossible to achieve; most decisions continue to be taken by conventional methods.

The second factor concerns a restructuring of the international economic order's architecture as a natural consequence of this methodological change. The positive impact of world economic growth in the 1990s masked the need for reform and the architecture of the international economic order, itself the product of the Bretton Woods system, was largely maintained. The expansion of globalization in the economic field more or less represented the high-water mark of the triumph of capitalism over non-Western systems. The term "Washington Consensus," which was first used by the British economist John Williamson in 1989, became a modern version of the Ten

Commandments for the global economic order.[11] Between the fall of the Berlin Wall in 1989 and the onset of the global financial crisis in 2007, the ratio of cross-border financial flows to world output quadrupled, reaching 21 percent; trade increased from 39 percent to 59 percent of world total gross domestic product (GDP); the number of expatriates jumped by more than a quarter.[12] Foreign direct investments remodeled the value chain of economic production, and the reign of multinational companies began.

This positive atmosphere led people to overlook the possibility of any crises emerging and the need to rebuild the economic-political order. The only fresh element was the formation of the G20, which included some developing economies in an effort to achieve broader-based financial policy coordination in the wake of the 1997 East Asia crisis. The 2008 global economic crisis showed how correct this step was; G20 meetings were elevated to the level of annual heads of state and government summits.

However, in spite of this positive step and claims during the first stages of the crisis that a new financial and economic architecture would be formed, it is hard to say that much distance has been covered in this regard. Apart from certain symbolic arrangements giving a comparative boost to developing countries' shares and voice in the IMF, structures acquired from the Cold War have for the most part been maintained while more wide-ranging reforms in line with governance principles taking the possibilities and risks associated with globalization into account have not been realized.

As for positive steps taken in the G20 framework, although this platform has gained greater representation and visibility, it has proven harder for assessments and resolutions taken on the voluntary, informal and consensus-based principles of summits to be effectively implemented. The absence of any functional institutional mechanisms to follow up resolutions taken by the G20 (especially the P5 countries) renders their concern and reservations about any shift in the ultimate decision-making mechanism in the international system away from the UNSC an obstruction to this platform playing a constructive role in the reconstruction of the global economic architecture. In most cases, global-scale consensus resolutions remain mere gestures of goodwill.

For example, resolutions taken at more or less every summit to overcome economic recession by freeing up trade, the growth of which had fallen back to the same rate as economic growth after a pre-crisis period of growing twice as fast as the world economy, have not been implemented. And the ever-growing protectionist trend looks set to induce world trade to grow at a slower rate than the world economy in the coming period. Domestic political concerns come into play when summit decisions revert to national capitals; resolutions on matters that require political will are sidelined or forgotten. Progress in the field of global financial architecture has focused on non-political technical procedures. In this context the establishment and functionality of the FSB (Financial Stability Board) represents a rare positive example.

One of the striking examples is the protectionist reflexes evidenced by customs duties and investment restrictions increasingly applied by Trump against China, paving the way for an approach based on shared global economic interests to be replaced by one in which every country prioritizes its own particular interests. The spread of such an approach promises to bring the efficacy of platforms such as the G20 into question. Just as the UN system suffers the negative impacts of the spread of the concept of a balance of power system in which every player has an influence in accordance with its raw power, an international economic-political environment where every actor strives only to maximize its own economic interests narrows the field of effectiveness of international economic institutions, especially the G20.

In addition, protectionist policies should not be seen as being limited to economic measures alone. One should keep in mind that the issue of protectionism is not of its nature restricted to the economic field; rather, it is a question of a method and mindset whose impact may spread to every field. Protectionist reflexes seen as being an essentially economic measure and method cannot be restricted to this area alone and begin to exert an influence in political and cultural fields over time. Looked at from this perspective, Trump's overall inward-looking, exclusionary political psychology and culture is an integral part of his protectionist economic approach.

The progressive spread of this increasingly exclusionary approach to all fields, along with its step-by-step spread to other countries from the United States, which claims to be the locomotive force of the global economy, will bring about the universalization of a singular exclusionary approach instead of the development of an understanding of a common global order. In such an international psychological atmosphere, the development of a concept of a global-scale order is beyond the realms of possibility.

The third factor is the profound impact the global economic crisis has had on the success story of intensifying regional economic integration processes. In this regard, the domino effects of developments in the Eurozone, which have profoundly shaken not only financial and economic structures but political stability as well, have exposed the operationally interactive and interdependent nature of the global economy for all to see. Rather than this process serving to boost growth through the adoption of positive approaches and methods, it has only caused the crisis to spread at an unexpected rate.

The EU, which became a region of prosperity with the expansion and deepening policies of the 1990s, succeeded in maximizing countries' comparative advantages via a single market, common central bank, and common unit of currency. While some European countries developed service sectors such as tourism and detached themselves from the manufacturing sphere, others (especially Germany) became central manufacturing hubs, just as other countries particularly in Central and Eastern Europe formed into peripheral manufacturing support zones. As the EU economy grew and appeared to have a significant functional division of labor advantage, countries that were focused on non-manufacturing areas found it difficult to resist this crisis with their national capacity. The political instability caused especially by contracting employment levels then led to social upheavals. The profound crisis in EU countries focused minds on the burdens rather than the advantages of EU membership, which in a sense laid the psychological groundwork for a process that would ultimately turn into Brexit. This global economic-political earthquake paved the way for its metamorphosis into an EU earthquake.

The fourth factor is that the global economic-political earthquake has given rise to outcomes that have brought nation-states' areas of sovereignty and legitimacy into question. Policy-makers seem quite willing to assume the benefits of globalization, but reluctant and sometimes quite hostile to releasing their grip over national policies, in part fearing a backlash from voters who have the final word in democratic societies. The introduction of EU control mechanisms over financial and budgetary issues that had for centuries been seen as within the purview of nation-states' sovereignty has induced serious debate. German–Greek tensions during the crisis were mirrored in the political rhetoric of these debates. While in return for the assistance given, as a result of Eurozone financial union, to bail out Greek financial structures

Germany demanded increased financial auditing and control and a narrowing in the budget deficit by various means (mainly a reduction in salaries), the Greek government saw such affairs as integral to its own political sovereignty and steered to a neo-nationalistic reaction. This played a significant role in the weakening of mainstream political parties in Greece and Syriza's rise to power.

In fact, the significance of Greek–German tension went beyond the stance of either country; it spilled over into the question of the delicate balance between economic integration and national sovereignty. Each party weighed up this process from the perspective of its own priorities. With the EU expansion process having gained Germany a huge market plus low production costs for its large-scale industrial manufacturing capacity, as well as the financial depth granted by the Eurozone's financial integration, the country begrudged paying the costs, preferring the closure of national fiscal deficits throughout the crisis.

On the other hand Greece, whose EU membership had benefited the national economy through an extraordinary flow of EU funds and the prospect of strengthening its banking system as part of the process of financial deepening, underwent a period in which it more or less completely withdrew from the area of manufacturing to indulge in the luxury of "production-free consumption" while seeking to cover up the consequent imbalances with statistical data; when the economic crisis exposed the cost of this policy, the country then sought to escape the cost of salary and budgetary pressures via a rhetoric of national sovereignty. All these debates constitute a litmus test that reveals how the area of national sovereignty can cause clashes during periods of crisis. It is still not clear what course this debate is going to take.

In brief, just as some of the damage wrought by the 2008 economic-political earthquake is beyond repair, it has also proved impossible either to bring the factors that caused this crisis to intensify under control, or to develop the doctrinal, methodological, and structural elements of a new international order. Increasingly populist policies propounded by President Trump – with their protectionist, inward-looking, populist, and unilateralist approach – constitute this economic-political earthquake's aftershocks that possess the characteristics to trigger fresh earthquakes. Thus, the rising unilateralist exclusionism may have an even further negative impact on these earthquakes due to the fact that "political ideology always affects economic policy and priorities."[13]

Structural Earthquake (2011)

Even before the Middle East region had been able to recover from the aftershocks of the earthquakes that had already occurred, every geopolitical, geoeconomic, and geocultural fault line ruptured to produce an across-the-board tremor harboring the impacts of all the previous quakes that made the region the scene of the bloodiest civil conflicts, tensions, and wars in the past hundred years. This earthquake was not restricted to any nation-state, regional sector, or area and paved the way for far-reaching structural devastation.

The comprehensive structural earthquake in the Middle East that accompanied the Arab Spring brought with it the most profound period of upheaval the region has experienced since the First World War, because it swept before it every stratum of society in Yemen, in Iraq, in Syria, and in Libya – from remote villages and tribes to their capital cities. In terms of scope it is cataclysmic, because unlike previous regional crises it has not been limited to one area or group of countries, but has taken the entire region by storm. For example, while the Iran–Iraq War of the 1980s only directly affected those countries and their neighbors, the emergence of Daesh with the collapse of the state structures in Iraq and Syria constituted a threat to the whole region from the countries of North Africa as far as Yemen, even beyond the Middle East and North Africa (MENA) region – including Europe and North America.

In fact, the demands and upright justifications given voice by the regional dynamism of the early Arab Spring generated a sense of enormous hope. When the self-immolation of the unemployed Tunisian university graduate and street vendor Mohamed Bouazizi triggered a well-warranted popular reaction directed at a universally felt global economic crisis as well as autocratic regimes that had lost all touch with the people, this mobilization gained support on a national, regional, and global level. There were no signs either of Daesh, or other terror groups, or ethnic and sectarian clashes, or of civil war in a liberated environment that subsequently mobilized mainly young people to form mass demonstrations against Mubarak in Tahrir Square, Qaddafi in Benghazi, and Assad in Homs to demand a participatory political structure, a flourishing economic life, and a state of law based on equal opportunities and fair income distribution.

We may talk about psychological, cultural, technological, economic, and political factors that mobilized the mass of people taking heartfelt part in these civil movements. The fundamental concept from the psychological perspective was the search for dignity. For the mass of people, who for decades had suffered the indignities of subjugation to autocratic regimes at the national level coupled with humiliation vis-à-vis Israel at the regional level, this movement was perceived as their chance to take ownership of their own dignity and destiny. In this context, the self-immolation of a young street vendor in Tunisia in reaction to police oppression was seen as an inspiring symbol of dignity.

The cultural factor, which demanded a free environment against an autocratic control that had insinuated itself into every area of life, was very much in line with the demands of the mass of people in Central and Eastern Europe in the post-Cold War period; indeed, looked at from this perspective it might even be counted as a delayed reaction. Both the expression of these demands and their reflection in the social arena gained huge momentum through extraordinary changes in the technological factor; the tools that assured these demands' social activation were social communication platforms such as the internet, Facebook, and Twitter. Autocratic regimes' conventional capacity for media control was simply not applicable to social media. As visible economic factors, rapidly rising youth unemployment brought by the global economic crisis combined with the quest for fair income distribution formed the basis upon which the masses demanded a better life.

The demand for political reform (which is both the source and the objective of all these demands) concerns the internal nature of Cold War structures whose ideological characteristics struggled to adapt to new conditions. Cold War regimes lacking ideological flexibility and functional productivity sought to maintain their existence through appeals to an inward-looking sense of social solidarity (*asabiyyah*) based on family, tribe, clan, and sect. The concentration of economic and political power of the Mubarak family in Egypt, the Qaddafis in Libya, the Assads and Makhloufs in Syria, and the Salehs in Yemen, and the attempts to cloak this concentration in an aura of heroism based on Ba'athist ideology and Arab nationalism, made it impossible for these political regimes to reform themselves to accommodate new conditions; this paved the way for confrontation between these regimes and the masses.

Indeed, it is as though all these factors emerged as the upshot of attempts to continue just as if the conditions pertaining to Cold War ideological, cultural, economic, and political structures still applied. In other words, the Cold War mentality carried on in the Middle East although it had ended in other regions a quarter-century before. The inability of these structures to renew themselves was a primary cause of the Arab Spring, and then, as this spring turned to winter, paved the way for the disintegration of all structures.

Contrary to expectations that the Arab Spring, which began with such great hope, would lead to the establishment of a stable national and regional order, it followed a destructive rather than a constructive course under the impact of a number of factors. We may talk of three critical thresholds and periods/processes. The first phase was shaped by the successive revolutionary movements of 2011 and resulted in the transfer of autocratic leaders' responsibilities to provisional governments by various means. Sections of society that desired change were encouraged in this phase; political, diplomatic, and military support was provided when necessary. However, it proved impossible to create an approach for the Middle East similar to the comprehensive strategy developed in Central and Eastern Europe in the 1990s to help societies to adapt to the post-Cold War era.

Societies without any previous experience of this kind of political process were caught unprepared to deal with such a comprehensive process of change. At the beginning of 2011 during Turkey's Presidency of the Committee of Ministers of the Council of Europe, we developed an action plan with Secretary-General Thorbjørn Jagland with a view to contributing to the transition process; in this framework we paid a joint visit to Tunisia, which had a leadership status in this process, where we held discussions with all parties to the revolution. Considering the positive contribution the Council of Europe had made to the process of structural change in Central and Eastern European countries in the 1990s, the perceived need for such steps was clear. Nonetheless, no international body, no regional actor, nor any individual country was able to put forward a comprehensive strategy designed to achieve the peaceful evolution of this process through the formation of new structures.

In spite of all these deficiencies this phase passed relatively peacefully and countries held elections for permanent governments in 2012 without difficulty. Although there was a degree of tension, elected governments started their terms of office in these countries, except in Syria. At the same time this constituted the beginning of a major test in terms of fulfilling the expectations of the revolutions that had occurred. At this point there were two principal challenges. The first concerned the maintenance of the internal unity of the revolutions' leading groups. Groups that had stood shoulder to shoulder against autocratic regimes lost their internal unity as they entered a power struggle without the prior development of any culture of peaceful political competition whatsoever. The second challenge concerned the question of meeting the urgent expectations of the pro-revolution masses for freedom, security, and prosperity. New administrations without the slightest experience of government were left alone on this challenge too; obliged to struggle against the opposition thrown up by *ancien régime* elements in their efforts to bring back the old order under other guises, they were unable successfully to deliver political and economic reforms that might meet expectations.

In the absence of the necessary economic infrastructure, security platform, and an appropriate international environment, this kind of transition process is in fact extremely hard to achieve. An examination of two successful transition processes from European history clearly shows the prerequisites. Europe's post-Second World War transition from the prevailing totalitarian structures to democratic structures was only made possible by means of the security platform that emerged with the formation of NATO coupled with funds such as Marshall Plan aid that brought wide-ranging economic reforms to life. And the post-Cold War transformation of Central and Eastern Europe was only feasible with the funds and the security umbrella afforded by the EU and NATO expansion processes.

As these cases show, this kind of comprehensive structural transformation requires the existence of three main elements – namely the provision of a proper security environment, material support to meet the costs of structural transformation, and an appropriate regional and international state of affairs. The inexperienced administrations that came to power in the wake of the Arab Spring lacked all three. Domestic security structures left over from previous regimes refused to provide the necessary support; as for the international community, it proved incapable of developing an overarching security strategy. Rather than developing new models to meet the inherent costs of this process, international and regional institutions and actors busied themselves with speculative efforts based on scenarios about how energy resources were to be distributed in this new era. The support that was provided, especially by Turkey, remained grossly insufficient to meet the gargantuan costs of restructuring. In the case of Libya, which could have been a major success story if only funds had been used rationally, even the country's own funds that had been frozen in international banks could not be deployed for the benefit of the Libyan people.

Following the difficulties experienced at these two thresholds, three developments that took place in the summer of 2013 served radically to alter the nature and course of the Arab Spring and turn limited fault line ruptures into an all-embracing structural earthquake. The first was the rapid progress of Daesh, which started life as an Iraq-based terror organization, in unifying the chaotic environments in Iraq and Syria, with their complex ethnic and sectarian composition, to seize control of both countries' sensitive security belt along the Aleppo–Raqqa–Mosul line. This development served to change the nature of the Arab Spring, transforming tension between the regime and an opposition that had risen on the back of demands for freedom into terror organization/regime tension, as well as terror organization/opposition tension. This naturally favored regimes that wanted to keep Cold War remnant governments in power, and faced regional and international actors with a choice between two evils rather than the formation of a new order of stability. In this context, the logistic support given to Daesh in this period through the bombing of anti-Daesh FSA (Free Syrian Army) units by the Syrian regime, which did not shy from using weapons of mass destruction against the civilian populations of Damascus, Homs, and Aleppo, is highly meaningful. Daesh's bloody acts of terror then spilled over from Syria to target major European cities, diverting international actors' attentions away from active efforts to establish a new and stable regional order towards a reactive struggle against terror.

The second significant development was the July 2013 *coup d'état* in Egypt, which exposed the fragility of freshly elected administrations and paved the way for autocratic *ancien régime* elements in almost every country to regroup and launch counterrevolutionary actions. The recognition by the international community of the coup in Egypt, the locomotive of Arab politics in every sense, signified its preference for static autocratic stability over dynamic democratic stability and dealt a heavy blow to the psychological and social resistance of those in the field calling for peaceful democratic change.

The third critical development at this threshold was the failure to impose any sanctions on the Syrian regime when in August 2013, emboldened by the signals it received from the other two developments, it crossed every red line to use chemical weapons against its own citizens. In its total destruction of the deterrent effect of international law and institutions, the failure after Srebrenica to punish this flagrant war crime effectively demolished the moral foundations of the regional and international order. In encouraging autocratic politicians on the basis that they shall never be subject to sanction regardless of their actions, this development also means their backers have a free hand. The evident acceleration in the activities of pro-regime countries and their militias in the field following this development is a natural outcome of the signals emanating from all these developments.

After crossing this critical threshold in the summer of 2013, the Arab Spring entered midwinter. The earthquake's destructive impact uprooted countries, institutions, cities, boundaries, borders, and civil groups, driving them to ruin. A consideration of the geopolitical, geoeconomic, and geocultural dimensions of this all-pervasive destruction in such a framework is of great significance in terms of understanding the damage wrought by this quake, and the capacity for rehabilitation.

The intensity of this earthquake has shaken the entire geopolitics of the Middle East, which in any case rests on exceptionally sensitive and unnatural structures. In my work *Strategic Depth*, first published in 2001, I seek to analyze changes in the post-Cold War geopolitical structure and describe the geopolitically unnatural formation of Middle East boundaries; how the removal of any stone in this structure, which brings to mind a very shoddily built wall, will unleash a domino effect to cause the entire edifice to collapse; and how the principle of immutable boundaries is thus a prerequisite for stability in the Middle East.[14] Unfortunately, so many years after the writing of this book, the dislodging of not just one but many stones first made the sensitive geopolitics of the Middle East even more fragile, and then threw it into utter disarray.

This geopolitical disintegration has been realized on several planes. First, and starting with Iraq, areas emerged that were beyond the control of the central government in the nation-state structures; areas of de facto power were formed. Today at least five countries (Iraq, Syria, Lebanon, Libya, and Yemen) continue to suffer the dire impact of this geopolitical fragmentation. In addition, an uncontrolled porosity has arisen on the Iraq–Syria, Syria–Lebanon, and Libya–Egypt boundaries where de facto buffer zones have been established. This geopolitical earthquake has been far bloodier and more traumatic than the one that took place in the Eurasian belt stretching from Eastern Europe to Central Asia in the 1990s. Today, the establishment of a new regional order of stability is prevented by the absence of interlocutors with control over the geopolitical area.

Looked at from the geopolitical perspective, national economic areas delineated by certain geographic regions have been lost. In this context, the domestic economic channels and tools of commercial transaction in countries in geopolitical fragmentation have become inoperative; their fiscal and financial integrity has dissolved. Countries' natural resources and infrastructures have been ruined; urban economies have suffered large-scale damage. Natural production areas have been debased by the fact that the agriculturally and industrially productive human factor has joined a refugee flow.

The geopolitical earthquake has given rise to a catastrophe that sadly serves to complete the picture. Cities like Baghdad, Damascus, Mosul, Basra, Aleppo,[15] Homs, and Sana'a, whose centuries-old multicultural, multidenominational, multifaith, and multiethnic personality gave them all the trappings of a living museum of the legacy of humankind, have had their very souls destroyed as their cultural legacies have been shredded.

The mosques, churches, synagogues, mausoleums, libraries, historic monuments, and ancient cities over which these countries claimed ownership have been irreparably damaged by aerial and terror attacks. This geocultural destruction has clearly been more ruinous even than the Mongols' sacking of Baghdad in 1258. As painful, perhaps even more painful, than the physical and material geocultural devastation is the slaughter and expulsion of the geocultural human resource. Today the region is witnessing the largest flow of refugees in its history. Instead of staunching their wounds, international actors and institutions strive only to keep this flow of people away from their own backyards. As countries in the region, especially Turkey, which is sheltering more than 3 million refugees, grapple with this tragedy, innocent people in the region are forced to pay the price of international (dis)order.

No doubt, this structural earthquake in the Middle East will reshape the geopolitical, geoeconomic, and geocultural texture of the region. It is set to be a highly dynamic, severe, and challenging process because, as Richard Falk correctly emphasizes, "the recent upheavals in the Arab World optimistically greeted as the Arab Spring suggested the limits of hard power as a means of permanently oppressing people, but also the strength of counter revolutionary tendencies to restore the established political and economic order, no matter how corrupted, unfair and ineffective it had become."[16]

3 SYSTEMIC EARTHQUAKE: FRAGILE NATIONAL, REGIONAL, AND GLOBAL STRUCTURES

The intense release of energy by these successive earthquakes and the aftershocks they have triggered has rendered seismic dynamism systemic. The most significant feature of this systemic earthquake is the "fragility" that it has fostered in every component of the system. Fragility is defined as the loss of internal harmony and resistance in the structural components of any order as a result of earthquake impacts.

In this context, fragility constitutes a period and process of transition between a state of order, and the collapse that absolute disorder entails. If the elements of fragility can be rehabilitated during this transition process, they can return to a state of order by regaining their internal harmony and their capacity to withstand quakes. Suffering further damage at each blow, and after losing all their capacity to resist, fragile elements that do not undergo such a process of rehabilitation collapse, sometimes gradually, sometimes by surprise.

The domino effect that exerts itself on other structures struggling to survive unexpected collapse occurs far more rapidly and decisively. In this respect, the collapse of all the structures that had been rendered fragile via a rapid domino effect between 1989 and 1991, a collapse that began by surprise and spread from the Warsaw Pact to the Soviet states, and from the Soviet states to nation-states during the process that ended the Cold War, constitutes a striking example. And finally, the successive collapse of structures that had become fragile over decades during and after the Cold War in the Arab Spring that unfolded in the aftermath of the surprise collapse in Tunisia, represents a further example of the domino effect unleashed by the collective fragility caused by systemic earthquakes; the impacts of these collapses continue. Structures unable to rehabilitate themselves in this process remain liable to the new, unanticipated collapse.

An analysis at the national, regional, and global levels of the fragilities caused by the systemic earthquake process currently under way is of critical importance with respect to developing the ability to conduct a damage assessment of these fragilities, preparing for the possibilities of a surprise collapse, and taking the necessary measures for rehabilitation.

The National Dimension of the Systemic Earthquake: Fragility in Nation-State Structures

Post-Cold War earthquakes have transformed the nature of nationhood, nation-states, and national politics, which constitute the building blocks of the international system.[1] With the Cold War triumph of Western democracy over the Soviet system in the 1990s, national structures adopted approaches that promoted liberal/democratic values in the political field, free-market economics in the economic field, and pluralism in the cultural field. While these approaches were put into practice as a transformation strategy in Central and Eastern Europe, they met resistance in other regions, especially the Middle East, because of the persistence of a Cold War culture.

The three pillars of democracy, free markets, and pluralism, which it was assumed would dominate national structures in the post-Cold War order, began to falter one by one in subsequent quakes. The security earthquake that accompanied 9/11 gave rise to the adoption of an approach focusing more on security than freedom based on introverted defense reflexes and control policies in nation-state structures, especially in the United States, which was recognized as the leading proponent of these values on account of its status as the superpower of the bloc that had emerged as the victor of the Cold War. The state-of-emergency psychology that developed as a reaction to the terror threat in the United States gradually spread by domino effect to other nation-states. In particular, authoritarian regimes saw this new psychology as an opportunity to legitimize their forms of government, leading to both rhetoric and measures that further narrowed the field of freedom.

As a result of the impact of the 2008 global economic crisis, instead of free-market principles in national economies and trade liberalization-based policies of interdependence in the international economy, a new state of mind held sway in which every national economy promoted its own self-preservation instinct and trade restrictions grew. The transformation from 1990s expectations that everyone would take a greater share on the back of growth in the world economy, to expectations of crisis, has driven national economies as a whole, as well as the economic-political elites within these economies as influential groups within the whole, to concentrate their efforts on solidifying their own economic power.

The self-preservation impulse has driven a process in which national economies have embarked on monopolization or oligopoly-based resource concentration instead of competition-based productivity.[2] And national political choices are beginning to fall under the sway of this economic reflex. The integration of such a state of mind with a pre-existing security psychology has induced the emergence of an economic-political understanding focused on security rather than freedom and liberal values.

Already injured by the 9/11 security earthquake, the cultural/political pluralism dimension has been entirely flattened by the regional earthquake that began with the Arab Spring. Internal tensions, wars, and massacres have weakened nation-state citizenship identities, culminating in the increased prominence of communal ethnic and sectarian identities and, over time, their taking on the characteristics of the ultimate safe haven. For example, a Syrian Alawite feels a stronger affiliation with a Lebanese or Iraqi Shiite than with a Syrian Sunni, while the Sunni masses excluded from the political arena in Iraq and Syria and living in fear of extermination have begun to give their transborder sectarian identity precedence over national identity.

Thus, rather than a new, fruitful, and expansive perspective of cultural pluralism synthesizing modern principles of freedom and human rights with ancient cultural diversity, events have given way to a narrow, sectarian and exclusionist cultural singularism. It is not only nation-states, but the cities, neighborhoods, and villages where diverse ethnic and sectarian communities coexist, that have been torn apart. In this sense, the Daesh that destroys Palmyra, the Shabiha militia that massacres Sunnis in an unremitting effort to change demographic balances through ethnic slaughter, and their backers, are actually adherents of the same dogmatic and sectarian approach. Their common feature is an endeavor to establish cultural and political dominance by eradicating cultural pluralism.

These developments are not exclusive to the Middle East. The 2017 acceleration of the pace of the decades-long ethnic cleansing against the Rohingya Muslims in Myanmar showed once again that these exclusionary policies are not restricted to one region.[3] Moreover, the fact that this ethnic cleansing, which has led to one of the greatest human tragedies of the past decades has taken place under the watch of Aung San Suu Kyi, whose non-violent struggle for democracy and human rights had earned her a Nobel Peace Prize, is a striking indication of the fragility of national structures when confronted with exclusionary policies. This ethnic cleansing, ruthlessly carried out in the face of UN resolutions in a manner that has impacted the whole of Southeast Asia through its creation of a flood of refugees, is noteworthy in terms of showing the regional consequences of fragilities that exist on the national level.

The refugee flows unleashed by all these exclusionary policies not only impact the national structures that are at the source of the crisis, but also have a profound effect on the national structures of the countries into which the refugees flow. In this context, recent developments in Europe are sounding alarm signals. The refugee crisis has intensified a sectarian and dogmatic exclusionism that was already on the rise in Europe. Refugees arriving for entirely humanitarian reasons have begun to be presented as a new barbarian horde or the "new Jews" destroying the identity of "Christian/White Europe" by racist movements that see Europe as a purely Christian/White continent.[4] Striving to make people forget that Islam has an authentic European identity not only in the present day but going back in history, an identity that stretched across the continent of Europe from Andalusia to the Balkans, these dogmatic trends, just like their equivalents in the Middle East, have engendered a political rhetoric that portrays cultural pluralism as a threat.

Movements that seek to scapegoat different cultural communities can emerge in any society and any period of crisis. The difference this time around is that these trends may emanate from a marginal socioeconomic group gaining the power to determine mainstream politics and deliver the necessary mass support. The election of Trump, whose campaign rhetoric showcased his vision of the United States as a White Anglo-Saxon Protestant (WASP) nation rather than a common homeland for groups with different religious, sectarian, and ethnic identities,[5] Le Pen's adoption of the purification of Europe around a Christian and White identity as a fundamental political principle,[6] and her emergence in France, and that of Wilders in Holland, as among the leading candidates for government, demonstrate that even countries recognized as the cradle of the liberal cultural pluralism that is seen as the founding principle of the post-Cold War order, are now under threat.

All these developments have been accompanied by significant challenges to the nature, legitimacy, and institutional functioning of nation-states. The main challenge to their nature concerns areas of domination and control capacity. The distinguishing feature behind the emergence of a nation-state onto the stage of history is its sovereign control over a certain territory. All these earthquakes have severely eroded the pillars of command that keep nation-states standing. A grave discrepancy between the UN-recognized borders of a number of nation-states and those nation-states' actual areas of sovereign control has arisen in the period from the first earthquake in the Eurasian belt to the time of major regional devastation in the Middle East. The nation-state authorities of Ukraine, Georgia, Azerbaijan, Moldova, Afghanistan, Iraq, Syria, Libya, Somalia, and Yemen have been deprived of their actual power to exercise sovereignty over all or part of their territory as a result of occupations or internal conflicts. As well as the ever-present risk of a new hot crisis, this divergence between recognized borders and areas of sovereign control renders it hard to establish a regional or global order based on the nation-states that remain the international system's keystones.

In addition, as witnessed in recent cases in Scotland, Catalonia, and the Kurdish Regional Government in Iraq, referendum demands for the division of nation-state structures and their potential domino effect have the potential to present fresh challenges to nation-states' areas of sovereignty. The sovereignty problem of the Palestinian State, recognized by the UNSC as a non-member state, is critically important both to resolution of the Palestinian issue and the reconstruction of regional and global order. The establishment of a sovereign Palestinian State will serve to remove an abnormality from the region as well as reviving hopes for the future of the international order by resolving an issue with global-scale ramifications.

The issue of nation-states' sovereignty and their capacity to control their own economies has taken on a new dimension in the wake of post-global economic crisis developments in Europe. One of the main parameters in the formation of nation-states is the right to sovereign control over financial policies, including the right to raise taxes. In this context, salary and budgetary conditions laid down in return for assistance, especially with respect to countries like Greece facing severe financial turbulence, have triggered controversy. Arguments over whether Greece's fiscal policy would be decided by the elected government in Athens, or Brussels, moved from the realm of technical issues to that of national honor and sovereignty. It is inevitable that the subject of national sovereignty, little discussed when it and other matters share in the fruits of economic development, shall continue to raise its head in a psychologically intense fashion during periods of crisis.

Recent developments have also brought critical facedowns with respect to concepts of the legitimacy of governance in nation-states. The legitimacy or otherwise of autocratic one-party and single-leader governments has in any case been under discussion ever since the Cold War. The legitimacy of governments that had come to power without popular consent through coups within the elite or the governing party became the subject of serious debate with the Arab Spring. The future stance of administrations like the Syrian regime, officially recorded by the UN as having used weapons of mass destruction against its own people, on issues of national and international legitimacy has become an open question.

However, an even more crucial issue faces the international order today, one that appears to be on an ever-rising trend in the political structure – namely populism – and the course that it will take. Setting off in the guise of autocratic populism then to become a pattern in the international system, this development has now begun to impact democratic societies as well. Certain common features may be identified in phenomena that have come to embody this trend such as Trump's Muslim travel ban and his attitude to the Mexican border, the anti-refugee stance of a number of European leaders, and the rhetoric, policies, and policy proposals of leadership candidates like Le Pen and Wilders.

This approach has promoted a concept of legitimacy based on an impulsive emotional identity rather than a rational legitimacy founded on a process of argument in the formation of political power and governments. Political rhetoric and discourse are thus dominated more by efforts to shape the mass perception of existential threats than any rational vision. First of all, a threat perception is developed; then this perception is whipped up in an effort to gain mass electoral support.

Although forming a government on the basis of autocratic populism may seem procedurally democratic inasmuch as it returns a government by popular demand, as a method it is intrinsically alien to any democratic culture because its impulsive nature, which forbids any rational discussion, is by definition closed to negotiation. We may discuss different political visions and projects, but debating dogmas that have become an existential threat is simply impossible. Politics is the art of being able to come up with intermediate solutions when necessary, but political conceptualizations based on impulsive dogmas cannot bear flexibility; they act on an "all or nothing" basis.

The populist understanding sees political and cultural diversity more as a risk factor that could turn into a threat at any moment than a right and a treasure that needs protection, presenting uniformity as the only way to ensure security. In this context, a Muslim arriving in the United States, or a refugee heading for Europe in a struggle for survival, is a potential risk and must be stopped, even if they have committed no crime. Considering the experiences of the past quarter-century, efforts to make new iron curtains descend along the Mexican border and at its airports in order to secure a democratic culture that feels such pride in the fall of the Berlin Wall and the original Iron Curtain, are thought provoking, to say the least.

At this point, two issues of concern to national and international order demand our serious consideration. The first is the motivation behind the autocratic populism of the masses and the beginnings of a transformation in democratic societies' mainstream politics under pressure emanating from these circles. The impulsive reactions of the great mass of people, and political elites' gravitation towards a rhetoric designed to satisfy these impulses in order to gain mass support, creates a self-perpetuating vicious circle. Mass impulses feed harsher rhetoric, harsher rhetoric feeds mass impulses. When mainstream political leaders are driven to satisfy this impulsive psychology in order to ensure mass support, it serves to block the exit routes from the vicious circle.

This vicious circle is horrifyingly reminiscent of the psychology of the 1930s. With the combination of an impulsive ideological rhetoric closed to negotiation, a superficial consciousness turned into a vehicle for a kind of politics that excludes history, a failure to produce alternative thinking, and the dearth of a visionary intellectual and political elite, a picture has emerged that should raise grave concerns about the future.

Another dilemma in this framework is the state of tension that exists between institutional decision-making mechanisms based on rational negotiation, and instant decision-making processes based on managing mass reaction. Striking instances of this psychopolitical institutional tension have abounded ever since President Trump first stepped into the White House. Differences of method and mindset between a president with a tendency to take impetuous decisions and who sees his popular mandate as giving him the right to announce such decisions not through institutional channels but over a personal Twitter account, and a civil service that defines itself within the Weberian bureaucratic tradition of being responsible for presenting serious policy options to the president and then implementing those decisions, rapidly led to a number of bureaucratic crises and dismissals.

This tension has led not only to a crisis of governance in the United States, but also to uncertainties about managing crises in the international system. Those who take heart from divergent messages to different parties are encouraged to instigate or intensify crises. For example, the differing messages given publicly and behind closed doors by the White House, Pentagon, and State Department, and the contradictory steps that were taken over the Qatar issue, evidently created a serious predicament of crisis management.

We can observe five trends or strands that differentiate autocratic populism's new style of decision-making and governance from those of conventional state structures. These may be listed as moves (i) from long-term strategic perspectives to short-term, even instantaneous, reflexes in the decision-making process; (ii) from the institutional to the personal in the decision-making process; (iii) from rational/professional mechanisms to amateur nepotistic networks in the decision-evaluation process; (iv) from formal relations to informal, back-door relations in the decision-implementation process; and (v) from a principled stand to transactional opportunism throughout all these processes. These strands lead to a greater degree of uncertainty and fragility in national, regional, and international orders than conventional methods.

It is hard to envision a predictable future in which the stones of national and international order have settled in place without first resolving ever-deepening tensions between democratic representation and institutional continuity. In this context, we are faced with a double-edged sword when it comes to the choice of options. If established bureaucracies regard elected governments' decision-making processes as irrational and choose to obstruct them, democratic representation and legitimacy will be dealt a heavy blow. If on the other hand governments coming into power with small margins of victory indulge in the personalization of those processes and restrict them to a small circle, this will bring institutional continuity, consistency in terms of principles, and the functional effectiveness of decisions into question.

In summary, the systemic earthquake process in which we now find ourselves is rapidly transforming the philosophical, political, cultural, economic, and structural features of nation-states that constitute the principal building blocks of the international order. Fragilities caused by these radical transformations are accompanied by a spiral of crises interwoven with regional and global fragilities. In order to be able to survive as founding elements of a new order in the face of these challenges and fulfill their proper role, nation-states need to implement a process of comprehensive restructuring.

The Regional Dimension of the Systemic Earthquake: Domino Effects and Fragile Regional Balances

Looking at things from a systemic perspective, we observe how profoundly post-Cold War earthquakes shook substructures and balances that had been built on bipolar foundations. Regional balances based on these foundations have dissolved one by one while fragile, temporary, event-based alliances have formed on the shifting sands of regional geopolitics. Even as the main earthquakes continue to rumble, aftershocks evincing diverse responses strike with varying degrees of intensity along four fault lines: Eastern Europe/the Balkans; Caucasus/ Central Asia; East Asia; and the Middle East.

The security umbrella provided by NATO membership coupled with economic development spurred by EU membership ensured relative regional stability in Eastern Europe and the Balkans in the first decade of this century,[7] after the Bosnia-Herzegovina and Kosovo wars. However, the economic crisis and the widespread unemployment of recent years; the refugee crisis stemming from the Arab Spring; the rising wave of terror in Europe and around the world; Russia's

intervention in Ukraine, annexation of Crimea, and subsequent intervention in Syria; Brexit; Trump's attitude towards NATO; and resur-
gent nationalism have caused the risk of increased fragility in regional
stability, previously restricted to Eastern Europe, to become a Europe-
wide phenomenon.

After the ceasefires that ended the armed conflicts in Nagorno-
Karabakh, Ossetia, and Abkhazia that came about with the geopolitical
earthquake in the *Rimland* belt after the Cold War,[8] attempts to preserve regional stability in the Caucasus and Central Asia have been
made within a continuum of political leadership and elites, except in
Georgia, Armenia, and Kyrgyzstan. The advantages conferred by
commodity-based economies have served to safeguard this continuity
and soften the extent to which the shockwaves of the economic crisis
have been felt. Yet it is clear that the post-9/11 intervention in
Afghanistan has failed to provide the anticipated environment of security and in this sense fragility continues to intensify. Instability in
Afghanistan, which constitutes a geographic transition zone between
the Middle East and Central Asia, also played a role in the growth of the
terror phenomenon that has developed within the security earthquake
by stratifying and deepening the links to Al-Qaeda and Daesh. If a just,
lasting, comprehensive, and consequential endeavor had been implemented in Afghanistan and Iraq, where the old regimes were militarily
toppled in the wake of the 9/11 security earthquake, the Arab Spring
that emerged on the basis of people's justified demands might not have
fallen under the shadow of Daesh.

Although East Asia appeared to be an oasis of calm in the initial
phase of the post-Cold War geopolitical earthquake, it has emerged as
another significant fault line in the ongoing systemic earthquake as a
result of the new dynamics introduced by the global economic crisis,
and now the reawakening of problems and rivalries especially with
respect to spheres of dominance in the East and South China Seas.

It is in the Middle East that the most devastating effects of the
earthquakes that took place in the wake of the collapse of the Cold War
order have been, and continue to be, felt. The Middle East region –
which geoculturally holds human history's most ancient civilizational
legacy, geopolitically its most deeply-rooted state traditions, and geoe-
conomically its greatest concentration of trade routes – has now become
a zone of internal tensions, external interventions, and bloody ethnic
and sectarian wars. The main reason for this is that the region has been

most directly and profoundly impacted by the five earthquakes we are addressing. These earthquakes have made the already fragile map of the Middle East and its political and economic structures even more fragile.

In fact, the Middle East region, which is the geographical intersection between the continents of Asia, Europe, and Africa, constituted a region of relatively stable order during the Ottoman State's ascendancy between the sixteenth and twentieth centuries at a time when Europe was undergoing an era of major tensions, wars, and turbulence. The last major war in the region, which determined the Turkish–Iranian border that remains valid to this day, concluded in the 1639 Treaty of Zuhab (Qasr-e Shirin). At that time, the region had not been exposed to any external intervention except for Napoleon's 1798 Egyptian campaign. These long centuries of stability served to preserve a culturally diverse urban life, develop natural economic links between intraregional basins, and maintain contacts between the region's basins, principally the Balkans, Caucasus, Mediterranean, and Black Sea.

However, starting with the First World War, the twentieth century witnessed periods of severe division and fragmentation after a period of stability that had endured for centuries.[9] The First World War divided the region into unnatural subordinate units attached to colonial empires. The natural links between Aleppo and Mosul, Jerusalem and Damascus, Baghdad and Dayr al-Zawr, Gaziantep and Aleppo, which for centuries had lain in the same geocultural and geoeconomic interaction basins, began to break down. This brought with it a process of internal alienation the likes of which the region had not seen since the Mongol invasions. So, the so-called "peace diplomacy" after the First World War disrupted the Ottoman *millet* system and via Sykes-Picot imposed artificial political entities on the region that reflected European colonial ambitions, and contributed to the political turmoil of the present period. As David Fromkin rightly underlines, "it was an era in which Middle Eastern countries and frontiers were fabricated in Europe."[10] The title of his book summarizes the main consequence of this "peace diplomacy" in a very clear manner: *A Peace to End All Peace: The Fall of the Ottoman Empire and the Creation of the Modern Middle East.*

This geography, which was supposed to be reunited with the disintegration of the colonial empires after the Second World War and the wave of Arab nationalism, turned into a field of rivalry between nation-states run by harsher and more combative regimes that reflected the sectarian character of Ba'athist ideology and the bipolar nature of the Cold War. Relations between many neighboring countries that had been frozen in line with the exigencies of the Cold War prevented the confluence of the region's human and natural resource potentials.

As with the artificial structures, the peace diplomacy after the First World War incorporated the Balfour Declaration into the British colonial mandate administration of Palestine. The Palestinian issue, which with the establishment of the State of Israel after the Second World War and the 1948 war had become a decisive factor in subsequent regional and global developments, began to manifest itself in all its dimensions. The migration to neighboring Arab countries of approximately 750,000 Palestinians as refugees, more than half of the Palestinian population at that time, severed from the lands in which they had lived for centuries, formed the first phase of the regionalization of the issue.[11] According to the United Nations Relief and Works Agency for Palestine Refugees in the Near East (UNRWA) figures, more than 5 million Palestinians are living as refugees today.[12]

Ever since this development, it has been impossible to conceive of any problem in the region separately and independently of the issue of Palestine. At the psychological and strategic heart of developments, including regimes' quests for legitimacy, the functioning of regional structures like the Arab League and the Organization of Islamic Cooperation (OIC), and matters of war and peace, the Palestinian issue always lurks. For example, Clause 8 of the Charter of the OIC, which was established after the attack on the Al-Aqsa Mosque, defines the establishment of a Palestinian State as one of the fundamental objectives of the organization.[13] The clause states that the organization's location of its headquarters in Jeddah is temporary and that they shall be moved to Jerusalem after the city has been liberated.[14]

The end of the Cold War created hopes and expectations in the region as throughout the world. The fundamental expectation in the Middle East was that there would be a resolution of the Cold War-legacy Palestinian issue and a reduction in the tensions inherited from a now-defunct bipolar structure. Yet it is in this region where the most destructive and lasting impact of the earthquakes of the past quarter-century has been seen. This exponentially growing impact has left the region's traditional social structures as well as its modern political institutions facing ruin. A domino effect has rendered the fragile state structures inherent in this picture, and regional balances, even more fragile.

At the beginning of the 1990s the geopolitical earthquake coursed along the Eurasian belt on a Balkans–Caucasus–Central Asia line running to the north of the Middle East. Yet the first major war of this earthquake took place in the Middle East. The intervention against Saddam Hussein, who wanted to benefit from the upheavals of the final years of the Cold War by occupying Kuwait, ended up with an Iraq effectively divided into three spheres of influence. To use a term from my earlier work *Strategic Depth*, a geopolitically critical keystone had now been dislodged from an anyhow extremely poorly constructed Middle East wall. Ever since then, Iraq has become both benchmark and symbol of geopolitical disintegration in the Middle East.

Just as the establishment of a Palestinian State, contrary to the objectives of the Oslo Peace Process launched with such fanfare in 1993, has been impossible to achieve, so the occupation of East Jerusalem and its surrounding area has hardened as the Palestinian drama has been compounded. The Palestinian issue thus maintains its status at the center of disorder and tension in the region.[15] In addition, the failure of the Oslo Process has become a symbolic indication that the Cold War has not yet ended in the Middle East.[16] From the perspective of the international community, the approximately twenty-five years from the ambitious rhetoric of the Oslo Process to Trump's declaration of Jerusalem as Israel's capital represents a story of unmitigated failure. As well as being one of the main reasons for a lack of confidence and trust in the international order, this story of failure has laid the psychological groundwork for the trend towards radicalization in the region.

The security earthquake ushered in by 9/11 triggered a process that would transform an already fragile state of regional stability into chaos. The Afghanistan and Iraq Wars had a transborder domino effect that destabilized not only those countries, but neighboring states and the region as a whole. The blurring of the Afghanistan–Pakistan and Syria–Iraq borders over time is a result of such an interaction. Tensions generated by ethnic and sectarian identities ossified by these countries' internal conflicts have ruptured cultural fault lines, turning geocultural earthquakes into bloody conflicts.

The impact of the global economic-political crisis has made itself especially felt in the countries which are not rich in natural resources such as Tunisia, Egypt, Syria, and Yemen. From this perspective, it is absolutely no coincidence that the Arab Spring was sparked by the self-immolation of an impoverished fruit vendor in Tunisia. This reaction soon expanded from a personal *cri de coeur* into a psychological state that gripped the masses throughout the Middle East.

To summarize, a list of the tensions, wars, and civil wars that have occurred over the past quarter-century reveals the fact that the most devastating impact of the earthquakes triggered by the collapse of the Cold War order have manifested themselves in the Middle East: wars between states (the Gulf War, 1990–1991; the Iraq War, 2003; the Israel–Lebanon War, 2006; Israeli attacks on Palestine, 2002, 2006, 2008, 2012, 2014), civil tensions and wars (Algeria, Iraq, Syria, Lebanon, Palestine, Libya, Yemen, Sudan, and Somalia), embargoes (Iraq, Iran, Syria, Sudan, Gaza, and most recently Qatar). This geopolitical earthquake has caused the death and displacement of millions of people, the waste of economic resources, and the destruction of historic heritage and cultural riches.

One can detect traces of the geopolitical, security, economic, and political earthquakes referred to at the beginning of this chapter in all these instances of tension, crisis, war, and embargo. These impacts have also begun to have a profound effect on subregional structures in the Middle East. The Gulf region has suffered two major wars, known as the Gulf Wars, brought about by geopolitical earthquakes in the post-Cold War era; been portrayed as the instigator of the 9/11 security earthquake; experienced the shocks of the economic earthquake from within; been both the subject and the object of the Arab Spring; and finally faces the challenge of intraregional tension because of the sanctions imposed on Qatar in 2017. The fact that the Gulf, whose natural resources bestow on it the potential to be one of the world's most prosperous regions, has now turned into the point of rupture on geopolitical, geoeconomic, and geocultural fault lines, strikingly exposes the extent to which the Middle East's subregions have been affected by post-Cold War earthquakes.

Looking at all these processes, it is not realistic to single out a particular event or country in isolation from the balances of the entire region. Events in the region unfurl in an extremely dynamic atmosphere in which all the key actors in international relations play an active role and every development triggers or influences another. Careful examination of Gulf crisis in 2017 shows how it distinctively reflects all the new balances and dynamics in the region formed by previous quakes, especially the political earthquake induced by the Arab Spring.[17]

In the wake of all these aftershocks, the Middle East harbors all the features of the ongoing systemic earthquake, while also paying a heavy price for it. In this context we may talk about five crisis-intensifying factors. The first is that the region's transboundary geocultural fault lines, activated by previous earthquakes, are continuing to rupture with ethnic and sectarian conflicts right down to village level. Ethnic and sectarian communities that coexisted for centuries are held subject to a state of mind that alienates them from each other before mutating into a psychology of enmity spread by sentiments of revenge.

The tensions and conflicts associated with this psychology also bring migratory movements that change the region's demography. As the concerned United Nations High Commissioner for Refugees (UNHCR) report elucidates, the region is currently witnessing global society's most widespread migrant flows and population movements: "In 2017, the region hosted just six percent of the world's population, but nearly a quarter of the global population of concern to UNHCR. This responsibility continued to stretch economies, public and social services, and civil and political structures to the limits."[18] Every flow of refugees or migration leads to a sociocultural fragility that destroys a demographic balance shaped over centuries. It will be extremely difficult to transition from a state of systemic earthquake to a new order of stability without going through a process of psychocultural rehabilitation to bring these affects under control.

The second factor is that the struggle for control over regional-scale geoeconomic lines, especially those that house energy corridors, are escalating tensions along these fault lines and fueling strategic conflicts of interest. The fact that every twentieth-century regional fragmentation and disintegration disconnected the trade corridors emanating from the ancient Silk Road economy has caused the rupturing of the lines of geoeconomic stability and interaction. The main factor that transformed these geoeconomic ruptures into geopolitical instability has been competition for oil and natural resources, and their transmission lines. Most recently, the impact of this geoeconomic rivalry has played a significant role in the Kirkuk crisis that emerged in the wake of referendum tensions in northern Iraq in September 2017 and which has drawn in national and regional players. Geopolitical, geoeconomic, and geocultural fragility stemming from the ongoing systemic earthquake underlies the fact that an economic potential which might be the basis for a stable regional economic-political order in which common interests and cooperation would work for the benefit of all has in fact paved the way for rivalries that threaten regional stability.

Thirdly, the influence of regional structures such as the Arab League, the OIC, and the Gulf Cooperation Council (GCC), which have performed poorly in crises proliferating throughout the region, is fading. The latest crisis within the GCC stands out as a striking and cautionary indication. Today there is unfortunately not a single problem-solving international organization or structure with the capacity or credibility to intervene to resolve any crisis that might arise either on a bilateral or regional scale. The vacuum created by this state of affairs hampers efforts to bring crises under control and causes even conjunctural crises to escalate rapidly.

The fourth factor is that the influence of powers from outside the region is being shaped not with a view to forming a new order but only in line with their own understanding of short-term national interests. The tendency of these interests to instigate the use of force by parties supported by powers from outside the region has turned the region into a fertile ground for proxy wars. For example, in Syria, US support for the PYD (Democratic Union Party – *Partiya Yekîtiya Demokrat*)-YPG (People's Protection Units – *Yekîneyên Parastina Gel*) groups and Russia's backing of pro-regime militias have effectively divided the country into different spheres of influence in which each actor is laying the groundwork for efforts to form an in-country order based on groups to which it is aligned.

Fifth, as both consequence and complement to all these factors, nation-states in the region are becoming fragile structures and losing their control and decision-making capacity in the field. As well as being a general phenomenon, the fragility of nation-states in the region is also accompanied by processes and challenges that are specific to the historic, geopolitical, geoeconomic, and geocultural characteristics of each nation-state. This has led to severe difficulties in finding counterparts to try to resolve crises and create a new order, and enlarged the role of non-state actors.

Considering all these factors, we see that there is no sustainable status quo in the region today. The fragility that is most intense in the Middle East also applies to varying degrees to regions such as the

Balkans, Caucasus, Central Asia, South Asia, East Asia, sub-Saharan Africa, and Central America. Today, a gradual, step-by-step, comprehensive process of rehabilitation in the international system's regional structures is required. And with an all-embracing vision of international order, such a process can be grounded in a meaningful framework.

The Global Dimension of the Systemic Earthquake: The Ineffectiveness and Fragility of the UN System

As both cause and reflection of this systemic crisis, one of the most striking developments we have witnessed is the decline in the capacity and reputation of international organizations, especially the UN, for establishing order and crisis resolution. These structures are normally expected to fulfill a dual role. One is to manage, de-escalate, and resolve potential crises; the other is to ensure the order's sustainability by means of a restructuring process without disrupting its internal equilibrium.

Today it is very hard to claim that the UN and other international organizations have performed well on either count. Due to conflicts of interest and structural problems within these organizations, crises over the last quarter-century have either been addressed too late in the wake of major human tragedies, or problems are postponed by solutions such as ceasefires that render them liable to flare up again at any moment. For example, an intervention was staged in the Bosnian crisis after the massacre of 250,000 people; however, the solution contained in the Dayton Agreement has prevented the functioning of a viable state and incubates a potential new crisis, which could ignite at any time. The ethnic slaughter of 800,000 people in Rwanda in 1994 (made even more egregious by being so close in time to the Bosnian experience) intensified and spread concerns about the future of the international order. The ceasefire in the 2008 Abkhazia and Ossetia crisis could not prevent war between Russia and Georgia, and the fragile Nagorno-Karabakh ceasefire agreed through the Minsk Process under the aegis of the OSCE, which remains subject to continuous breaches along the ceasefire line, could erupt as a serious armed conflict at any time.

These examples may well multiply. Events in Syria over the past seven years have wrecked the effectiveness and reputation of international organizations, especially the UN. One of the main factors fueling this spiral of systemic crisis has been the loss of reputation inflicted by the inability of the P5 veto-stymied UNSC to take any resolution in the face of a situation in which all kinds of war crimes, including the use of chemical weapons, have been committed, hundreds of thousands have been killed, and millions have fled their country as refugees, while millions more who remain lack even basic human needs. Today, any UN intervention in an international crisis depends more on the ability of the P5 countries to reconcile their interests than any urge to defend the guiding principles of the international order.

In international relations it is entirely natural for countries to have differing interests, and for them to use diplomatic means to defend these interests. However, if we are to talk about an international level at all, and when it comes to the international order's parties having a set of common principles as the normative base for international legitimacy,[19] the need for them to show a common stance is perfectly clear. To give an example, it is perfectly natural that different parties have different perspectives on the Syrian crisis and its course; however, it was expected that at least two issues would be excluded from the field of conflicts and clashes of interest as a requirement of the international conventions and principles to which all parties have signed up: namely, humanitarian access and war crimes (especially the use of weapons of mass destruction). Yet the UNSC has been unable to formulate a single resolution to prevent, or impose sanctions against, the use of chemical weapons, air and missile attacks on schools and hospitals, the starvation of civilians under siege, mass murder in prisons, and all the other crimes that have been committed. Moreover, agreements on humanitarian aid access and refugees have not been implemented on the ground.

Quite the reverse, these issues, which constitute the very foundation of international order, have been treated as negotiating cards to achieve tactical superiority in the field. This approach has become the prevailing trend, which has led to a shift away from the idea of an international order based on the international system's common principles and institutional structures first to a "balance of power"-based process and then to a state of chaotic uncertainty. This chaotic uncertainty and unpredictability have activated adventurist tendencies and unmanageable actors. The quest for balances based on short-term reconciliations of interest has hampered efforts to establish an enduring long-term order.

In general terms, the sustainability of any international order rests on four main conditions: (i) *guiding principles*: the existence of a set of principles to guide the order, and the recognition of these principles as a reference point in concerned parties' decisions and resolutions; (ii) *representativeness*: the representation of the order's legitimate actors in international institutions; (iii) *participation in the decision-making process*: the existence of a decision-making process that ensures the fair participation of these actors in decisions and resolutions; (iv) *institutional reflection of the power structure*: the existence of a power structure capable of implementing decisions and resolutions based on these principles, and the reflection of this structure in international institutions.

No one looking at the present state of affairs can plausibly claim that the international system fulfills these four conditions in practice. Inconsistencies over the principles we addressed in the previous paragraph have largely eroded the international order's *guiding principles*. Criteria that change according to the balances of power in each area of crisis have relegated the international order from having a value-oriented status to that of a passive, fragile structure that mirrors projections of force.

The *representativeness* condition apparently met by member states' representation in the UN General Assembly has been rendered merely symbolic by the functional inadequacy of an institution that reflects no genuine representation of humanity. Indeed, it is very hard to say that any comprehensive representativeness exists in international structures, especially the Security Council, in terms of regional, cultural, and economic development criteria. It is a striking paradox that there are no permanent representatives of the Islamic world or the continent of Africa on the UNSC even though the greatest human losses of the crises of the past quarter-century have been suffered by Muslim societies and Africa.

Nor is it feasible to assert that there is fair *participation in the decision-making process*. When it comes to decision-making, non-P5 countries are all equally powerless and bereft of authority. The non-representation in decision-making processes of countries that are directly affected by any crisis completely upsets the responsibility–authority balances in the international system. This gives rise to a situation that works against the countries that end up paying the cost for the prolongation of crises. For example, the cost of the veto-driven incapacity to enact any UNSC resolutions on Syria continues to be paid by neighboring countries who are obliged to accept millions of refugees fleeing the crisis.

As for the *institutional reflection of the power structure*, although the political, economic, and military balances of power have drastically changed over the past fifty years, the UNSC, which remains the final decision-making and enforcement body, still reflects the post-Second World War power structure. Yet it has proven impossible to reflect changes in that power hierarchy in institutional structures. In this respect, it is not only relatively powerless countries who have been involved in attempts to reform the UN, but states that have grown in power in the postwar era such as Germany, Japan, India, and Brazil. And countries in a leading position in their own regions, continents, and cultural basins (Turkey, Indonesia, Egypt, Iran, Pakistan, Nigeria, South Africa, et al.) continuously draw attention to power–representation imbalances in the functioning of the UN system.

In spite of all these efforts, the UN continues to prop up the post-Second World War settlement and its balances. The principal reason for this is that UN reform requires a resolution of the General Assembly, and all General Assembly resolutions are subject to the veto power of the P5 countries, which means the system effectively precludes reform simply because no P5 country wishes to surrender its veto-based absolute decision-making power. The existence in the UN of a closed system resistant to change prevents the implementation of measures that are necessitated by a dynamically changing international conjuncture. To make an economic comparison, just as productivity in oligopolistic markets controlled by a few companies declines over time, it is inevitable that UN productivity will continue to fall.

The failure to meet the prerequisites for the sustainability of the international order has brought problems of functionality as well as legitimacy. Without the reinstatement of these four conditions, the international order's tendency to self-regulate is making it extremely difficult to find a solution to a progressively deepening systemic crisis. This difficulty has resulted in the ever-accelerating evolution of the system towards multiple balances of power.

4 SYSTEMIC EARTHQUAKE: GLOBAL POWERS AND THE "MULTIPLE BALANCES OF POWER" SYSTEM

In the bipolar world of the Cold War era, power shifts that might have impacted the international system were generally regulated to the context of US–USSR summits and negotiations, with decisions taken at the superpower level cascading down to the lower strata of the power pyramid. International crises and ways to resolve them were shaped by the ability of superpowers to balance each other and exercise control over the players in their own pole. Large-scale tensions, proxy wars, ceasefires, nation-states' internal balances, and regime changes were also determined through a pyramid-like network of relations, at the top of which sat the two superpowers.

Crises that emerged in this pyramidal power structure, with the two superpowers at the summit, major powers in the upper section, regional powers in the middle and other actors lower down, were resolved by reciprocal balances grounded on relations established by the apex superpowers with players lower down the pyramid. In any case, although tensions were ideologically deep-seated and global in scope, the balance was static and its mechanisms had defined roles.

The Cold War structure had actually begun to be shaken to some degree by divergences between the pyramidal relationships in the power balance, and these powers' relative global economic share. Considering the balance between the superpowers, the loss of the USSR's capacity to finance the global competition incumbent on a superpower at a time when the US economy upheld the productivity and technological superiority required to meet the cost of that competition was one of the fundamental factors that brought an end to the Cold War. In a sense, this was a reassertion of the rule that applies to all great empires and political orders: powers that prove unable to meet the cost of hegemonic expansion through economic productivity and efficiency end up experiencing decline and eventually face disintegration.

On the other hand, as countries like Germany and Japan, whose defeat in the Second World War deprived them of a position of legitimacy and influence in the international power pyramid, rose in the economic power hierarchy, Britain and France, with their colonial imperial legacies, underwent a relative decline in the pyramid of economic power while maintaining their position in the political power pyramid. China, on the other hand, chose to open its economy on a global scale while consolidating its political order in the post-Cold War era.

In the meantime, regional powers such as India, Brazil, Turkey, Iran, Pakistan, Egypt, Indonesia, Malaysia, Australia, South Africa, and Nigeria found opportunities to take advantage of the vacuums and gaps that arose in their own regions as a result of the dissolution of the bipolar Cold War structure by means of various power factors including population, territorial scale, strategic position, military power, and economic capacity. These countries began at different times to expand their own spheres of influence and maneuverability through policies that exceeded those of regular regional powers.

In summary, the end of the Cold War shook the pyramidal relationship networks of that era's static balance of power, paving the way for new equations and balances of power. In a sense, the stances and power rivalries of the global powers within this dynamic network of relationships during the post-Cold War earthquakes have laid the seismic substructure for the systemic earthquake that rumbles on today. The movements these countries have undergone within themselves during this process and their attempts to adapt to the new era have had a direct impact on the direction and force of the tides and turbulence in the international system.

US Strategic Discontinuity: From "New World Order" to "America First"

With the disintegration of the bipolar structure inaugurated by the end of the Cold War, all eyes turned to the United States, as the absolute victor of the Cold War,[1] with regard to regulating the system. Those who characterized the end of this war as the end of the flow of history through the ultimate victory of liberalism and its institutions to proclaim the glad tidings of a new world order, as well as the casualties of the ever-flowing course of history, looked to the United States as the new world order's principal agent in anticipation of its assumption of this role.[2]

In the context of a state of affairs marked by such expectations, there were two possible strategic orientations open to the US administration in the post-Cold War era: to try to construct a new world order through unilateral interventions as the dominant player exploiting its apparently indisputable global supremacy whatever the gains and costs; or to lay the groundwork for a new order with more participatory, cost-sharing decision-making mechanisms by recalibrating the authority–responsibility balances within the system.

Taking an overview of what has transpired from 1990 to the present day, we may observe that the United States seemingly chose the former course in the early years after the Cold War, and when the costs inherent in this choice become evident, rather than switching to the second option, it has been seen to leave developments to fluctuate. This stance of wavering between absolute unilateralism and vacillation, and the uncertainties to which it gives rise, has not only led to the intensification of ongoing earthquakes but has also diminished the possibility of the emergence of a participatory, representative international order based on an appropriate authority–responsibility balance.

At a time when the international system needs to be rebuilt with the benefit of a long-term strategic perspective, these oscillations, sometimes the result of a change of administration, sometimes conjunctural change, have served to increase the level of uncertainty and unpredictability both within the United States and globally. The intermittent implementation of divergent approaches has strengthened the development of an understanding of sustainable order. For example, while action was immediately taken against Saddam Hussein upon his invasion of Kuwait, it took three years after the occupation of Bosnia-Herzegovina, which resulted in the slaughter of a quarter of a million people, for any action to be taken against the Milošević administration that had flagrantly carried out such savage acts of ethnic cleansing. The United States, which invaded Iraq in 2003 on claims of Iraq's possession of weapons of mass destruction based on evidence that even those claims' proponents subsequently admitted was unreliable, barely raised an eyebrow against the Assad government whose use of chemical weapons against civilians in 2013 was officially acknowledged by the UN, preferring to negotiate with the regime that deployed such weapons.

Other examples abound. If a conceptualization of the policy pursued by the United States over the past quarter-century is needed, the most accurate would be one of "strategic discontinuity." Radical changes and fluctuations in psychology, political rhetoric, strategic priorities, and tactical *modus operandi* have occurred in the wake of each quake. The United States' dominant global position has caused these fluctuations to spread throughout the world through the domino effect.

Possessed of an assertive, self-confident psychology as a result of having emerged as the victorious power from the geopolitical earthquake that ended the Cold War between 1989 and 1991, the United States settled the "New World Order" concept at the heart of the consequent political discourse.[3] In this context, we may refer to a course of events in three phases. During the first phase between 1989 and 1993, there was an endeavor to transform the new world order conceptualization into a strategic area of application around three developments: (i) the introduction of a new order of stability in Central and Eastern Europe starting with the unification of Germany; (ii) the reestablishment of Kuwait's sovereignty through UN resolutions and with the support of the international community after Saddam Hussein's violation of international law in his invasion of that country; and (iii) the creation of an expectation that the most pressing problem area of the Cold War would be resolved with the assertion that the Palestinian people would gain their own state within the framework of the Oslo Process. The first was a strategic priority, the second a projection of power to safeguard the international order, and the third a diplomatic initiative addressing the most heated problem of the Cold War era.

The second phase (1993–1997) was one in which the United States' status as the lead actor in establishing a new order in all three of these areas was shaken. While efforts to establish a space of reform and stability in Central and Eastern Europe were progressing, the greatest devastation witnessed in Europe since the Second World War unfolded in the Balkans, especially in Bosnia-Herzegovina, as a result of which that country became, and continues to be, a politically fragile structure at the mercy of other spheres of influence. And although Kuwait's sovereignty was indeed restored, Iraq was divided into three de facto zones of sovereignty that threatened regional order, particularly the stability of Iraq's neighbors. The Oslo Process, its objectives dimmed by interminable negotiations, has still failed to reach the goal of a two-state solution. In addition, the occupation of one-fifth of the territory of Azerbaijan by Armenia in 1993 and the escalation of the Abkhazia and Ossetia issues have paved the way for an era of frozen crises that threaten the very concept of sustainable order. The ethnic slaughter that led to the massacre of some 800,000 souls in Rwanda in 1994 exposed the vulnerability of the international community in the face of an imminent large-scale systemic earthquake.

All these developments shook the United States' psychology of self-confidence that had marked the first phase; the ambitious "New World Order" discourse was replaced by crisis-laden, responsibility-shirking "Clash of Civilizations"-like rhetoric. Strategic priorities have shifted from the objective of establishing an enduring and sustainable order towards crisis-containment. This concentration on efforts to contain crises has led to a status quo of long-standing ceasefires that carry on in a number of regions in a framework of frozen crises.

The greatest delusion on the issue of establishing a new international order today lies in the difference between a law-based order of enduring peace, and an order that merely interrupts conflicts through ceasefires. The main reason why interim ceasefires in various crisis zones from Abkhazia to the Transdniester, Karabakh to Crimea, and Ossetia to Palestine have been impermeable to any conversion into lasting peace on the basis of international law is the inconsistency in diplomatic and strategic methodology pursued in the early years of the post-Cold War era. And today, this fragile status quo constitutes the main minefield facing the international order.

In the third phase (1997–2001), which coincided with President Clinton's second term of office, efforts were made to establish a stable order grounded on the development of a range of alliances and multilateral measures through the expansion of NATO and the new strategic concept adopted by the Washington Summit,[4] the parallelism achieved between the EU and NATO expansion processes, the Kosovo intervention and the transformation of the G7 into the G8 with Russia's membership, and the formation of the G20 in the wake of the Asian economic crisis, with discourse and priorities being shaped accordingly. In spite of President Clinton's domestic difficulties, these efforts revived expectations that a more visionary and participatory course would be pursued on the question of the international political and economic order.

The 9/11 US-epicentered security earthquake radically altered all these psychological, discursive, and strategic priorities. In a sense, this security earthquake also triggered another earthquake in strategic perception and approach. A reflexive psychology based on preserving the existing status quo replaced a self-confident psychology based on a belief in the possibility of the establishment of a new order.[5]

As a result, "New World Order"-oriented idealist and visionary discourse was abandoned in favor of the adoption of a purely realist and conjunctural strategic rhetoric centered on "preemptive strike" principle; the emphasis on democracy, human rights, and humanitarian intervention of the 1990s lost its position in the conceptualization of US strategy. Such rhetoric deployed by George W. Bush was aimed at legitimizing the Afghanistan and Iraq Wars rather than promoting a genuine democratization process, and laid the groundwork for unilateral interventionist approaches towards the region.

This radical change was mirrored in strategic priorities and policy methods. While the Afghanistan intervention had been carried out within a system of alliances, the invasion of Iraq was performed as a unilateral intervention without the full support of UN resolutions or the NATO alliance system. The only serious support for this unilateral intervention came from the British government led by Tony Blair.[6] The experience of both interventions once again demonstrated the scale of the destructive power of US military might; yet it also represented a serious test of its ability to establish order.[7] Attempts have been made in both Afghanistan and Iraq to establish the institutional and political structures of new nation-state orders. However, even a cursory glance at the point we have reached today makes it obvious that both interventions have given rise to internal conflicts, political instabilities, institutional deficiencies, power vacuums, and disorders that risk spilling over to neighboring countries at any moment. The Iraqi State structure that was dissolved by Paul Bremer, appointed after the Iraq War as the head of an interim administration, in the manner of a colonial governor, has still not been able to take shape as a sustainable political order capable of standing on its own feet.[8]

Failures to pass these tests led to serious questions being raised both by the American public who bore the human and financial costs of the war, and by world public opinion that had believed in the United States' capacity to intervene effectively in every kind of turmoil and disorder. The profound security crisis experienced in New York and Washington for the first time confronted American public opinion, which apart from the nuclear threat had seen itself as living in a secure continent far from the dangers of war throughout the Cold War, with the reality that the security problem was not a national or continental issue, but one that threatened the entire world. And world public opinion as a whole, seeing the dawn of a new era of risks and threats in which the United States itself might have security vulnerabilities, began to question the validity of the idea of a new world order in which the United States would play a decisive role.

In addition, the Guantanamo judicial process, which breaches even the most fundamental principles of law and justice,[9] has set an example that has effectively granted the governments of other countries the privilege of countering any risk factors that pose a threat to them on the basis of motivations of revenge and prestige rather than any values of law or justice. The essential condition of the existence and perpetuation of any order – on whatever level and scale – is the set of fundamental ethical and legal values upon which that order is based. In the event that a de facto state of order is established in the absence of a set of values of this kind, that order cannot be sustained. The experience of the state of lawlessness in Guantanamo that became one of the leading agenda points during President Obama's election campaign laid the groundwork for the spread of a new psychology and approach that rendered "New World Order" conceptualizations utterly meaningless.

President Obama came to office in this psychological environment, and at a time when the initial shockwaves of the third great tremor – namely the global economic earthquake – were making themselves felt. Choked by the unilateral interventionist stance of the Bush era, the international community saw Obama as the proponent of a kind of Wilsonian approach and the harbinger of a more participatory new order. These circumstances instigated a period of fresh expectations not only in US society but throughout the world.

Underlying everything was a redefinition of the shared values that bind the conscience of humanity and its adaptation to real life because, in the twenty years since the much-heralded end of the Cold

War, events have unfolded that have inflicted deep wounds on that conscience. Post-Cold War events from Bosnia to Rwanda, Palestine to Lebanon, Abu Ghraib to Guantanamo, have given rise to a picture that pains the conscience of all humanity, including that of US administrations claiming to be rebuilding the international system on the basis of freedom and human rights. There was a perceived need for a new voice to activate this conscience, and with his African heritage, his critical reaction to the policies of the Bush era, and his peace-promoting rhetoric, Obama was seen to have the potential to respond to this need. The Nobel Prize he received even before having put his name to any concrete accomplishments was the symbolic embodiment of this new discourse and expectation.

And Obama's election as president was indeed a symbolic success for US sociocultural pluralism. Barack Obama's election may also be viewed as an *inclusive multiculturalism*-oriented response to the "Who Are We?" question that had been raised by Samuel P. Huntington some four years before Obama's election.[10]

Indeed, President Obama presented a clear definition of American identity in a speech to a group of young people in Istanbul during his first foreign trip as president: "We're also a country of different backgrounds and races and religions that have come together around a set of shared ideals. And we are still a place where anybody has a chance to make it if they try. If that wasn't true, then somebody named Barack Hussein Obama would not be elected President of the United States of America. That's the America I want you to know."[11]

The United States was in fact undergoing the internal test of all past imperial structures that became more heterogeneous as their imperial areas of control expanded. It was for this reason that I stressed in a conference address I gave at Princeton University on 18–19 April 2002, after 9/11 but before Obama's name had gained much recognition, that the trauma being experienced by the United States could not be overcome through the exclusionist attitude envisioned by a rising wave of WASP nationalism, but rather by an inclusive perspective, and that this could best be achieved by an African-American president:

> Today, the United States of America feels the need not for a new Caesar to pursue military triumphs through the imposition of unilateral decisions, but for a philosopher-president able to keep a diversified society together with shared values and send

the right messages to the international community – that is, a new Marcus Aurelius. And this may best be accomplished by an African-American president.

Hence, the observation and analysis of Obama's foreign, and in particular regional, policy is more than a matter of mere analytical or political curiosity for me. It is also very personal. I became Foreign Minister of Turkey very soon after Obama took office: on 1 May 2009, to be precise. As this background implies, Obama's election and his inaugural messages awakened in me too an expectation concerning the regulation of the international system that I believed was overdue.

This expectation was essentially based on three factors concerning global psychology, diplomacy, and political values. The first, as I mentioned above, was that the election of an African-American president for the first time in US history was of itself a symbolic manifestation of the perceived need for an inclusive politics and understanding of order not only in the United States but on a world scale. This development, which mirrored an inclusive approach in the United States, could have laid the ground for a new inclusive global culture at a time when domestic and foreign policy psychologies were so closely intertwined. A change of direction of this kind towards an inclusionary approach might have served to rehabilitate the exclusionary approach founded on an ascendant WASP nationalism in the wake of the social trauma wrought by 9/11, as well as deliver a clear message to the entire world in the same direction.

The second factor concerned diplomacy. The expectations that Obama, who had come to power highly critical of the Bush administration's stance of militant unilateral interventionism, would steer towards a new, embracing form of multilateralism, gave hope for the restructuring of the international order. And during the first years of the Obama presidency, he did indeed take a stance in line with those multilateralism expectations, as evinced in the example of his assembling the G20 at summit level in the wake of the global economic crisis. However, the debasement of consequential multilateralism based on active diplomacy into a policy of passive diplomacy and inconsequential engagement led to the dashing of these expectations.

The third factor, which concerns political values, was the expectation that Obama's emphasis on democracy and human rights would go beyond mere rhetoric and that these values would be put into practice in US foreign policy, especially in the MENA region. This was no mere idealist hope. For it was also clear that an approach grounded on these values would make a real world contribution to US foreign policy by changing negative perceptions of the United States in the region. In addition, the establishment of a new order based on democratic stability instead of the Cold War-remnant authoritarian regimes in the region was significant in the context of releasing a number of areas of tension inherited from the Cold War.

The messages given in the speeches President Obama delivered in Turkey[12] and Egypt[13] shortly after coming to office were designed as comprehensive responses to these expectations and included rhetoric on a new, more participatory and inclusive international system. Coming to the presidency at a time of transition from the global economic earthquake to the structural tremor triggered by the Arab Spring in the Middle East, Obama could have taken decisions at this critical juncture to lead a process capable of addressing the quest for a new international economic, political, and strategic order. Such leadership required three fundamental conditions to be met: (i) the integration of human conscience with common values, (ii) the correct methods and mechanisms to facilitate the taking of decisions to put these values into practice, and (iii) the determination to implement these decisions boldly, and, when necessary, with the use of force.

However, the age-old contradiction between idealism and realism began to manifest itself over time. The tests brought to the agenda by the impact of the earthquake caused by the Arab Spring were also accompanied by severe challenges in terms of tensions between rhetoric/discourse and politics, ideals and reality, theory and practice.

Obama, who at the beginning of the process took a stand in line with the justified demand of the Arab masses through his appeals for democracy and freedom, began to hesitate when the time came to make the bold decisions required by these appeals, and chose to let events take their course. A comparison of events between 2011 and 2013 presents a clearer exposition of this picture. The Obama administration, which had already declared the illegitimacy of the Syrian government in the summer of 2011 on account of its excessive use of force against its civilian population, and regarded the diplomatic efforts we in Turkey were carrying out at that time as an unnecessary waste of time, remained silent in the summer of 2013 when the same civilian population was being massacred by weapons of mass destruction, and chose the path of negotiation. The same Obama who took the lead in activating NATO against Qaddafi's aerial bombardment of Benghazi in March 2011 saw no harm or contradiction in turning a blind eye to the slaughter of hundreds of thousands of people in all kinds of bombardments, including the use of barrel bombs, and millions of Syrians being forced to become refugees from 2011 until his departure from office in 2017. And the Obama who backed democratic demands at the time of Mubarak's resignation at the beginning of 2011 then took a stance that legitimized the coup that toppled the first president freely elected by the Egyptian people in the summer of 2013. To use Huntington's term, "the paradox of democracy" concern prevailed over moral and political values: "In accordance, 'the paradox of democracy,' the introduction of democracy in other societies also often stimulates and provides access to power for anti-American forces, such as nationalistic populist movements in Latin America and fundamentalist movements in Muslim countries."[14] Thus, in the post-Cold War period, the fundamental rights and freedoms recognized as the natural rights of the peoples of Central and Eastern Europe and as the ethical and political values of the new world order were seen as things that could be ignored or that were even surplus to requirements when it came to the peoples of the Middle East.

The international system thus took on an air of chaos as Bush's exaggerated unilateral interventionism was replaced by Obama's underwhelming "whatever happens, don't intervene" policy. The peoples of the Middle East paid the heaviest price for both approaches. When Obama finally left office, a state of chaotic disorder partitioned between autocratic regimes and areas controlled by terror organizations had taken the place of any notion of a regional order based on democratic stability.[15]

The Trump administration's first year of domestic and foreign policy brought a strategic rupture that transgressed any sense of strategic continuity. It was as if the US elections at the end of 2016 had caused a radical change not only in the presidency and administration, but the regime itself. Trump's political understanding and rhetoric changed the axis in terms of both its essence and methodology in a way that would only be possible in other countries in the wake of revolution. His successive reversals of the largely unmet expectations of the Obama era left international perceptions of the United States, and the already weakened belief in the international system's capacity to produce solutions, in tatters.

First and foremost, an exclusionist form of populism began to take over the whole of domestic and foreign politics. In domestic politics, an exclusionist understanding of American identity identified with WASP ideological interpretations has replaced an inclusionary American identity shaped by the arrival of immigrants in difficult circumstances from all over the world ever since the founding of the republic.[16] Trump's "America First" slogan is in fact perceived as "ideological WASP First." Thus, the transition from an era in which the Oval Office was presided over by an African-American president to an era in which no one without a predominantly WASP-ish ideology (let alone black) has been appointed, has begun to be seen as an existential change in American identity more than a political preference.

The dominance of such a polarizing and discriminatory identity-based rhetoric has not been seen to this extent since the days of the American Civil War. Extreme anti-black, anti-immigrant racist tendencies had been evident until the middle of the twentieth century but the White House generally adopted a rhetoric and method designed to soothe rather than incite these trends. The initiation of such rhetoric from the White House itself, and from the very top, has caused a state of profound disillusionment both in peripheral groups within the United States as well as throughout the world, especially in Africa, among peripheral communities who had been anticipating their participation in the system with the accession of Obama.

In this context, the discourse and policies around the Muslim ban and Mexican immigrants constitute manifestations of a permanent mindset that transcends a mere passing political preference. Such an exclusionary mentality has encouraged the development of a state of mind that threatens not only American cultural pluralism but global pluralism as well. Such an exclusionary domestic policy in the United States towards its citizens, residents, and people living on US soil sets a dangerous path and precedent for far-right parties to pursue further afield. It will tarnish the US image globally, and destroy the foundation of its soft power, which has formed a significant chunk of overall US power and standing in the world over the past century.

It was rather a paradox that the new US administration ordered the Pentagon to devise a plan to deal a death blow to Daesh in Iraq and Syria at the same time as it was instituting the Muslim ban. There can be no greater gift to Daesh than such an ill-conceived measure. It was also a bitter twist and irony of history that President Trump signed the Muslim ban on International Holocaust Remembrance Day. A commitment never again collectively to stigmatize any people, religion, or society should have been the guiding principle for this remembrance. Likewise, the idea behind 9/11 was to drive wedges between diverse peoples, religions, societies, and civilizations. 9/11 attacked first and foremost societies' inclusivity, the idea of coexistence, and the phenomenon of multiculturalism. If insisted upon, the Muslim ban will reward these perpetrators with a gift beyond their wildest dreams. It will constitute the institutionalization of Islamophobia as the official policy of a superpower. This will intensify polarization worldwide and activate sociopolitical fault lines between societies, religions, and civilizations. As history has shown so many times, fear, and especially fear of "the other," should not be manipulated for political gain. Such policies have never ended well.

Inclusivity, respecting human dignity, and upholding rights and liberties would be the most powerful means to counter the twisted ideology of the perpetrators of 9/11, and the cowardly brutality of Daesh. Betraying these principles and values will in contrast be tantamount to administering the kiss of life to these perpetrators' decaying and dying ideology. The treatment of Islam and Muslims as a security issue or threat will drive a further wedge not only between the United States and its own Muslim population, but also between the United States and the larger Islamic world.[17]

Secondly, the militant excesses of the Bush era's counterproductive unilateralism have now taken the place of Obama's multilateralism, which disappointed so many expectations. And this time, unilateralism has not been limited to a diplomatic method adopted only by the United States as a country. A White House – even an Oval Office – that has eliminated coordination between domestic institutions has begun to exercise a direct impact on unilateral decision-making processes.

This unilateralism in the decision-making process is set by a strategic discontinuity based on day-to-day, instantaneous reactions. Subjecting policies that have been formulated through prolonged analyses and bureaucratic processes to U-turns and radical changes on the basis of the president's momentary reactions and tweets is driving domestic and foreign counterparts into a state of insecurity and uncertainty aggravated by the unpredictability of such an approach. And the fact that vital decisions are being taken by a close family member – someone without relevant background and experience – appointed to an advisory position has destroyed the institutional rationality and continuity of decisions.

The controversy swirling around the unilateral termination of the agreement signed with Iran during the Obama administration, which would abrogate the *pacta sunt servanda* ("agreements must be kept") obligation of states that constitutes one of the main principles of the international order strikes the heaviest possible blow against the very idea of international order. Thus far, and under pressure from other parties, no such termination has occurred, yet even the discussion of its possibility shows the capacity of militant unilateralism to undermine international law. A state of affairs in which *pacta sunt servanda* has lost its validity is not a state of international order, but the law and the chaos of the jungle.

Thirdly, Trump's stance towards NATO and the EU, which was after all the front that won the Cold War, has led to the serious questioning of traditional alliance structures. Trump's belittling of the European integration project and his downplaying of the significance of NATO will shake the bonds between the transatlantic community, which again will be counterproductive to US national interests. In particular, as well as courting populist movements across the European continent, his praise of Brexit and encouragement of its repetition in other contexts invites security challenges of all kinds, be they political, economic, or social.

The reversal and unraveling of the European integration project would be one of the gravest mistakes since the Second World War, and its consequences would be deep and far-reaching. Such a process could also revive the long-buried issue of the balance of power in Europe. This would not only be tragic news for Europe, it would also directly and immediately undermine the global standing of the United States. Joschka Fischer, who served as the Minister of Foreign Affairs and Deputy Prime Minister of Germany (1998–2005) in a period of consolidation for the Transatlantic alliance by means of the EU and NATO enlargement processes, commented that Trump's view of the new global role of the United States created an existential problem for the entire West. "But we should not harbor any illusions: Europe is far too weak and divided to stand in for the US strategically; and, without US leadership, the West cannot survive. Thus, the Western world as virtually everyone alive today has known it will almost certainly perish before our eyes."[18]

Trump's "America First" approach marks the advent of one of the most profoundly testing periods for the Atlantic Alliance, described by Henry Kissinger as "The Troubled Partnership" even at its inception in the middle of the twentieth century, when he wrote, "Both sides of the Atlantic would do well to keep in mind that there are two kinds of realists: those who use facts and those who create them. The West requires nothing so much as men able to create their own reality."[19] Today, the place towards which the "alternative realities" conjured up by Trump may drive the Atlantic Alliance is set to influence the future not only of the Alliance but the international order as a whole.

Fourthly, regional instabilities are being intensified by one-sided, short-term, conjunctural and contradictory approaches. The decision to move the US Embassy from Tel Aviv to Jerusalem, which would only serve further to intensify the Palestinian problem and make any reasonable solution impossible, constitutes the most striking instance of discontinuity and unpredictable fluctuations in US strategy. The impact of this step has not been limited to endangering the Middle East Peace Process. The overwhelming UN General Assembly vote (128/9) rejecting this move, declaring "null and void" any actions intended to alter Jerusalem's character, status, or demographic composition and calling on all states to refrain from establishing embassies in the Holy City,[20] has further undermined the already fragile reputation of the United States.

In the meantime, the opportunist stance pursued during the embargo process against Qatar has left the GCC, a bulwark of Middle East stability, at risk of disintegration. And the United States arming its ally the YPG on the basis of claims it is fighting Daesh in Syria, although the YPG threatens Turkey as an extension of the PKK (*Kurdistan Workers' Party – Partiya Karkerên Kurdistanê*) terrorist group officially listed as a terror group by the United States itself, represents a profound contradiction that negates the principle of consistency, coherence, and alliance relationships on the issue of countering terror. The US's lack of an empathetic capacity to grasp the concerns and anxieties of its allies is preventing the development of common attitudes to mitigate the impacts of the systemic earthquake.

In a nutshell, the existing international "order" supposedly upheld by values such as democracy, the rule of law, and the free market with the support of institutions including the UN, G20, IMF, World Bank, and World Trade Organization, but kept standing to a large degree by US power, is coming under the direct effect of fluctuations and uncertainties in US strategy. This strategic discontinuity so prevalent during the post-Cold War era is serving to intensify the impacts of the systemic earthquake.

The occurrence of radical changes not just in micro-policy choices but in basic strategic orientation at almost every change of presidency causes the spread of a psychology of uncertainty and insecurity. The fact that the divergent changes turn into widening gaps at every turn brings to prominence transactional alliance relationships limited to particular presidential incumbents rather than substantial alliances with the United States as a country and prevents the development of enduring policies.

The divergences in the transition from the first Bush presidency to the Clinton presidency widened upon that from Clinton to George W. Bush, becoming a change of course towards a fully fledged policy of unilateralism. This change may be explained with reference to the 9/11 trauma. Yet the radical political differentiations brought about by the Bush–Obama and Obama–Trump transitions have reached an extent that cannot be explained purely in terms of external factors. The interpretation of Trump's stance as expressed in his "America First" slogan as the abandonment of the traditional approach that saw stability in the international system as being aligned with US interests, and a sign that international disorder may be the preferred option when US interests require, are among the most grave and current manifestations of the ongoing systemic crisis.

The European Union: From Success Story to Strategic Ambivalence?

One of the most striking reflections of the crisis in the international system is the difficulty being witnessed in the continental and regional-scale unification and integration processes that constitute the building blocks of the architecture of the international order between the UN and nation-states. As pillars of the underlying order, continental and regional unions form both an internal order between these associations and member states as well as tools to prevent potential crises and to resolve emerging crises before they turn global.

In this context, the most prominent and successful example of the international order's continental/regional building blocks in the modern era is the EU. European history is in fact the product of a long-term integration–fragmentation dialectic. In ancient times, the Mediterranean-centered union forged by the Roman Empire was shaken by Germanic incursions. Then in the Middle Ages, Carolingian Roman–Germanic tensions were overcome under the aegis of the Holy Roman Empire, but the partitioning of the Carolingian Empire between the three surviving sons of Emperor Louis I under the Treaty of Verdun in the year 843 initiated a process of division that subsequently determined present-day German–French boundaries. After the failure of the Vatican's attempt to unite Europe around a holy mission of religious war in the Crusades (1096–1291), the continent faced another destructive and bloody disintegration with the European Hundred Years War (1337–1453) fought principally over the succession to the French throne. The final major unification effort of the Middle Ages, attempted by Charles V under his title as Holy Roman Emperor, ended up as a milestone in the transition to the modern era with the Thirty Years War and the Westphalian Treaty consigning the Holy Roman Empire to history. Viewed today from another perspective, the Thirty Years War and the Westphalian Treaty that marked the beginning of the nation-state system led to severe social, economic, and political tensions and sowed the seeds of new conflicts.[21] But the key distinction of these wars was that they were based on national and secular causes, not religious ones.

In the modern era of European history, two nationalist leaders tried to establish the ideal of the Holy Roman union with modern ideological frameworks and military means, one centered on France, the other on Germany: Napoleon and Hitler. Napoleon's assumption of the title of Emperor in 1804 and his attempt to unite Europe under a single authority riding the wave of the French Revolution triggered counterreactions; the seeds of the Napoleonic Wars' great and bloody process of disintegration were then sown. While Hegel exalted Napoleon as a heroic figure and the symbol of the new order under the soubriquet "this world-soul,"[22] two countries stood against this new unification effort to forge a united hegemonic order: Britain and Russia. While Russia saw itself as continuing the mantle of the Roman Empire, Britain acted on a traditional attitude based on the instinct that any union created on continental Europe would challenge Britain's own dominion. Both countries' diplomatic initiative to convince the Ottoman State not to recognize Napoleon's imperial title remains noteworthy in terms of a line of historic continuity that continues to this day from the perspective of Turkey's relations with the central powers of the EU (Germany and France), Britain, and Russia.

Europe's integration–division dialectic was reactivated in opposition to this endeavor of Napoleon and the new rules of the game were set at the Congress of Vienna, which formed the legal basis for the balance of power structure grounded on balances between the European powers' areas of autonomy. On the other hand, Hitler's Third Reich order, which sought to unify Europe upon the new dynamics arising from the paroxysms of the First World War using the bloodiest means history had witnessed within an exclusionary process of total domination,[23] represented an effort to resuscitate the Holy Roman-Germanic ideal through modern ideological and military means.[24]

The failure of both these efforts to unite the continent of Europe under a single authority benefited the powers surrounding the continent. The balance of power forged in the Congress of Vienna after Napoleon's defeat at Waterloo boosted the influence of Britain and Russia in Europe and the international order, while the balance of power formed after the defeat of Hitler in the Second World War boosted that of the United States and the USSR in the same arenas. As well as the devastation it wrought, the Second World War also divided the continent into two spheres of influence between two non-continental powers (the United States of America and the USSR). Symbolized by the Iron Curtain, this division manifested itself right down to the level of a city on the scale of Berlin and opened up a major wound in the European consciousness.

The EU is a work of shared rationality arising from this wounded consciousness. This time, the endeavor was to overcome the immense trauma of the Second World War not by means of a strong leader or dominant power, but through a process of unification centered on common values and mechanisms. This integration/unification effort rested on four main pillars: (i) shared values and a consciousness of citizenship based on democracy and human rights, (ii) a common market and customs area formed by national economies on the basis of the free-market economy, (iii) political mechanisms such as the European Parliament and the Council of Europe, and (iv) the legal *acquis* constituting the legally formulated framework of all these principles, mechanisms and structures. This process of integration was an alternative to the integration of the Eastern part of Europe under the

Soviet bloc's socialist economic models based on authoritarian one-party regimes that ran parallel to the bipolar international structure of the Cold War era. Indeed, the Cold War manifested itself in Europe in the form of a clash between these two models of integration based on contradictory ideological frameworks and models of society.

The evolutionary transition during the Cold War from the ECSC (European Coal and Steel Community) to the EEC (European Economic Community) and then to the EC (European Community) opened the way to a step-by-step process of institutionalization. In the 1974 Paris summit, the leaders of the member states resolved to meet three times a year in the format of the Council of Europe;[25] the transition from the Joint Assembly of the ECSC to the European Parliament was completed with the first direct European Parliament elections held in 1979,[26] which then formed the legislative and operational buttresses of this institutionalization process. In this sense, this experience represented a highly successful example of a transition from a sector-based community to models of economic and political union.

This process made rapid progress in deepening and expanding in the wake of the end of the Cold War. This is also the story of the transition from the EC to the EU – that is, from a community to a union.[27] The 1992 Maastricht Treaty, the transition to the Single European Market in 1993, the introduction of the Schengen Agreement in 1995, the consolidation of the Common Foreign and Security Policy (CFSP) in the Treaty of Amsterdam in 1997, and the adoption of the 1998 European Central Bank set out a road map for efforts to establish order on a regional and continental scale.

From the enlargement perspective, the integration of non-Soviet bloc countries was first completed in the 1990s. The accession of ten member states in 2004, followed by Bulgaria and Romania in 2007 incorporated most of the area to the east of the Iron Curtain into the EU. This enlargement strategy continued with the accession processes – starting with majority-Catholic states – of countries of the former Yugoslavia that formed a buffer zone between the two Cold War blocs, with the accession of Slovenia (2004) and Croatia (2013).

This process of deepening and enlargement represented a major accomplishment in terms of driving the integration–disintegration dialectic towards integration. Above all, what was foreseen was unification based on common institutions and the formation of integrated power, rather than on the domination of raw power as envisioned by

Charlemagne, Charles V, Napoleon, and Hitler. In addition, robust bridges were established between principles and institutions; a common economic, political, and strategic area of power was created in which all parties' interests were assured on a "win–win" basis.

On the other hand, The *Charter of Paris for a New Europe* adopted by the *Commission on Security and Cooperation in Europe* (CSCE) in November 1990 defined democracy as the fundamental reference measure for the new Europe that emerged after the Cold War as well as declaring democracy the common political system for the entire continent of Europe: "Ours is a time for fulfilling the hopes and expectations our peoples have cherished for decades: steadfast commitment to democracy based on human rights and fundamental freedoms; prosperity through economic liberty and social justice; and equal security for all our countries ... We undertake to build, consolidate and strengthen democracy as the only system of government of our nations."[28] This framework of democracy, which defined the new Europe of the post-Cold War era, was approved by the United States and the USSR, the two superpowers of that period, laying the groundwork for the consolidation of the European continent around the idea of the EU (at that time the EC). The countries at the vanguard of this development underwent the transition processes to democracy in Central and Eastern Europe in the face of the economic costs of the geopolitical earthquake of the early 1990s and scored remarkable successes in post-earthquake rehabilitation.

Having consolidated its institutional integrity during this process, the EU suffered a less severe impact from the 9/11 security earthquake that posed such a formidable test for the United States: its role was largely limited to providing support for US operations. The wary approach of the central powers led by Germany and France to President George W. Bush's call for support in the Iraq intervention and the fact that the bulk of support came from Britain and new EU member states or Eastern European states still in the accession process presented a severe test for the CFSP and led to a problem of trust between the United States and the EU[29] – especially between the US and France[30] and between the United States and Germany[31] – together with the emergence of a dual structure in which the US administration drew a distinction between "old Europe" and "new Europe."[32] The fact that the authoritarian and populist tendencies that have arisen in Europe in the recent period have found it easier to gain a foothold in

Eastern Europe showed that this differentiation in political culture remains valid.

However, the real political stress test for the EU began with the 2008 global economic-political earthquake, which came in the immediate wake of the accession of most of the former Warsaw Pact countries. This test was only made harder in 2011 with the regional earthquake that shook the EU's neighboring regions. And the Brexit referendum decision of 2016 turned the EU, up to then a successful project to establish a post-Cold War order, into one of the epicenters of systemic crisis.

Initially, the global economic-political earthquake rattled psychologies. And divided destinies began to emerge in the EU, whose member states had up to that time all enjoyed the benefits of membership to a large extent. Historical experiences show that when actors within the continent of Europe disconnect from their common continental destiny to focus on their individual interests and plans, this not only leads to an intra-European crisis but also lays the ground for wider tensions. It seems that we have strayed far from the line drawn by Helmut Schmidt, German Chancellor during the most critical phase of the Cold War (1974–1982) in his generalized vision for the West as the Cold War drew to an end in 1985: "In any form it is a delusion to suppose that individual western nations can be successful on a purely national basis. And it is equally a delusion to imagine that, even if they seek to act in cooperation, they can do without having an agreed or accepted Grand Strategy."[33]

While the trend within the EU away from common values and objectives was exposed by the 2008 global economic earthquake, the lack of a Grand Strategy manifested itself especially in the structural earthquake that struck the Arab world and Ukraine at the same time. When the transformation of the global economic-political crisis into a European crisis gave rise to questions over who was responsible for the crisis, how the economic costs were to be covered, the respective roles of national and EU institutions in decision-making processes, and, most significantly, how to bring the political consequences under control, member states surrendered to a mindset that prioritized individual over common interests. While the governments of countries undergoing economic crisis saw the potentially high political costs and fiscal policies as lying within their sovereign domain, other states, especially Germany, were disturbed by being in the position of having to meet the costs of the crisis through financial support demanded by EU institutions. On the other hand, countries that had become detached from the field of manufacturing or had become economically peripheral as a result of the domination of the single market and the Eurozone by countries (again, Germany in particular) with strong manufacturing strength, were overtaken by concerns about how they would survive alone in the face of fresh shocks.

This psychological transformation led some countries to start viewing the union as a burden rather than a field of beneficial interest. Countries outside the Eurozone, who were outperforming Eurozone members, and the ability of non-EU states such as Norway to develop alternative policies with closely linked countries presented the option of being an autonomous area without entirely disconnecting from the EU.

The regional earthquake set off by the Arab Spring that activated all the EU's neighboring areas, and the Ukrainian crisis, led to a fragmentation not only of economic but also political preferences within the EU. In this sense, the refugee crisis that developed within this cycle of crises, and which accelerated the pace of both economic and regional quakes, presented a real litmus test. The aspect that I particularly noticed during my discussions with EU leaders during my tenure as Prime Minister of Turkey in late 2015 and early 2016 was that the political divergence under way in the EU had taken on a dimension that far surpassed the considerations of a technical migration issue. At that time, I observed at close quarters the corrosion not only of the European common political decision-making process, but of its infrastructure of shared political values.

The reactions of certain Central and Eastern European countries, conspicuously and depressingly exemplified how a humanitarian problem at the very heart of Europe could be posited in an ideologically exclusionary context. Removing the refugee issue from its human and humanitarian context to posit it as a Muslim invasion of Europe and propounding a rhetoric proclaiming the need to defend and protect Christian Europe against this imagined threat[34] constitutes an approach that entirely negates the fundamental principles of the EU, principles to which these countries put their name in the 1990 Charter of Paris before they were EU member states. Such a polarizing approach recalls the Thirty Years War born of sectarian conflicts, the exclusionary ideological frameworks of the period between the two World Wars, and ultimately the environment of the Cold War's iron curtain. The fact that barbed-wire fences along borders might form new iron curtains across Europe, that rising Islamophobic rhetoric might once again cause exclusionary racist ideologies to grip people's minds, and that rising racist parties may become viable alternative governments constitutes a highly cautionary tale in terms of the evident capacity of this extreme discourse to gain a mass base.

Moreover, the effects of the Arab Spring and the Ukrainian crises on the EU have shown that the regional/continental order is not sustainable in isolation from developments in neighboring regions. Safeguarding the stability and order of areas of prosperity surrounded by zones of economic and political crisis is very difficult. Especially today, when regional interaction has intensified via new means of transportation and communication, it is impossible to isolate even the best-run regional structures from this interaction.

We have now reached a point when the EU, a great success story in terms of establishing regional/continental order in the post-Cold War era, has transmogrified into one of the main centers of the ongoing systemic crisis. There are three striking symptoms of this crisis that could have a profound impact on the continent's political order: Brexit, the sociodemographic change wrought by migratory movements, and the ascent to the status of alternative governments in elections held in 2017 of political trends and leaders who are diametrically opposed to the EU's founding principles.

Brexit cannot be viewed merely as the departure of a single member state whose effects will be limited to this single event. Examples from Britain's history make it evident that it cannot circumvent unification movements on the continent of Europe by forever keeping its distance. However – and many historic, geographic, and cultural elements verify this analysis – the timing of the process leading up to the separation of a central member like Britain is noteworthy. Winston Churchill's call to build "a kind of United States of Europe" at an address at the University of Zurich in 1946 should not be forgotten:

> We must build a kind of United States of Europe ... The structure of the United States of Europe will be such as to make the material strength of a single State less important. Small nations will count as much as large ones and gain their honour by a contribution to the common cause. The ancient States and principalities of Germany, freely joined for mutual convenience

in a federal system, might take their individual places among the
United States of Europe ... Therefore I say to you "Let Europe
arise!"[35]

This was a call for the formation of a new future for a Europe squeezed
and divided between two poles under the leadership of the two emergent
superpowers.

Today, Brexit, being undertaken at a time when the EU's
sustainability as a strategic power is under challenge, is not a mere
technical process of departure, but a strategic rupture. The manner in
which Britain's separation from the Union affects the common foreign-
policy-making process will also influence the EU's status in the international order. The fact that the P5 membership of the UNSC has up to
now had two EU members means that following Brexit the EU will only
be represented on this council, which remains of such vital importance
for the international order, by France. While this new state of affairs
increases the strategic and diplomatic weight of France within the EU, it
could also lay the groundwork for Britain for a more flexible stance
between the EU and the United States. Therefore, the future shape of
post-Brexit UK–EU coordination will have an impact on the EU's
general strategic influence in every field, especially on UN platforms.

Brexit also carries the risk of setting a new example, or even
a new pattern. In the event that countries that do not see their national
interests in the EU, or countries that perceive a deterioration in
the cost-benefit balance, follow this example, the diversion of the
integration–disintegration dialectic in the course of European history
towards disintegration could gain pace. Historic experiences of different
periods in European history have shown that as soon as the disintegration dialectic prevails, it is impossible to predict the future, pace, and
timing of the process. Like a stone thrown into a pool, intracontinental
disintegration processes create unpredictable ripple effects.

Disintegration on a continental scale threatens to bring the
risk of nation-state fragmentation by further shaking the pliability of
intertwined boundaries that have in any case lost their validity in EU
processes. The processes and mechanisms of the EU, regarded as
building-blocks of nation-states, might be profoundly affected by issues
such as the 2017 Catalonia crisis, continuing demands for Scottish
independence, and political problems in multilingual and multiethnic
nation-states, especially Belgium. Although the Catalonia crisis appears

to have been overcome through the EU's backing for the central government in Madrid, this cannot remove the groundswell facing some nation-states. The fact that supporters of Scottish independence have long brought EU membership to the agenda as an alternative to membership of the UK presents a serious challenge with respect to how the EU will posit this groundswell on a principled basis. How the EU, which rejected Catalonia's demands for independence in order to prevent the break-up of EU member Spain, approaches the issue of Scotland, some of whose population wish to break off from Brexit Britain to integrate into the EU, and the possible effects of this on the continent, conjures up some significant question marks.

On the other hand, the likelihood of a change in perspectives of the Atlantic system in the Trump era in the United States, which has been the lead actor in the security umbrella in the Cold War and then in the integration process in Europe, could also lead to growing uncertainties. The Old Europe–New Europe dichotomy developed in reaction to the hesitant stance of Western European countries towards George W. Bush's intervention in Iraq has left its mark in people's memories. The impact over the continent of future US–EU strategic incompatibilities will be directly influenced by the strategic choices taken from now by Britain, which sees itself as a bridge between the two continents.

The fact that the departure of Britain, a part of the European identity for centuries, from the EU, and the mass movement of migrants and refugees with different geographic and sociocultural identities towards Europe from a massive area extending from the interior of Africa to the Middle East and as far as Eurasia has occurred at the same time signals a dynamic historical process that is set to have a long-term impact. To return to our earthquake analogy, as Britain enters a process of distancing itself from the continent of Europe with Brexit based on the impact on the English Channel of the fault lines thrown up by the systemic earthquake, the faults on the Africa, Mediterranean, MENA, and Eurasian line are driving these regions' human element towards Europe.

In this dynamic process, the EU will either choose to fall into a romantic and nostalgic nationalism that harks back from the nineteenth century to the middle of the twentieth century, or understand the nature of this change and promote multicultural European values over narrow and exclusionary nationalist templates in order to rebuild the European identity. The first option will serve to distance the continent of Europe, the leading actor that helped shape human history from the sixteenth to the twentieth centuries, from global trends by narrowing identity references in an even more exclusionary manner and constricting the EU's internal integrity and values system. The second path will require the redefinition of the European identity in a value-referenced fashion. This necessity, which seems hard to digest socioculturally, will bring the continent of Europe into global processes and make it an active and decisive element in the flow of history once again.

In fact, the most instructive guide on this subject is European history itself. Looking at the continent of Europe from the perspective of ethnocultural identity change, the decisive impact of movements of people and migrations is hardly new. The ethnocultural basis of the very Europeans now trying to withdraw into themselves are the product of historical processes similar to those upon which current trends are based. Most of the countries now putting up an exclusionary resistance to migratory movements were formed from the historically transformative impacts of tribal migrations on the settled Roman order. In this context, they need to appreciate that the crossing of the Danube River by German groups was regarded as an existential threat, and those who resisted by defending the status quo of the Roman order had to accept this historical flow in the long term and that European history and identity – and German identity – was shaped within a change of this kind. Likewise, the impact of the entry of the Huns into Rome (AD 452) on Hungarian history, the transformative effect of flows of Vikings on the settled order of the Anglo-Saxons (who had themselves migrated to the island of Britain centuries before), the establishment of the first French kingdom (AD 481 – the Merovingian dynasty) as a result of the transformation of the order handed down from Rome by the Germanic Franks who flooded into present day France, and similar cases, were all the result of the interaction between the dynamism formed by large-scale migratory movements and settled orders.

The basic difference between these examples and today's migratory movements is that current flows are mobilized by socioeconomic factors, and are unarmed. This modern migration to Europe was initiated on the will of European countries as a way to close the workforce deficit that emerged in the economic reconstruction of Europe after the Second World War and gained pace in the process of enlargement to the east after the end of the Cold War. It is clear that the latest migratory and refugee movements have had a profound impact on European political culture because of a failure to draw sufficient lessons from the accumulation of experience from the Middle Ages to the modern period and to develop inclusive policies around common values.[36]

There are two key reference points to resolution of the refugee and migrant issue currently having such a profound impact on the EU's political agenda and processes: the accumulation of historical experience, and multicultural European values. However, it seems that the extreme right-wing anti-refugee and anti-migrant nationalist movements now on the rise in Europe are unaware of the fact that their own national formations are the product of migrations to Europe and that one of the most important values in the founding of modern Europe is multiculturalism.

To give an example from my own experience, I had the occasion to give a speech in my hometown and parliamentary constituency of Konya as Prime Minister at a time of growing anti-refugee rhetoric in which I said:

> Let not those who are coming out against the refugees forget our great world-changing thinker and poet Mawlānā Jalāl al-Dīn Rūmī came to Konya in the 13th century as a refugee fleeing Mongol oppression. No one who respects the words of the Mawlānā when he uttered those immortal words *"Come, come again, whoever you are, come! Heathen, fire worshipper or idolatrous, come! Come even if you broke your penitence a hundred times, ours is the portal of hope, come as you are"*, can come out against the refugees.

This historical example impressed the conservative base, which held the Mawlānā in enormous respect. Social leadership in great and critical historical processes is not about going along with the emotive flow of social processes but requires the steering of these processes by rational historical experience and fundamental human values.

Unfortunately, however, the winds in Europe are blowing the other way. The simultaneous course of Brexit and refugee and migrant issues brings with it pressures on the EU for a dual solution. As well as Brexit constituting a significant factor in terms of the systemic crisis's reflection on the EU, the real danger in this context is the destructive impact of rising extremist tendencies, xenophobia, and racism on the collection of liberal, participatory, and multicultural principles that constitute the philosophical foundations of the EU's formation process. In the past, differences between political parties in the EU were about policy preferences; care was taken to safeguard the groundwork of common political principles. Elections in 2017 show that this feature has changed and divergences have now shifted to the ground of principles. The possibility of Le Pen winning the last presidential elections in France is as significant of itself as it is in terms of her ability to find a mass popular base for such a concept of political philosophy.

Today, the ability of the EU to overcome this systemic crisis depends on intellectuals, opinion leaders, and policy-makers who share the visionary characteristics of the EU's founders redefining and re-establishing the common principles and ideals of the EU. However, just as indications of such a struggle and quest are unfortunately hard to detect today, we are faced with the fact that the very people who have the capacity to undertake such an effort are themselves caught up in the populist *Zeitgeist* of the age.

Russia: Challenges of Reconsolidating Power

The end of the Cold War had its deepest impact on the USSR, which lost its superpower status, and its successor state Russia. In this process, Russia took over five main elements of powers from the USSR that gave it the ability to maintain its status as a global power: (i) the continuity of state institutions, experience, and know-how, particularly intelligence and security structures; (ii) the inherited international status and privileges granted to the USSR as a superpower, in particular P5 membership status; (iii) its sphere of influence in its Cold War hinterlands, especially the new republics that had separated from the USSR; (iv) an accumulation of scientific and military technology, in particular nuclear capacity; and (v) a wide territorial expanse extending into the depths of Eurasia, home to the world's richest energy resources.

As it happened, during the quarter-century since the end of the Cold War, Russia has witnessed periods of tension and dynamism veering between the risk of fragmentation and its key objective of gaining a new global power status based on these sources of power. Every earthquake that has rocked the post-Cold War international system has added new dimensions to this tension and dynamism. Russia has grasped the opportunity to regain the international status and power lost in the dying years of the Cold War by taking strategically systematic advantage of these new dimensions.

The geopolitical earthquake inflicted its most profound impact on Russia. A three-phase rupturing of fault lines led to profound psychological, strategic, political, and economic effects. The first phase was the USSR's loss of depth in Central and Eastern Europe and its withdrawal from the Baltic–Vistula–Danube line to that of the Baltic–Dniester–Black Sea as the geopolitical consequence of the dissolution of the Warsaw Pact in 1991. This meant not only a territorial loss, but the loss of a continental center of gravity. This withdrawal actually meant the changing of hands of the Eurasian line of transition between these two lines that had formed the critical threshold of German–Russian and Ottoman–Russian balances throughout history, in favor of the Brussels–Paris–Berlin-oriented EU.[37]

Subsequently, its efforts to exert influence in the depths of Eastern Europe through traditional Slavic solidarity over the Bosnian and Kosovo issues were only possible by virtue of the advantages its P5 membership in terms of enabling Russia to keep its foot on the international brake pedal. Having already lost predominantly Catholic and Germanic societies and countries, Russia's concerns about losing its influence over Slav and Orthodox societies and countries caused it to see its UNSC veto not as a requirement of a status based on international law, but rather as a strategic card. This geopolitical earthquake and its consequences were accompanied by a severe convulsion in a Russian geopolitical conceptualization based on its influence over the Baltic–Danube–Adriatic line inherited by the Soviets from the Tsarist era.

The second phase of the rupturing of geopolitical fault lines occurred with the dissolution of the USSR as a state and subject of international law on 26 December 1991 based on Declaration No. 142-N of the Soviet of the Republics of the Supreme Soviet of the USSR. During this process, the Russian Federation that formed the successor state to the USSR[38] began an endeavor to adapt itself to a new situation in an area in which it had lost significant sea lanes on the Baltic shore, withdrawn to the Dnieper and Don line, suffered a narrowing of its Black Sea and Caspian shore lines, been disconnected from the Southern Caucasus, and lost its Central Asian depth.[39] This withdrawal was seen as a withdrawal from the sphere of influence in the Russian geopolitical conception to its historical line of existence and led to Russia–Ukraine relations being attributed a significance and meaning beyond that between two independent countries. Looked at from this perspective, the political change in Ukraine in 2013 may be viewed as the aftershock of the geopolitical earthquake of 1991. The concentration of today's clashes in Ukraine in the region between the Dnieper and the Don is a result of the fact that this is the region where geopolitical lines and ethnodemographic areas overlap.

The risk of disintegration centered in the North Caucasus, especially Chechnya, represented the third phase of the geopolitical quake. Accompanied by the geopolitical earthquake, these successive shocks led to a severe psychological loss of confidence in Russia. In this context, Russia's strategic priority in the 1990s was concentrated on maintaining its internal integrity and consolidating power within the country. President Putin, with his background of accumulated experience in the Soviet Russian security and intelligence bureaucracy, took office in such a psychopolitical environment in the year 2000.

The 9/11 security earthquake that occurred a year after Putin came to power, and the profound shockwaves that accompanied it, brought with them certain international conditions that were conducive to this consolidation of power. The shift from freedom to security in international discourse, from humanitarian intervention to combating terror and preemptive strikes in strategic priorities, and from legal norms to unilateral intervention in strategic methodology, created the international environment that Russia needed for the internal consolidation of power. Indeed, crisis regions in the country (Chechnya in particular) have been brought entirely under control on the basis of an anti-terror strategy, as the country has been consolidated under a politically robust central administration.

In the meantime, Russia's staying out of the Afghanistan and Iraq Wars as well as the active areas of crises and tensions on the Middle East–Central Asia line facilitated a rehabilitation of international perceptions. For Russia, a period during which NATO and the United States have been preoccupied with the costs and consequences of their respective interventions in Afghanistan and Iraq has been a time for recuperation and the accumulation of power. In a sense, Russia did not directly feel the shockwaves of the security earthquake. On the contrary, it gained the chance to recover from the damage inflicted on the state structure during the geopolitical earthquake by means of security-oriented policies afforded by the psychological atmosphere induced by the security quake. And the experience that President Putin had gained in the security apparatus ever since Soviet times allowed him to take full advantage of this opportunity.

In a period when the Putin administration has been highly successful in terms of maintaining internal political stability and gaining international prestige, Russia's self-confidence has risen significantly and found reflection in more assertive foreign policy rhetoric and practices. Putin's address to the 2007 Munich Security Conference heralded this new psychology and approach. The three principal emphases in his speech showed that Russia had emerged from the impact of the geopolitical earthquake to stake its claim as an active party in reshaping the international order: its sharp criticism of the United States' unilateral methods,[40] strong underlining of multilateralism as a method of resolution,[41] and references to the changes in global economic-political balances in terms of comparative GDP's leading to a transition to a system of a multilateral balance of power.[42] These emphases reflected the basic elements of a new Russian strategic orientation and the nucleus of a new balance of power system that was emerging in the wake of the failure to transit from bipolar Cold War balances to an understanding of unilateral order. Different aspects of this orientation manifested themselves in subsequent foreign policy moves.

2008 witnessed two key developments in terms of Russia's burgeoning strategic perspective. The first was the intervention in Georgia, which showed that Russia had regained the capacity for operational military intervention beyond its borders and indicated that the country had in a sense overcome the loss of self-confidence suffered during the period of the geopolitical earthquake. This intervention signaled a reaction to the wave of "orange revolutions" that presented a security risk to the consolidation of power as well as Russia's determination to preserve, and if necessary exploit, the advantages it had gained from frozen crises in the early post-Cold War years.

The second major development was the rising trend of natural gas and oil prices in the wake of the 2008 global economic crisis. While this crisis caused severe turbulence within Europe, for Russia it provided an income stream to finance power consolidation and new strategies. The vacuum that developed with the transition in the US presidency from the assertive policies of Bush to Obama's more deliberative policies, and the beginning of a period in which the EU had to focus more on its own domestic issues, also expanded Russia's maneuverability.

Natural gas and oil prices rose further with the turbulence of the Arab Spring, reaching a peak with the intensification of the movement in 2011–2012. Apart from its opposition to the Libyan intervention and its support for the Syrian regime in the first phase of the Arab Spring at the UN, Russia generally pursued a policy of following developments. Russia initiated a more active and assertive strategy in 2013 parallel to the escalation of the Ukrainian crisis and the use of chemical weapons in Syria; Russia's military intervention in Syria in 2015 was the first time in the post-Cold War era that it had instigated a military operation beyond its near-abroad. The ineffective diplomatic efforts of the EU in Ukraine, and the United States in opposing the use of chemical weapons in Syria, laid the groundwork for a further expansion of Russia's area of maneuver. The annexation of Crimea on 18 March 2014 and the fall of Aleppo in December 2016 as a center of resistance to the Syrian regime under heavy aerial bombardment were only made possible by means of the effective exploitation of this area of maneuver.

In summary, from Russia's perspective, the security earthquake facilitated its political consolidation, while the global economic crisis provided the necessary conditions for a more active strategy. These opportunities compensated for the destruction wrought by the geopolitical earthquake in the early years of the post-Cold War era and this consolidation paved the way for the pursuit of a more assertive strategy during the Ukrainian and Syrian crises between 2013 and 2017, which constituted the second phase of the structural earthquake of the Arab Spring.

In this context, we are now in the throes of a comprehensive systemic earthquake with a reconsolidated Russia. This has played a significant role in Russia's political stability from 2000 to the present day. During this period, a state of strategic continuity and consistency has prevailed under Putin's leadership that originates from a state of political stability in marked contrast to the strategic discontinuity emanating from US presidents deploying extremely divergent political rhetoric and strategic priorities. The executive order of 7 May 2018 on the national goals and strategic objectives of the Russian federation through to 2024 clearly reflects an assertive strategy of power consolidation as a global power in a multipolar world, including the objective of taking Russia into the top five largest economies.[43]

That said, Russia faces significant challenges with respect to how this consolidation of power affects the systemic earthquake, and the role it might play in the transition to regional and global order. We may thus discuss three key problem areas in the transition processes from crisis to order.

The first relates to the fundamental principle of the legitimacy of strategic and military operations. In this sense, Russia's interventions in the crises in Ukraine and Syria harbor a severe internal contradiction with regard to the sovereign rights of nation-states. Russia, which opposes any military intervention in Syria without the consent of its UN-recognized regime and has thus encouraged the unsanctioned use of chemical weapons, which is recognized as a crime under international law, has in the case of Ukraine given its backing to separatists against that country's legitimate UN-recognized central government, and has suffered no consequences in its annexation of Crimea, a territory defined as part of Ukrainian territory according to UN norms. As a permanent member of the UNSC and an influential power from the Balkans to the Pacific and from Eastern Europe to the depths of Asia, it is both natural and necessary that Russia should play an important role in our emergence from the systemic earthquake that holds us in its grip. However, this role depends on a consistency of principles in the country's contribution to a new global order.

The second issue relates to how Russia will meet the costs of a strategy that involves flexing its muscles with cross-border operations and proxy wars in Georgia, Ukraine, and Syria for the first time since the end of the Cold War. It is clear that the Russian political elite, which is well aware of the risks inherent in the country lacking the might of the USSR's economic infrastructure to finance global interventions, needs to exercise extreme caution in this matter. By the same token, the United States, even with its overwhelming economic production capacity, has direct experience of the negative effects it suffered through its interventions in Afghanistan and Iraq and everyone was able to observe how it was caught off guard and unprepared for the global economic crisis.

The third, and related, problem concerns the structure of the Russian economy, which is more of a commodity than a manufacturing economy and whose sources of revenue are largely dependent on the cycle of international crisis–order. It is at this juncture where the most critical area of tension between Russian strategy and its economy lies. Statistics over many years show that commodity prices tend to rise during periods of international crisis. Yet these hikes are more cyclical than structural in nature. In this context, Russia's assumption of an order-forming mission may give rise to a paradoxical decline in economic revenues. In addition, falls in the demand for energy are likely consequences of international economic crises in particular.

This picture is directly related to the sustainable growth balances of commodity-based economies. As a general principle, while manufacturing economies can maintain sustainable growth within a political order that facilitates their products' access to markets, commodity economies are able to increase their reserves through conjunctural, crisis-fed cyclical price hikes. And beyond the Russian context, one of the key areas of tension concerning the economic basis of the current international order lies in this tension and conflict of interest between manufacturing and commodity economies. This state of affairs presents an even more contradictory situation for countries and groups of countries like Russia where the features of a commodity economy intersect with those of an economy that exports military technology. The fact that international crises tend to lead to price rises in both these sectors raises the issue of the optimization of the international order. The effectiveness of Russia's power potential in the context of regional and global order also depends on this optimization. Such an optimization can also help to ensure a transition from revenue increases arising from escalating crises to those emanating from the increasing productivity associated with regional and global order.

Russia faces a significant challenge in terms of the likely impact of an increasing supply of alternative and renewable energy sources on the prices of conventional energy sources such as natural gas and oil. The way in which the diversification of these resources influences the economic strategic balance is also important in terms of its impact on Russia's recent strategic action.

In any circumstances, if we wish to avoid a return to a new Cold War or a balance of power situation that increases uncertainty and destructiveness from the perspective of all players, and if an enduring and predictable international order is to remain a possibility, one of the key elements is the role that Russia is going to play and the nature of its engagement with other global and regional powers. Russia's contribution to establishing a new international order is also vital in terms of resolving issues on the *Rimland* shaken by the geopolitical earthquake, as well as in controlling global-scale risks and threats, particularly nuclear threats.

China: The Balance between Economic Power and a Global Role

With about one-quarter of the world's population and a very deep-rooted political tradition, China has risen to the status of the most important global power to have achieved a consolidation of power in the post-Cold War era. Just as some saw China as a new global power challenging the hegemonic power of the United States in this context, certain analyses tried to define a shared vision between China and the United States.[44] Some studies emphasized that, being motivated by China-specific impulses, China's influence in terms of constituting a global power was "more broad than deep" and suggested that in the future China would constitute a "partial power" rather than a full rival to the United States.[45] Henry Kissinger, who played such a key role in the softening of US–China relations and the initiation of the period of dialogue, makes particular reference to the cooperation of these two powers in efforts to establish a new world order: "When Premier Zhou Enlai and I agreed on the communiqué that announced the secret visit, he said 'this will shake the world.' What a culmination if, forty years later, the United States and China could merge their efforts not to shake the world, but to build it."[46] The trade wars between the two countries begun in the Trump era represent a test of this well-intentioned prediction.

Whatever the direction of all these commentaries and projections, they all agree that in the post-Cold War period China's distinctive strategic road map has been based on long-term transformation within the status quo rather than short-term reflexive reactions. In this context, each of the post-Cold War earthquakes has been a significant transformational junction in China's long-term strategy.

The first striking measure of this strategy of transforming over time within the status quo manifested itself during and after the Tiananmen demonstrations, which took place in the period when the Cold War was ending and demands for democracy were widespread. With its harsh response to the Tiananmen demonstrations, and its adoption of a strategy of opening up its economic structure to the rest of the world while preserving its political structure in a manner that differed from the approach taken by the USSR at the end of the Cold War, China endeavored to adapt to the conditions of the new era while preserving its state institutions and the main backbone of its political system.

The Prime Minister of Singapore Lee Kuan Yew, who as well as being of Chinese origin successfully steered a regional nation devoted to the pursuit of liberal economic policies during these critical times, sought to explain that in the post-Cold War era China would maintain its centuries-long political experience of strong centralized administration against the trend towards democratic change in the world and stressed that Western-style democracy would never be realized in China: "For 5000 years, the Chinese have believed that the country is safe only when the centre is strong. A weak centre means confusion and chaos. A strong centre leads to a peaceful and prosperous China ... Some in the West want to see China become a democracy in the Western tradition. That will not happen."[47]

This approach, which preferred continuity through transforming existing role definitions rather than radical change, manifested itself in both the rhetoric and the implementation of foreign policy.[48] There was to be no Perestroika- and Glasnost-like change in rhetoric for Chinese leaders in this period.

In the framework of this strategic method, which envisaged change within a continuum, China knew how to turn the impacts of successive earthquakes to its advantage. Remaining beyond the fault lines of the geopolitical earthquakes that took place in the 1990s, China devoted its efforts to economic growth, predicating its strategic superiority on its economic competitiveness at a time when Russia was suffering a severe loss of power and the United States and the EU were preoccupied with crises under way along the geopolitical seismic line. Using its status as a UN P5 member as a balancing factor against growing US power at that time, China barely felt the effects of the geopolitical quake along the European *Rimland* belt (with the exception of the 1999 bombing of the Chinese Embassy in Belgrade) and pursued a stance that focused heavily on its central objectives of consolidating its own power and opening its economy to world markets. The fact that East Asia enjoyed a regional atmosphere of relative calm without armed conflict in this period facilitated China's consolidation of its economic hinterland and turned the country into the economic locomotive of the region at an ever-growing pace. China's status was also heightened by the slowdown in Japanese economic growth and the influence of the Chinese diaspora in the economic structures of countries in the region.

The transformation of China from an inefficient, uncompetitive, closed economic structure into a rapidly opening global economic area enabled the country to achieve a consolidation of power that proved resistant to post-Cold War crises. Annual growth rates rose from 3.907 percent in 1990 to 9.294 percent in 1991 and 14.216 percent in 1992 and, apart from during the Asian crisis, this double-digit growth trend was largely maintained, never falling below 7 percent until 2016 (6.7 percent), including during periods of crisis.[49]

The 9/11 security earthquake created an international environment that, as in the case of Russia, legitimized China's resolution of its own internal problems using more authoritarian methods. The replacement of a prevailing discourse of freedom and democracy in the more secure international atmosphere of the 1990s with a rhetoric of security and control allowed the trauma of Tiananmen to be overcome and internal problems, especially the Tibet and Uygur issues, to be presented within a security context. This strengthened the *controlled politics with an economy open to global competition* adopted by China in the post-Cold War era and paved the way for sustained double-digit growth. During these years, when the attention of the United States was concentrated more on Iraq and Afghanistan, like Russia, China too was given the opportunity to expand its regional influence.

The impacts of global economic shocks on the Chinese economy have also been limited. The growth rate dipped from 14.23 to 9.4 percent from 2007 to 2009 but recovered to 10.63 percent in 2010.[50] The decline and stagnation in competing economies in these years has boosted China's relative advantages.

The effects of the structural earthquake that accompanied the Arab Spring in 2011 on energy supplies and prices has also led China to take a greater interest in other regions. Uncertainties in the regional and global arena have revealed the limits to China's growth, a major manufacturing power whose economic superiority has been achieved by means of the access of its manufactured goods to international markets; China's growth rate slowed from 7 percent in 2012–2015 to 6.7 percent in 2016, the lowest level in the twenty-six years of the post-Cold War era.[51]

The process of the systemic earthquake, accompanied by international uncertainty, regional crises, and global security risks, is facing China with fresh challenges. China can no longer be excluded from areas of international risk and liability, as it was in previous earthquakes, in a region where regional and global fault lines have been so profoundly ruptured. These challenges, which are reflected in the policies of Chinese President Xi Jinping, may be summarized under five headings.

The first is the need to reform the internal political structure that has been maintained throughout the post-Cold War era, one consequence of which was the measures promulgated at the Nineteenth National Congress of the Communist Party of China held on 18 October 2017, especially with regard to corruption. The fact that President Xi, who has himself come from within the Chinese Communist Party apparatus, focused on this issue during his address, reveals the perceived need for a generational and conceptual change in Chinese domestic politics today. Xi's process, which was given the name "Chinese dream of national rejuvenation," was in fact the definition of a new vision based on post-Cold War experiences.[52]

The second is the fact that the impact of uncertainty of the systemic earthquake has now also begun to affect the East Asia region. The central position of the nuclear threat on the international agenda; US military concentrations and maneuvers in the region; tensions between South Korea, China, and Japan; struggles for domination in the East and South China Seas;[53] and the consequent escalation of nationalist discourse in almost every country in the region could alter the prevailing regional state of affairs that has set the stage for China's economic ascendancy over the past quarter-century. When we then take the existence of US naval power in the region into consideration, the stance that China takes over regional stability may give rise not only to regional but also global consequences. China's efforts to become a dominant regional power may lead to the formation of opposing alliances with the capacity to give rise to a new regional Cold War environment. On the other hand, China's use of soft power to reduce tensions and play an active role in resolving the North Korea crisis could serve to bring the regional impacts of the systemic earthquake under control.

Thirdly, the security of transit and transport corridors connecting different regions and seas has risen to the top of the list of strategic issues for China, which is well on the way to becoming the leading supplier country in global commerce. The *Belt and Road Initiative* crossing Eurasia announced by President Xi, coupled with China's investments in critical sea ports in Africa and Asia coupled with road-building projects in their hinterlands, reflect this strategic perspective. Today, Russia's strategic interests pass through energy corridors, China's through trade and transit corridors. The security of these corridors can be guaranteed by the sustainability of stable regional orders. The link established between regional order and economic corridors in President Xi's speech at the opening of the Belt and Road Forum (BRF) on 14 May 2017 in Beijing reflected this perspective:

> [W]e should build the Belt and Road into a road for peace. The ancient silk routes thrived in times of peace, but lost vigor in times of war. The pursuit of the Belt and Road Initiative requires a peaceful and stable environment. We should foster a new type of international relations featuring win-win cooperation; and we should forge partnerships of dialogue with no confrontation and of friendship rather than alliance. All countries should respect each other's sovereignty, dignity and territorial integrity, each other's development paths and social systems, and each other's core interests and major concerns.[54]

Moreover, China's acquisition of large expanses of agricultural land in a number of African countries and its permanent projects in that continent will lead to a growth in its interest in more distant regions and the importance it attaches to regional stability here. This will lead to an increase in China's interest in the security and stability of regions beyond its immediate geographical area in the coming period. This interest will bring new opportunities as well as new risks.

Fourthly, the position and share in the global economy that China has now reached will necessitate the reduction of disorder and geopolitical risks that might impact global economic flows. With the world's largest manufacturing and trade volume potential, China's interests lie in the reduction of any geopolitical risks that could increase energy production costs and the establishment of a secure order to guarantee the flow of trade.

Regional and global uncertainties will lead to increased energy costs as well as a slowdown in trade flows. The most significant strategic priority difference between Russia and China lies in the fact that the former is a commodity economy, the latter a manufacturing economy. The fact that the 2011–2012 spike in energy prices that accompanied the Arab Spring coincided with an increase in Russia's reserves while slowing China's economic growth represents a noteworthy example in this respect.

Fifthly, all these factors brought about by the ongoing systemic earthquake will require China to play a more active role in the quest for regional and global order. The crucial point is what priorities and which methods will be deployed in the fulfillment of this role, especially in the UNSC. The regional and global strategy that China adopts will be highly significant in terms of the future of efforts to bring the systemic earthquake under control.

In summary, the state of global power relations today shows that neither the bipolar structure of the Cold War era, nor the structure based on a single dominant power of the immediate post-Cold War era, prevails. Successive earthquakes in the international system and their impacts on changing processes within the global powers themselves have led to an extremely dynamic and changeable environment.

The strategic positions taken by global powers in the wake of the aftershocks of these earthquakes and the conjunctural relations that have developed through reciprocal balances have turned the international arena into a multiplayer chess board in which a number of games are being played at the same time. This multiplayer game of chess has of its nature given rise to a network of international relations operated on the basis of tactical steps rather than strategic vision. This state of affairs has driven global powers to focus their attention on increasing their concentrations of power to take advantage of the existing chaotic environment rather than committing themselves to an endeavor to establish an enduring and sustainable international order. This environment, which we might call *multiple balances of power*, leads to the corrosion of the basic principles upon which international order must rely and prevents the development of common positions to counter the systemic earthquake.

Part II

A NEW VISION: INCLUSIVE GOVERNANCE

5 FUTURE PROJECTIONS AND BASIC PRINCIPLES OF A NEW ORDER OF INCLUSIVE GOVERNANCE: THE FIVE I'S

One of the most significant consequences of the fragilities created in national, regional and global structures by the ongoing systemic earthquake process is unpredictability. Whatever the subject matter of these successive and dizzying seismic shocks, and at whatever level they occur, they do not facilitate our ability to make future projections.

The surprise effect and unpredictability mostly impacts the psychology of decision-making processes. Actors unable to make future projections and see far ahead are induced to accumulate power and take precautionary measures according to negative scenarios. This leads in turn to the weakening of the value dimension of national, regional, and global mechanisms and the proliferation of a general sense of pessimism.

Alternative Future Projections: Possibilities and Ideals

Looking at the general trend, we may state that we are walking towards the possibility of three different futures. The first possibility is a state of global chaos to the extent that the inability of actors to develop a common will leads to the disintegration of fragile structures in the natural course of events, and a large-scale and comprehensive war resulting from rivalries between powers taking account of this disintegration. In this projection, which means a repetition of the scenario between the two World Wars, tensions and the effects of seismic shocks progressively intensify and a new global war becomes inevitable. In such a scenario, a new world order will only be established after this war, shaped around the principles adopted by its victors.

The second possibility is a global autocracy involving the establishment of an autocratic order or orders high in the power to control and low in participation levels by a group of countries or leaders exploiting the struggle to escape from an escalating and spreading state of chaos and the psychology of pessimism, and using the extraordinary possibilities presented by the technological communications revolution to bring their own populist and exclusionary claims to life. The globalization of an authoritarian tendency of this kind, buttressed by the "worst state is better than no state" argument favored by traditional state structures to demonstrate the drawbacks of chaos and the importance of the continuity of order, means the delayed realization of Orwell's *1984* conceptualization. This scenario could occur as a single autocratic Leviathan, or the creation of a widespread and hierarchic order by a number of Leviathans resembling one another.

The third scenario, which we might call global democracy, could be the product of the motivational will of policy-makers, politicians, thinkers, and opinion leaders with the backing of society, based on the centuries-long and bitter experiences of humankind and bestowed with the participatory virtues of shared values. The sole prerequisite for such a participatory, embracing, and inclusive approach on the national, regional, and global scale is that it is realized this time without entering a new world war.

The truth is that when we examine the available data and the general stance of today's politicians and policy-makers, a realist would predict a future in a space where there is some kind of combination of the first and second scenarios. However, when asked what the scenario *should* be, the same observers would point to the third.

We thus find ourselves once again facing the most time-weary problematic of all, stemming as it does from the ideal–real, theory–practice dichotomies of humankind's political quest down the ages. When our mental balance is weighted to the "real world" end of the scale, we are led to waiting for our inevitable fate, while when the balance swings to the ideal end of the scale we find ourselves at risk of being trapped in the idealist boundaries of our imaginary world. The first stance would detach us from our will, the second from the realities we experience. The state of shock induced by successive earthquakes threatens to imprison our will; an escape from existing realities, our mind. Therefore, what we need to do is release ourselves from the psychology of pessimism, establish a healthy balance between a normativism attached to reality and a realism that takes values into account, and then to create a new projection of order within the harmony of this balance.

In order to elicit a new order's doctrinal basis, one needs to define the fundamental principles that will constitute the intellectual substructure for international, regional, and national-scale endeavors and guide practical applications. In this and the following chapters, we shall first determine the principles of such a projection of order, before moving to a discussion of the prospects for adapting these principles to the national, regional, and global structures, and what needs to be done.

The systemic earthquake process in which we now find ourselves calls for principles that are processual rather than piecemeal, integrative rather than disintegrative, feasible rather than hypothetical. Based on the experiences of the post-Cold War era and the requirements that have surfaced, we may assert the existential nature of five key principles in the reconstruction of national, regional, and international order: *inclusiveness*, *internal consistency* (the harmonization of values and mechanisms), *interest optimization* (the optimization of individual and common interests), *implementation* (of the power structure), and *institutionalization*.

The first two of these principles (inclusiveness and internal consistency) define the idealist foundation, the following two (interest optimization and implementation) the *realpolitik* framework, while institutionalization provides the bridge and transitivity between them. Experience shows us that while an approach defined by ideal values alone struggles to find implementational grounding, a *realpolitik* that is detached from values undermines its doctrinal grounding. A new understanding of order is attainable by overcoming the idealism-realism tensions experienced throughout human history. In this regard, the extraordinary communications potential that has now reached every level of society presents encouraging opportunities as well as serious challenges.

Basic Principles: The Five I's

Inclusiveness

I believe that when we consider these principles one by one, the principle of inclusiveness is of primary importance, because any order that is not integrated into the system and fails to include all actors and elements – be it on a national, regional, or international level – cannot be effectively run or sustained. Every actor excluded from or rendered inactive by the order either seeks out an alternative order in alliance with similarly excluded parties, or becomes an element of potential chaos.

This principle has shown its impact not only in the modern era but at all stages of history. A look at the traditions and orders of the great empires shows that the Germanic tribes who were not included and internalized in the Roman order first disrupted this order and were then influential in establishing the Holy Roman-German order, which did include them. The Protestant princedoms excluded from the Holy Roman-German order shaped the course of history that led to the chaos of the Thirty Years War and then to the Westphalian order.

This phenomenon finds reflection in the geography of the Middle East with the leadership of the non-Arab Muslims (*Mawālī*), who were unequally treated in the clannish *asabiyyah*-based Umayyad order,[1] in the emergence of the Abbasid order.

The non-Arab elements that had been excluded from the system for a period then took control of it, thus positioning themselves at the center of the political order. Ibn Khaldūn, who had placed the concept of *asabiyyah* at the heart of his theory of political order, described this change as follows: "Then, the days of Arab rule were over. The early generations who had cemented Arab might and founded the realm of the Arabs were gone. The power was seized by others, by non-Arabs like the Turks in the east, the Berbers in the west and Christian Europeans in the north."[2]

As we have emphasized before, the concurrent use of the four titles symbolizing the past orders of the classical age by Ottoman sultans who had drawn lessons from this historic experience (Caliph/Islam, Khān/Tūrān, Pādishāh/Iran, Caesar/Rome) was designed to emphasize their status as the continuation of the great orders of the past and therefore that all these different elements had legitimate authority. In this way, they symbolically demonstrated that their own orders had internalized and integrated all the communities that had previously been under the domination of different political traditions. As Amy Chua underlines, "the Ottomans derived great benefits from their strategic tolerance."[3] Indeed, when the Ottoman State lost its inclusive capacity, it initiated a process of chaotic division.

This dialectic of inclusiveness also played a significant role in the dissolution of the colonial empires, which by their natures observed no such principle or purpose. The main impetus of the independence movements in India and Algeria was the incapacity of the governing elite, who remained differentiated from the indigenous society in every respect, to incorporate an inclusive philosophy into their governance. This also applied in the case of the Apartheid regime, one of the last representatives of the logic of exclusionary colonial governance brought about by a lack of inclusiveness. And once again, it is the inability to be inclusive that lies at the root of the existential tensions in Israel, a state founded on a colonial rationale.

This same dialectic, which has defined the fate of attempts to establish new orders throughout history, also applies to the nation-states that constitute the building blocks of today's international order, and to the regional and international struggles for order that have shaped them. Nation-states that had been sustained by static external balances associated with the bipolar Cold War structure faced a severe test of their inclusiveness when these static balances began to lose their hold. States pursuing an inclusive approach embracing the entire range of identities within their boundaries as part of their concept of citizenship passed this test to enter the new era in a stable condition while those who were unable to do so fell prey to a chaotic course marked by division and conflict, as we have seen in the cases of Yugoslavia, Iraq, and Syria.

The inclusiveness principle influences more flexible regional structures as well. It is true that the EU has scored successes through its capacity for inclusiveness towards Central and Eastern European countries after the Cold War. Yet its postponement of Turkey's full membership on the pretext of issues like Cyprus that are not directly related to Turkey, and its promotion of countries that are further from fulfilling EU economic and political membership criteria than Turkey based on an exclusionary resistance to Turkey's accession process have exposed weaknesses in the EU's capacity for inclusiveness, as well as laying the ground for Turkey to develop a psychology of distancing itself from the EU. If it had been possible to complete this process of inclusiveness in the first decade of this century before the global crisis and the Arab Spring, the course of history would doubtless have taken a different path; neither the Islamophobia now growing in the EU nor the anti-European sentiment now growing in Turkey would have found such fertile ground in which to flourish.

For the international system overall, the most serious sustainability challenge stems from weaknesses in its capacity for inclusiveness. The profound differences in structure and authority between the UN's representative and decision-making bodies (the UN General Assembly and UN Security Council respectively) constitute a striking manifestation of this weakness. The inclusive nature of the General Assembly is rendered meaningless by the oligarchic decision-making mechanism resulting from the veto power of the five permanent members of the Security Council. For example, the veto of a single country on the Security Council renders decisions taken by the overwhelming majority of human society on the Palestinian issue entirely symbolic and bereft of any scope for implementation. The most recent example of this was on stark show in the UNSC and UN General Assembly procedures in the wake of President Trump's declaration of Jerusalem as the capital of Israel. Similar situations have arisen as a result of other countries' veto powers, especially with respect to the Syrian crisis. In terms of the sustainability of the international order, the frailty of inclusiveness in the international system is currently one of the most fundamental challenges facing not only the UN but the system as a whole. Today, the most significant obstacle to any future efforts to establish order are exclusionary methods and approaches in the international system and the geopolitical tension they generate.[4]

To be able to establish a new, sustainable order we should never forget this basic lesson of history: excluders get excluded.

Internal Consistency

The second principle directly related to inclusiveness is internal consistency. The idea and implementation of order harbors within it a condition for internal consistency. No order can be formed and made sustainable by a concept or structure lacking in internal consistency.

There are two minimum conditions for achieving internal consistency; the existence of an internally consistent system of values jointly espoused by the order's actors, and mechanisms to ensure the practical implementation of these values. Even with an agreed system of values, in the absence of a proper mechanism they will remain abstract ideals without the capacity to form the philosophical/ legal/ political substructure from which an order is constituted. On the other hand, when there is no agreed system of values, or when the essence and influence of these values is lost, any kind of mechanism turns into an interest-dependent tool.

Today, both the national and international order face weaknesses arising from a severe lack of internal consistency on both counts. First of all, values have been hollowed out by weaknesses in implementation mechanisms while the legitimacy that these values bestowed on the international order was undermined. Every value violation that occurred in front of the international community stretching from the genocide perpetrated in full view of UN forces in Srebrenica in 1995 to the use of weapons of mass destruction in the Ghouta area of Damascus in Syria on 21 August 2013 served to destroy the meaning of those values. In spite of the UN Secretary-General's clear call in stating that "The international community has a moral responsibility to hold accountable those responsible and for ensuring that chemical weapons can never re-emerge as an instrument of warfare,"[5] no sanctions were applied against those who had committed war crimes in violation of international law and values. The apathy of the international community laid the ground for the subsequent and frequent repetition of these crimes. The failure to protect shared values has hollowed them out and led to a lack of internal consistency that has shattered the very soul and spirit of the order.

Moreover, the international principles and conventions that are primarily the reflection of shared values are applied selectively. This selectivity is generally shaped by the national preferences of the P5 countries. For example, the United States, which with an international coalition has fought the Daesh terror organization, sees no issue in arming the YPG, which is organically linked to the PKK, a group the United States itself defines as a terrorist organization. By the same token, Russia, which legitimizes its military intervention in Syria through the thesis that it was invited in by the UN-recognized government of that country, is also able to grant itself the right to support separatist groups against the UN-recognized government of Ukraine. The same P5 members who call on all countries to comply with the nuclear Non-Proliferation Treaty (NPT) and the Chemical Weapons Convention (CWC) and, if necessary, apply sanctions to enforce compliance, turn a blind eye to Israel's remaining beyond such conventions. On the other hand, the nuclear weapons states, led by the United States, insist on compliance with non-acquisition of nuclear weapons while failing to comply with the Article VI obligation to seek nuclear disarmament in good faith, an obligation unanimously confirmed by the International Court of Justice in 1996.[6]

These value-action and value-mechanism contradictions are also apparent in the internal structure of a number of nation-states, leading to problems of legitimacy. The ethnic, religious, and sectarian discrimination seen in various countries claiming to be founded on principles of common citizenship and the values of the rule of law constitutes one of the most significant risks to the sustainability of the nation-state order.

To summarize, the double standards present at every level today erode shared values and promote a lack of trust and confidence in the existing order. This state of distrust and insecurity leads to a "jungle order" in which everyone takes a stance based on their own interests and power rather than shared values, a path that only serves to intensify the systemic earthquake. What is needed is a reappraisal of the existing conventions and body of knowledge that comprise the foundations of our shared values in a way that responds to new challenges. The attainment through such a reappraisal of a totality to create internal consistency in an updated system of values through appropriate mechanisms is one of the essential conditions of the struggle for a new order.

Interest Optimization

It is in the nature of the national and international order that concerned actors struggle to maximize the realization of their own interests. Shaped by all kinds of negotiation, reconciliation, tension, and war, the flow of history emerges in the area of competition and rivalry of these maximization struggles. Envisaging a new order that will eradicate this area is unrealistic. Yet the existence of a competitive environment of this kind does not necessary entail a state of value-destroying chaos. Values determine this environment's rules, define its boundaries, and fix its points of reference. The relationship between an idealist approach that highlights values and a realism based on the irreconcilability of conflicts of interest is itself determined by the relationship between the naturalness of a differentiation of interests and the rule-making characteristic of values.

When values lose the power to determine the rules of competing interests, rivalries first turn into tensions, then escalate into clashes, and ultimately wars. The substance of national and international order is measured by its capacity to prevent such escalation. In environments where order is functional, this area of competition is determined by peaceful means with diplomatic tools. In the transition from a state of order to one of disorder, the rules defined by these values first become blurred, then lose their effectiveness and finally start turning into a state of nature in which the concept "man is wolf to man" (*homo homini lupus*) prevails.

The key point here is to create an environment that optimizes mutual interests by keeping competing interests within the scope of rational negotiation. The performance of national and international mechanisms in terms of establishing and conserving order is about ensuring this approach and environment, guaranteeing the sustainability of the order by providing the opportunity for rational negotiation that optimizes individual and common interests.

There are three options in the struggle to maximize interests, each of which has a different impact on the course of the competitive environment in the national and international system: the win–win, win–lose, and lose–lose options.

When the concerned parties achieve a win–win optimization of interests as a result of rational negotiation, confidence and trust in the rules grows and everyone experiences the satisfaction of getting their fair share under the order's arbitration. Every time this option is repeated, the order consolidates itself and its sustainability is boosted. The success story of every diplomatically achieved resolution has a positive impact on the functioning of the order and the performance of its mechanisms as a growing atmosphere of optimism comes to fruition.

When the win–lose option recurs, the consistently losing side starts losing trust and confidence in the order. And when this loss of trust leads to alienation from the order, the losing party tends to bypass the rules it believes operate consistently against its interests. On the other hand, the winning party starts to develop a cavalier attitude to the binding nature of the rules, an attitude based on a psychology of excessive self-confidence and superiority and seeing the optimization of its own interests as a natural right without even feeling the need to negotiate with the other side. Thus, as a result of the winning party's excessive self-confidence and the loser's loss of confidence and trust, a tendency not to conform to the order's values and the system's rules manifests itself to such an extent that any shared belief in the sustainability of the order is destroyed.

In lose–lose cases, the order's gravitational force begins to fade. The extensive recurrence of this situation entices the parties either to relapse into a state of disorder or to advocate a new set of rules that they believe will maximize their interests. The increasing occurrence of this situation in national orders is observed in fragile states where de facto areas of dominance take shape. Nation-states that constitute the center of power of the common order thus begin to unravel, leading to the emergence of a chaotic process that also has an impact on the international order. By the same token, the recurring "non-success story" of the lose–lose option in international relations first shakes trust in the order and then leads to the domination of an ever-expanding psychology of pessimism over the process.

When we look at the actual functioning of the national and international order today, we observe that the first (win–win) option is the exception, the second (win–lose) is dominant and the third (lose–lose) is on a progressively rising trend. This has led to a growing sense of pessimism about the functioning of the current order as actors lose hope that they will emerge as beneficiaries. Such a state of pessimism and insecurity drives every actor to act unilaterally to protect their own interests to the extent that their power permits. Attempts to optimize interests through unilateral action rather than rational negotiation first stretch the rules, then render them meaningless, and ultimately invalidate them. We may discern four phenomena as both cause and reflection of this spreading sense of insecurity and pessimism.

The first is the almost total absence of any success story in terms of reaching final resolutions, in spite of the accumulation of dozens of problems in the wake of the earthquakes that have shaken the world in the quarter-century that has passed since the end of the Cold War. Efforts to reach such resolutions have achieved either provisional ceasefires (Nagorno-Karabakh, Abkhazia, Ossetia, et al.), fragile states of peace (Bosnia-Herzegovina, Kosovo) or limited conjunctural deals (the Iran nuclear deal). Concerns that fresh chaotic developments might take place even in the event that conflicts are somehow halted, and that one side might act to attain a win–lose position to its own benefit if appropriate circumstances arise, only increases fragility in the order.

The second phenomenon is the prevailing sense that parties have been treated in a discriminatory manner in efforts to resolve crises arising from conflicts of interest in the operation of the international order. And in a manner of speaking, the theoretical value that "all parties are equal in the international order" has become a case of "some are more equal than others" when it comes to practical implementation. In negotiations the "more equal" side is protected and rules are interpreted in such a way as to protect that side's interests. This leads the protected party to disengage from agreement until such time as a solution that maximizes their own interests in absolute terms is fashioned.

The most striking case of this kind is the inability of the Oslo Process, launched with the hope that the Palestinian people would finally be free to live in their own country, to achieve the objectives it set itself at the outset of a process that began a quarter-century ago. In spite of the fact that the Declaration of Principles (Oslo I) clearly refers to "a transitional period not exceeding five years, leading to a permanent settlement based on Security Council Resolutions 242 and 338,"[7] this transitional period has not been completed in the intervening twenty-five years. Nor is it expected to be completed in the foreseeable future. The fundamental reason for this is that this is not a situation in which the two parties have an equal negotiating position that might force a win–win position. Underlying this is one party's belief that it has the support of a veto that will prevent the imposition of any penalty or sanction come what may, as well as that same party's exploitation of all the advantages of being a state. Israel's knowledge from the very beginning that any decision or resolution contrary to its interests will be vetoed by the United States encourages that country to say no to any solution that fails to maximize its own interests while miring the Palestinian side in an ever deeper sense of pessimism and despair. The trauma inflicted on the objective functioning of the international order in this process has spilled beyond the Palestinian side, having led to an intensification of mistrust in the international system first in the Middle East and then in the Muslim world as a whole. The effects of the psychopolitical trauma resulting from Muslim societies' belief that they have been marginalized from the international system are manifest in almost every field.

A similar imbalance in the Cyprus issue, of all the problems left over from the Cold War the closest to a lasting solution, has prevented the emergence of an otherwise feasible success story. Following the successful conclusion of rational negotiations under the coordination of then UN Secretary-General Kofi Annan, the permanent peace settlement signed by the parties in Bürgenstock in April 2004 was approved by the Turkish Cypriot population but rejected by the Greek Cypriot population in a subsequent referendum; a potential success story was stillborn.

A successful negotiation process took place with the contributions of all parties, especially the UN with a view to achieving the resolution of the Cold War-legacy Cyprus issue both for itself and as a precedent and example for numerous other frozen crises; my own cold-blooded assessment of events – as someone who participated in negotiations in advisory and ambassadorial capacities – from the past to the present day is that the most significant factor in the ultimate failure of this process as a result of its rejection by the Greek Cypriot side is the state of inconsistency and inequality that stemmed from the inability of certain international actors, the EU and the UNSC in particular, to adopt a balanced stance between the two sides.

The main factor in the Greek side's rejectionism was the effective manipulation in the referendum by opponents of the peace settlement of a sense that "the Greek side won't lose anything if they say 'no'; they can get peace on more favorable terms for themselves when they join the EU." While the Greek side went to the polls safe in the knowledge that they would lose nothing if they rejected the Annan Plan, the Turkish side voted under the threat that ongoing embargoes might be tightened even further. The Greek side encountered no sanction whatsoever in the wake of their saying "no" but was rewarded with membership of the EU the following month. On the other hand, the embargo implemented against the Turkish side which had said "yes" was maintained unchanged despite the report of UN Secretary-General Kofi Annan on the process, which clearly suggested lifting sanctions and restrictions against Turkish Cypriots:

> The Turkish Cypriot leadership and Turkey have made clear their respect for the wish of the Turkish Cypriots to reunify in a bicommunal, bizonal federation. The Turkish Cypriot vote has undone any rationale for pressuring and isolating them. I would hope that the members of the Council can give a strong lead to all States to cooperate both bilaterally and in international bodies, to eliminate unnecessary restrictions and barriers that have the effect of isolating the Turkish Cypriots and impeding their development.[8]

This privileged status has induced the Greek side to steer clear of a permanent settlement until their interests are maximized in the next rounds of negotiation. Had a balanced approach achieved a lasting solution to the Cyprus issue in 2004, the upbeat momentum of this success story would have had a positive domino effect on the search for solutions to other problems.

The third phenomenon is that the emotional political atmosphere dominating today's international environment has led to reflexive position-taking based on emotional impulses instead of a rational negotiation psychology. This has rendered rational interest optimization impossible and caused parties to focus more on which of their supporters' emotions can be satisfied than on what they might achieve rationally. In a sense, "interest optimization" has given way to "emotion maximization." Escalating heroic rhetoric combined with micro-ethnic and micro-nationalist emotions have completely bypassed any negotiation psychology based on rational give and take and laid the ground for the spread of a polarizing "all or nothing" approach that raises tensions.

The fourth phenomenon is that even areas of shared values and interests impacting on the future of all humanity have been sacrificed to the confrontational language of national positions. As we have previously underlined, continuing to take positions that are reduced to individual national interests even in matters that concern the common future of mankind, such as climate change and nuclear armament, threatens not only the international order but also the living spaces of future generations.[9] Yet unfortunately today, the prioritization of highly individual interests even in global issues that concern all our futures is making it impossible to entrench a benevolent consciousness of international order. It is not possible to develop an understanding of international order that embraces all humankind without a harmony and balance between the shared destiny of mankind and individual national destinies.

Implementation of the Power Structure

One of the important *realpolitik* principles of national and international order is the need to maintain a power structure that ensures the protection of values and the enforcement of rules. In the event of a failure to combine internal consistency of values with the power structure in a meaningful and integral manner, there will either be no implementation area for values and rules, or it will become impossible to form a control mechanism that will keep power elements within legitimate boundaries. The former condemns the national and international order to remain on paper as an unrealized utopia; the latter makes it inevitable that all kinds of power relations will influence and transform the order in an uncontrolled manner.

Looked at from the perspective of the international order, three issues are significant in terms of power–order relations; (i) the legitimacy of uses of force designed to protect or restore order, (ii) the reflection of national power structures on international institutions, and (iii) how power–representation and power–justice balances are to be achieved in the international order.

The use of force is one of the order's main parameters that will take shape on every plane. But the questions of how the decision to use this force is taken, the processes by which it is legitimized, and how it is reflected in the field have a decisive influence on the character of the order. Legitimacy is brought into question as the number of participants in the process that decides on using force to protect the order decreases.

For example, there was a significant difference in the legitimacy of the use of force between the processes that led up to the first (1990–1991) and second (2003) Gulf Wars, be it in terms of the decision-making or implementation processes. In the First Gulf War, twelve resolutions were adopted by the UNSC between 2 August 1990 when Iraq invaded Kuwait and 29 November of the same year; UN Resolution 678 finally decided on the use of force in order to end the occupation of Kuwait and return to a legitimate state of affairs.[10] The Resolution authorized member states cooperating with the government of Kuwait to use "all necessary means" to restore international peace and security in the area unless Iraq fully implemented the previous eleven UNSC Resolutions relating to the invasion and occupation of Kuwait, by 15 January 1991. In this way, the intervention to restore the pre-existing order was legitimized.

The implementation of the second intervention against Saddam Hussein in 2003 without any such UNSC resolution on the use of force led to a debate on the legitimacy of the use of force that continues to this day. While the first intervention, carried out after gaining international legitimacy, achieved the ending of the occupation of UN member Kuwait and the restoration of the pre-existing order, the second intervention laid the ground for developments that were to threaten the regional order as well as shake the national order in Iraq to its core.

The fact that the international institutions charged with maintaining the international order reflect the power hierarchy between nation-states to some degree may be seen as natural or even essential, as these are the only means by which measures to protect the international order can be implemented. However, this reflection needs to be sensitive to changes in the balance of power and should not contradict the principles of representation and justice.

Looking at the power structure in the international order today, it is obvious that a serious gap has developed on these issues. With respect to the UN structure, the post-Second World War "victors' balance" has been preserved intact in spite of the passage of three-quarters of a century since then, with two distinct power categories: the privileged P5 equipped with their veto power, and other countries. The failure to reflect changes in the economic-political and military power hierarchy over this time in institutional structures has challenged the ability of emergent powers to contribute to the restructuring of the world order. In addition, while Europe is represented by three of the five permanent members of the UNSC (Britain, France, and Russia), Africa and Latin America lack any representation at all; with the exception of China, the non-Western and non-Christian cultural and civilizational basins that represent vast sections of humanity have been more or less totally ignored.

As we emphasized earlier, even though efforts have been made to close this gap with the G20, the platform where the world's economic order is discussed, it offers no representation whatsoever to the least developed countries (LDCs). And while the holding of an LDC meeting parallel to the 2015 G20 Summit hosted by Turkey in 2015 – based on the principle of inclusiveness[11] – represents a sensitive and sensible exception, the creation of a permanent consultative mechanism like the G8/LDC or G20/LDC that oversees justice and representation, as had been planned, has remained beyond the realms of possibility.

It will be extremely hard to form an inclusive order unless the principles of justice and representation are implemented in the power structure reflected in the international order today. This topic inevitably brings us to the principle of institutionalization.

Institutionalization

One of the indispensable principles and qualifications of any order, at any level, is institutionalization. Values find their practical manifestation through institutional structures. In the absence of institutionalization, values remain at the personal and subjective level and cannot be transformed into an order that functions through objective rules.

The most important point to note during periods when the national and international system is on a dynamic course is that institutionalization needs to be based on a dynamic process of restructuring, not a static perception of order. When the flow of history picks up speed, institutionalization's continued reflection of the old order's features and its adoption of a static character eventually render it anachronistic and out of tune with history. The dynamic flow of history challenges static structures and in the event that institutional resistance persists, cracks appear at first, followed by severe fissures.

The functioning of states is akin to that of the musculoskeletal system in people. In order for a person to be able to adapt to external impacts, the musculoskeletal system that gives the body form, support, resistance, stability, and movement needs to have precisely the optimum gold-standard degree of flexibility. Excessive flexibility in the musculoskeletal system (hypermobility syndrome) restricts the body's ability sufficiently to withstand external impacts and gives rise to problems of continuity and sustainability, while a rigid, inflexible musculoskeletal system risks being suddenly fractured by external impacts. Likewise, the survivability of institutional structures is endangered if they are overly flexible to international shocks and earthquakes, while excessively rigid institutional structures face the risk of collapse as a result of sudden fracture. The collapse of the Soviet system, which had an extremely rigid institutional structure, is a striking example of such a phenomenon. The key factor here is that institutional structures should have sufficient flexibility to facilitate the restructuring process that is required for their adaptation to new conditions.

One of the underlying causes of the earthquakes under way in the national and international system today is the fact that no restructuring process has been instigated with the capacity to adapt these structures to the dynamic course of history. The fundamental dilemma for nation-states during the Arab Spring also stemmed from this. Culturally it was anyhow difficult for harsh, exclusionary ideologies such as Ba'athism, based on a Cold War rationale, to sustain themselves in an environment where revolutions in technological communications are forcing the societies of regimes that rely on tight economic-political control to open up to the outside world. The ultra-conservative struggle of these states to preserve the old order while reform processes restructuring their institutions were needed to adapt to the flow of history, led to a considerable degree of destruction.

The international order has been prone to a similar dilemma. In spite of the earthquakes of the past quarter-century, the institutional structure of the international system has not undergone any serious process of reform and restructuring. If an evolutionarily progressive process of institutional restructuring had been undertaken starting from the geopolitical earthquake of 1991, the damage wrought by subsequent earthquakes could at least have been kept under control. However, the fact that any decisions on this restructuring process can be vetoed by the leading actors of the old order has made the system highly status quo-oriented and closed to internal change. This leads the international institutional architecture to shake even more violently with every new earthquake. Like bones in a musculoskeletal system that have lost their flexibility, institutions that lack the flexibility to absorb shocks start to fracture. As a result, crises began to arise not from external factors but elements from within the system itself. This is why we call the widespread state of crisis in which we find ourselves a "systemic crisis/earthquake." The institutional resistance that supported the status quo has rendered the post-Cold War crisis structural and systemic.

Institutionally, both the national and international order today perceive the need for a serious process of restructuring. Any further delay may well pave the way for an intensification of the systemic earthquake and the proliferation of destructive tensions and wars. The infrastructure for a lasting order is prepared with the presentation of a new concept of participatory, inclusive institutional architecture with a visionary perspective.

Keeping three things about this process of institutional restructuring in mind during intellectual and operational endeavors will increase the chances of success. The first is to draw the necessary lessons from past historic experiences. There are many examples of long-established imperial orders unable to adapt to and take the pulse of the dynamic currents of history being abruptly shaken. And in the modern era, it is evident from the experience of the League of Nations that weaknesses caused by inadequate institutionalization made it unable to thwart the build-up to the Second World War.

The second thing is that the new institutional architecture must reflect current balances of power, not those that prevailed in the middle of the last century, and be flexible enough to meet today's needs. Institutionalization that fails to reflect current balances of power cannot be effective and functional in establishing order and managing crises. Likewise, an institutionalization that lacks the flexibility to include all elements in the order can hardly be all-embracing. It follows that the architecture of the new institutionalization must have the flexibility to incorporate all elements within its decision-making processes as well as providing a reflection of current balances of power to ensure the implementation of those decisions.

The third thing to bear in mind is that institutional restructuring must possess an intellectual infrastructure capable of anticipating potential challenges to building the order, and the operational tools to withstand them. Proactive crisis management is only possible by means of an institutional infrastructure of this kind.

One of the underlying causes behind today's systemic earthquake is the fact that national, regional, and global institutional architecture has lost the power to withstand fresh tremors. National and international orders whose institutions have been hollowed out and rendered meaningless are like edifices made of cardboard. No matter how impressive they may appear from outside, the slightest quake leaves them in ruins.

Every step taken towards the creation of a new order requires a new institutional architecture. Instances of institutionalization that have the capacity to build sound theoretical and practical bridges between ideal values and living reality constitute the most robust buttresses for the establishment and protection of a new order. And today, efforts to establish a new order through a process of institutionalization grounded on values and made functional by living realities maintain their prospects for success.

6 INCLUSIVE NATIONAL GOVERNANCE: FROM SURVIVAL TO SUSTAINABILITY

Nation-states are the fundamental building blocks of the modern international order. Order problematics and order systematics also originate from these building blocks. Today, these keystone nation-states are undergoing a severe test. The fragmentation of identities in the cultural dimension, arguments over sovereignty and legitimacy in the political dimension, the problematics of sustainable development in the economic field, and the ecological consequences of climate change present national orders with serious challenges. The assumption that "the nation-state as the ideal form of political organization and the nationality as the source of all creative cultural energy and of economic well-being"[1] that gained general recognition in the middle of the twentieth century is facing wide-ranging challenges within a dynamic process.

As legally recognized sovereign domains, nation-state structures play an essential role in providing individuals and communities with a political order within a secure space, as well as in the functioning of regional and international order. A crisis at the nation-state level thus soon triggers problems of order at the international level. And transformations at the nation-state level induce further transformations by virtue of their impact on the nature of the international order.

Likewise, the overall nature and balances of the international order directly impact nation-state orders. Nation-states do not exist in a vacuum, but within a dynamic process marked by their reactions to challenges that emerge within the international order's features and balances. Therefore, the relationship between nation-states and the international order is not a one-way subject/object relationship, but a two-way interactional one.

Although it narrowed individual nation-states' scopes of action, the static balance-based bipolar nature of the Cold War era also presented them with the opportunity to sustain themselves without feeling any need for very significant change. As a consequence of the security umbrella provided by the superpowers at each pole of the Cold War balance, the fact that challenges to nation-states were dealt with at a higher level allowed nation-states, especially those in the lower tiers of the hierarchy of powers, to enjoy a certain sense of existential comfort. Challenges emanating from within nation-states themselves were suppressed within the ideological framework upon which the Cold War was based, while external challenges could be overcome by being transferred to balances established at a higher plane.

This state of static equilibrium led states' ruling elites to take stances designed to preserve and protect the status quo; the need for reform and transformation was barely felt. Leaders with a sufficient level of mastery over these balances were able to remain in power for long periods of time on account of both poles' preference for long-term stability. Examples of such leaders, Ceauşescu in Romania, Tito in Yugoslavia, Zhivkov in Bulgaria, Saddam Hussein in Iraq, the Assads in Syria, Ben Ali in Tunisia, and Mubarak in Egypt, where the survival of the state became more or less synonymously identified with that of their individual leaders, were largely the product of this state of static equilibrium.

Two great transformations that have unfurled over the past quarter-century have exerted a significant and comprehensive influence on the nature of nation-states. The first is the severe endurance test imposed on nation-state structures by the quartet of global-scale earthquakes that jolted the world in the aftermath of the end of the Cold War. The geopolitical earthquake shook and tested the territorial existence of countries within its seismic zone; the security earthquake, the basis of states' legitimacy; the global economic earthquake, states' sustainability in terms of economic resources; and the structural earthquake, their institutional fabric. Secondly, political culture was left exposed to turbulent waters on the micro- and macro-scale by the eradication of state monopolies over the means of communication caused by the general technological revolution brought about by globalization. While the new communications tools introduced by this technological revolution increased states' control capacities, they also eliminated the state monopoly on horizontal communications between individuals.

These impacts, which faced each national state structure with challenges of a different nature, linked the existence and survival of states to their ability to adapt to new conditions rather than their capacity to preserve the status quo. States that proved able to adapt to dynamic conditions through a process of continuous self-renewal gained strength, while those unable to read this dynamic change correctly and demonstrated a static reflex faced the risk of losing even the powers they had accumulated during the Cold War era.

Today, state structures are undergoing perhaps the most rapid and comprehensive process of change and transformation ever experienced in history. As with any process of this kind, it contains both the symptoms of a state of crisis and the constructive elements of a process of restructuring. The simultaneous occurrence of recent analyses trying to show that nation-states are in a state of crisis, and viewpoints arguing that they are gaining strength, should be considered from the differing perspectives of this two-way effect.

However, the aspect over which we need to exercise the greatest caution is to avoid our minds being held captive by the generalizing nature of the category labeled "nation-state." Yes, nation-states are typologically equivalent and share a status as individual subjects under international law. However, the basic nature of every nation-state, its historic formation, its sources of power, geopolitical environment and sociopolitical fabric are different, and these differences confront every nation-state with divergent challenges in the dynamic conditions in which they now exist.

These divergent challenges make it difficult to treat the nation-state category as a large, single cluster. For example, in terms of geographic size, continental-scale Russia, Canada, the United States, India, China, Brazil, and Australia are nation-states, just as are the island states of the Pacific and the Caribbean. The first group faces the challenge of having to oversee a massive territory while the second face the tests of being narrow strips of land in the middle of an ocean. From the perspective of population density, countries like China and India, each of which hosts one-quarter or one-fifth of the world's population, are nation-states; yet there are also nation-states with a population in the hundreds of thousands. Countries containing a wide diversity of ethnic, cultural and sectarian identities like the United States, Russia, China, and India are nation-states, just as are culturally homogeneous countries containing more or less a few families or tribes. Countries whose histories have been filtered through deep-rooted state traditions like China, Turkey, Egypt, Iran, Russia, Japan, Italy, Germany, Britain, and France are all nation-states, as are countries that were born in the wake of the disintegration of the colonial empires after the Second World War, which continue to undergo the pains of the processes of statehood. Countries such as Germany, France, Italy, and Britain that were born out of the natural historical processes of the nation-state are nation-states, as are the Asian and African countries that emerged after this system had developed on the basis of decisions taken by central elites who moved from traditional structures to the nation-state system and the wholesale top-down importation of this system.[2] With their sophisticated production structures and developed economies, the United States, Germany, China, and Japan are nation-states, as are countries with commodity economies concentrated on a single sector. Luxembourg manages to create a very high *per capita* income in its miniscule territory thanks to a market-friendly environment, enabling her to host financial institutions, law firms, and accounting and advisory firms as a nation-state, whereas countries with enormous territories that fall into the category of LDCs can only generate a very much lower *per capita* income.

We do not cite these differences to create a hierarchy of importance or value between nation-states. Rather, our aim is to draw attention to the fact that when we refer to the crises or challenges of nation-states, we are talking about a huge category differentiated by highly divergent characteristics. From this perspective, for example, the most fundamental challenge facing nation-states containing numerous ethnic, religious, and sectarian identities is about how to form a coherent link between the concept of *nation* that defines the *state* and its subordinate identities. As countries with developed economies enter a struggle over how to make their economic growth sustainable on the one hand, they are facing the inclusivity problematic presented by issues of harmonization and integration within their own society of waves of migration stemming from international chaos and uncertainty on the other. While countries with long-established state structures find themselves facing a continuity/reform dynamic in terms of adapting to new conditions and reforming the traditions and institutions upon which these structures rely, some of which have become ossified, countries with newly acquired nation-state identities are suffering from institutionalization shortcomings and a dearth of political experience.

Nation-state structures, which represent the political units of modernity's concept of international order, face the new challenges of globalization in different areas and in different ways. This encounter includes elements that will affect not only the structures of the concerned nation-states, but the very future of regional and global order. We may treat the fundamental problematics of order shaped through the interaction of the determinant elements of national-scale political, cultural, and economic structures under five main headings: (i) the human component of national order: the issue of cultural and political belonging; (ii) the geographical component of national order: its geopolitical basis; (iii) the legitimacy component of national order: the freedom–security balance and justice; (iv) the economic component of national order: efficiency, productivity, and income distribution; and (v) the organic component of national order: institutionalization and structural harmony.

The Human Component of National Order: Cultural and Political Belonging

Throughout human history, one of the most prolific challenges that distinguishes humanity from other living creatures has been the human need to establish a balance between the features that define us as a common species and the diversities within our own species. The entire history of humankind has been marked by bitter experiences when this balance is unhinged, from the emergence of the caste system in Indian civilization and its existential discrimination between different kinds of people in the ancient era, to the slavery and feudalism that dominated the Middle Ages, to the racism that has lain at the root of wars that have caused the deaths of millions of people in the modern era.

In terms of existential characteristics, one of humankind's most significant distinguishing features is the diversity that we possess as a species. Three different approaches have been taken in quests for an order based on a balance between these characteristics. The first approach represents an effort to establish order on the basis of a monolithic culture and belief by eradicating diversity, which has led not to order but to chaos, despite all military superiority, since this approach, typified by the Nazi movement, runs absolutely counter to the intrinsic diversity of the human species. These "orders" manifest the domination of a group that sees its own sense of belonging as superior to others. The sense of belonging that dominates the political field is also expanded into the cultural arena. Divergent cultural identities are subject to forced assimilation, driven into exile, or liquidated. Balance is thus attempted not through the fulfillment and fusion of cultural diversity, but through direct or indirect annihilation.

The reference point of this exclusivist approach is the socio-political imagination of "the enemy within." The striking experiences and observations of Sayeeda Warsi, the UK's first Muslim cabinet minister, demonstrate that such a conceptualization is widespread even in democratic countries where multiculturalism has been declared as a basic sociopolitical value:

> Britain has often found groups within its border whom it does not trust, whom it feels have a belief, culture, practice or agenda which runs contrary to those of the majority. From Catholics to Jews, miners to trade unionist, Marxists to liberals and even homosexuals, all have at times been viewed, described and treated as "the enemy within." The Muslims are the latest in a long line of "others" to be given that label, from those like my parents who sweated and toiled in the mills of Yorkshire half a century ago to successful, integrated British citizens who now make up the growing Muslim middle class, it was a phrase used to describe me in government. As the granddaughter of two men who both served in the British Indian Army, I felt it was probably one of the worst insults to be directed at me. It told me that I did not belong in Britain. This book is my way of fielding the insult, by owning and dismantling the label "the enemy within."[3]

The second approach involves the preservation of this diversity, allowing it to follow its natural course in the absence of any legal regulations; yet while this utopian approach can succeed in small-scale societies, it is extremely difficult to sustain at a larger scale. This approach, generally applied to homogeneous communities, attempts to preserve the social order by tolerating minor differences without any formal regulation. However, when a community grows there is always a need for comprehensive formal arrangements. Notable examples include: the perceived need for a new formulation of inclusive identities and their symbolic reflections as well as for more wide-reaching urban and legal regulations that took account of the cultural characteristics of those areas as the dominions of Alexander expanded beyond the confines of Macedonia;[4] the transformation of the Roman Empire under its first African-origin emperor Septimius Severus (193–211);[5] the extension of Roman citizenship to all free subjects of the empire in 212 under his son and successor Caracalla; and the fact that the transformation of an act[6] establishing a city order defining the rules of coexistence between the Jews and various tribes living in Medina as a religious community into a self-standing legal order over expanding boundaries became one of the principal elements in the history of Muslim societies.

It follows that the third approach is to maintain these diversities within a legal order based on shared human values. The lifespan of political orders is largely dependent on the harmony that can be achieved between political sovereignty and cultural diversity. It is therefore very hard for states that prove unable to foster natural pluralism based on a consciousness of cultural belonging under the umbrella of a consciousness of shared political belonging to transform themselves into bodies that will sustain themselves over generations.

When we examine the pre-modernity traditions of political order of antiquity, it is evident that their continuity was achieved by means of a state of harmony and tolerance established between diverse senses of cultural belonging over large territories, and a sense of belonging based on political sovereignty. Cultural pluralism-based conceptions of order are sometimes based on deep-rooted customs and conventions, sometimes on traditions spreading over centuries, and sometimes on legal rules settled on equitable and just measures. In this context, we should look for the secret of the centuries-long perpetuation of the domination of the Ottoman State, one of the last examples of ancient political order that stretched from the Eurasian steppes to the interior of Africa and from Iran to Central Europe, not in its military might, but in the inclusivity of the *millet* system that granted some sort of legal autonomy to diverse identities and groups.[7]

Modernity and Identity

In the modern era, nation-states endeavored to define the subject of national order by organizing themselves on the basis of an identity of citizenship that formed an umbrella over cultural identities. In this way, they strove to develop political identities transcending sectarian/ethnic identities by turning the subjecthood and vassaldom of imperial order into the citizenship of the nation-state. Partial structures formed during the transition from the Holy Roman Empire to the Westphalian order were reintegrated under a superior national identity with the unifications of Germany and Italy.

As Peter Watson rightly underlines "[German-ness], as we now understand it, emerged in the late seventeenth and early eighteenth century" as a reaction to the exhaustion of the Treaty of Westphalia that "hammered out a new political reality, a loose confederation of states of very unequal size and importance: 7 (later 9) electors, ... 94 spiritual and temporal princes, 103 counts, 40 prelates, 51 free cities, all equally sovereign (or semi-sovereign) and around 1000 knights, all claiming authority but ruling collectively barely 200,000 subjects."[8] The transformation of this German-ness to a national identity leading to the unity of Germany was based on a "romantic national sentiment ... through admiration of the Middle Ages as high time of German history"[9] as well as on new socioeconomic factors such as establishing a customs union as an all-German institution of economic integration. In brief, national identities have played a role in unifying fragmented political entities in modern European history, especially Germany.

On the other hand, national identity took a different course when it came to the basins dominated by the Ottoman State and Russian Empire in the east of Europe. The Russian Empire was transformed into a socialist empire that strove to establish a new political order based on an ideological definition of identity of a "new man" transcending ethnic or national backgrounds which was "the cornerstone of Soviet civilization," according to Andrei Sinyavski in his reference to Mayakovsky's poem "That is not enough, comrades; Go on, turn yourselves inside!"[10]

The call to "turn yourselves inside" was in fact a call to cleanse oneself from historical identities and first to forget, then eradicate, different cultural identities. Supported by Stalin's brutal methods, this call was envisioned as forging the creation of a new "Soviet man." However, the post-Cold War geopolitical earthquake reintroduced various identities to history, a fact that showed the impossibility of liquidating identities formed by historical formations through ideological diktat. Ironically, the grandchildren of those who had conformed to that call returned to their historical identities by "turning themselves inside" once again. In other words, the self-perception fed and transmitted by historical processes entered a period of revival in opposition to modern ideologically based definitions of identity.[11] This led to the emergence of new national identity issues that spread to the most micro-levels in the post-Soviet era.

The Ottoman State entered a process of disintegration under the weight first of the nationalist waves accompanying the Balkans Wars, and then the emergence of new nation-states. Subsequently, the remaining areas of the Ottoman State that lay beyond the Republic of Turkey were divided up between the colonial empires in the aftermath of the First World War. In terms of the geopolitical division and the fragmentation of sovereignty in territories within the Ottoman State, the First World War had a similar impact to that of the Thirty Years War. The key difference in this process is that the division was defined not by its internal dynamics but the spheres of influence of colonial empires.

Political entities that had shredded cultural identities in an absolutely artificial manner thus took their place in the grand stage of history. Along with the post-Second World War dissolution of colonial empires, which were not based on any enduring link between cultural and political citizenship identities, nation-states and their citizenship identities were defined in line with colonial structures' spheres of influence. The impact created by the dissolution of the colonial empires was similarly observed in Asia, Africa, and Latin America.

When we look at the earthquakes that have struck in the wake of the Cold War, we can state that they have occurred along the main fault lines within the domains of the Russian Empire and the Ottoman State a century ago. The geopolitical earthquake in the early 1990s was mainly observed in the Russian-Soviet Empire basin. In this sense, Yugoslavia, where the disintegration in the Balkans hit hardest, essentially bore the features of a diminished Ottoman regime under Slavic control. The north–south fault line from Syria to Yemen and the east–west fault line from Iraq to Tunisia that started to shudder in the subsequent quakes and totally ruptured with the Arab Spring occurred in the Middle East and North Africa, which had lived within the Ottoman order for about 400 years.

In this context, one can hardly argue that the imperial structures that began to dissolve a hundred years ago transitioned to soundly functioning nation-state orders. In conjunction with these earthquakes, the territorial nation-states formed in the geopolitical and geocultural basins that disintegrated after the First and Second World Wars have entered a state of existential crisis. The fact that the sectarian, religious, and ethnic identities underlying the citizenship-based identities of "being" Ukrainian, Syrian, Bosnia-Herzegovinian, Iraqi, Yemeni, etc. have reached a state beyond the possibility of any process of inclusiveness necessitates the intellectual and institutional restructuring of nation-states. It is also impossible for nation-states that constitute the building blocks of regional and international order to form larger-scale regional orders without building internal national orders.

In this framework, it is necessary first of all to establish a meaningful connection between the fabric of cultural identity and the structures of political identity. Citizenship-based political identity structures lose their meaning over time if they do not include and embrace ethnic/sectarian-based cultural configurations. If cultural identity configurations cannot be attuned to political identity structures, they become a yardstick in a process of disintegration.

In this sense, the structural earthquake that led to such political fragmentation in the Middle East, especially after the Arab Spring, led to striking examples and agonizing processes. It is very difficult to place recent ethnic-sectarian tensions and conflicts in a meaningful context without an understanding of the historical background that separates the Middle East from other regions. Sometimes the most constructive feature within a region's flow of history is its capacity to instigate extensive challenges in another region or historical context.

Examined from this angle, the Middle East leads the ranks of those regions where the diversity of the human species is most intensely manifested on the stage of history. The culture of coexistence and cultural pluralism in this region, which has been the cradle of the most deep-rooted civilizational legacies of human history – the first agricultural communities, the most widespread religious faiths that have ever been inherited, and the most complex ethnic formations shaped by great migrations – is one of the key prerequisites in the search for a regional order. The longevity of ancient state traditions in the Middle East, where the most intricate cultural identities – from local tribes to state traditions – have coexisted, has depended on the extent to which these traditions were able to exhibit an inclusive stance towards these cultural identities. It is this fundamental deficiency that underlay the inability of political entities such as the Mongols and the Crusaders, who lacked the capacity to accommodate diverse cultural identities, to establish any enduring order.

One of the most fundamental dilemmas of the efforts of the nation-states that emerged after the First World War as a result of the dissolution of the Ottoman State, which was the final representative of an ancient state tradition founded on cultural diversity, to establish order either within themselves or regionally, concerns the question of how monolithic nation-state identities can be sustained in conjunction with a cultural diversity stemming from the depths of history. No state in the region today is identifiably homogeneous with a single ethnic/sectarian identity. Nation-states founded on assumptions of such homogeneity face severe challenges in how to manage the diversity of regional-scale identities that transcend borders.

In this context, the tension-filled process suffered by Iraq represents a noteworthy and shocking case in point. Saddam Hussein saw Kurdish and Shiite cultural identities as a threat to Iraq's nation-state identity and excluded them; in fact, he prepared the ground for the next process of fragmentation by his own hands. After Saddam Hussein, the Iraqi sense of identity has shifted to a Shiite orientation and an exclusionary approach to Sunni and Kurdish identities has made it impossible for Iraq to be rebuilt through a citizenship-based identity. This tension between the fabric of cultural identity and the political identity structure has led to exclusionary definitions of the identities not only of citizens, but of cities and towns. Starting to define Basra as a Shiite city, Mosul as Sunni, and Erbil as Kurdish, and the intensification of identity-based tensions in Baghdad and Kirkuk, which have been symbols of multiculturalism throughout history, has also begun to destroy a shared urban identity that constituted a way-station of a citizenship identity that unified the nation-state.

One may assert the following as a general principle: the fate of nation-states in the coming period will be determined by the ability of city identities to be inclusive. The loss of cities' characteristics as sociocultural and socioeconomic environments embracing a diverse tissue of cultural identities will have an unraveling impact on nation-states. The "Iraq is a little Middle East, Kirkuk a little Iraq"[12] argument that we used in order to explain the need not to break up this mosaic in the context of the Kirkuk issue during the Iraq War strikingly exposes the interaction and transitivity between local, national, and regional orders.

Different Nation-State Experiences and a Test of Inclusive Citizenship

In this framework, the principle of inclusivity that we have cited as a principle of a new order has a central role to play in the restructuring of the nation-state. Without strengthening their capacity to include diverse cultural identities in their citizenship-based identity, nation-states will find it extremely hard to overcome the crises they face. As we have seen in the case of Iraq, the monopolization of any cultural identity by a political identity of citizenship to the exclusion of other identities has a corrosive effect on nation-states. This threatens not the identity itself but its very ability to function, and the monopolization of identity that the nation-state imagines will protect it severs the bonds of belonging between the nation-state and a section of its citizenry. And as the Iraqi example has again made abundantly clear, today's *exclusionist* identity turns into the *excluded* identity of tomorrow.

It is therefore necessary for nation-states to be restructured not on the basis of monolithic identities but on a sense of citizenship identity that includes individual identities. This embracing citizenship-based identity should be viewed as a protective umbrella for diverse cultural identities. In terms of different cultural identities, the identity of citizenship should be considered as a bridge of belonging established by the political order, not as a rival or alternative to cultural identity.

The political order of nation-states is established via a bridge of belonging such as this, fortified by a representational capacity. In order to be able to establish some kind of order, even having achieved a sense of belonging through bonds of citizenship, nation states lacking the ability to give representation to diverse social segments are effectively driven to the use of hard power that leads only to polarization, then tensions, and finally deep conflicts.

As occurred in the Balkans and the Caucasus in the 1990s, and in the Middle East in the past decade, when tensions over people's sense of political and cultural belonging combine with geopolitical shifts, outcomes arise that increase nation-states' fragility, even their disintegration. Yet these tensions do not only apply to countries in areas enmeshed in geopolitical impacts. Today, almost every country, large or small, rich or poor, homogeneous or heterogeneous, modern or traditional, is affected by this tension.

As a result of this tension, countries with a historic heritage of deeply rooted political traditions such as China, India, and Russia that have expanded over vast swathes of territory and therefore contain a highly complex mix of ethnic, religious, and sectarian groups, have tried to overcome the turbulence of the post-Cold War era with controlled regimes and charts showing ever-growing economic accomplishment. It would be extremely hard to claim that the reinforcement of the security dimension of national order through Russia's hard-power-backed policies in the North Caucasus, China's similar policies in Tibet and the Xinjiang Uyghur Autonomous Region, and the Indian approach to its Muslim minority, especially in Kashmir, have been matched by any strengthening of people's sense of belonging. The impact of these policies on the long-term stability of national order will depend on how a meaningful bridge can be established between cultural and political identity consciousnesses. The question of how Russian, Chinese, and Indian national identities can include extremely diverse ethnic, religious, or sectarian groups will be decisive in terms of the long-term political order of these countries.

Turkey, which is akin to this group of countries in terms of owning a deep-rooted state tradition, faced similar challenges as it strove to maintain this legacy in a diminished territory after the dissolution of the Ottoman State. Fostered over long historic processes, Turkish political identity came to be used first for all elements of the Ottoman State,[13] then for the Ottoman State's Muslim elements, and finally, after the First World War, for an identity based on citizenship of the newly established Republic of Turkey. This had a significant influence both on the internal order of the new nation-state as well as the regional extensions of these elements with respect to countries in the surrounding region.

Turkey's intervention in issues that arose in the Balkans, the Caucasus, and the Middle East regions in the post-Cold War era, and their impact on Turkey itself, is related to these perpetuations of cultural identity. The fact that there are more Bosniaks in Turkey than in Bosnia-Herzegovina, more Albanians than in Albania, more Kosovars than in Kosovo, more Chechens than in Chechnya, more Abkhazians than in Abkhazia, almost more Georgians than in Georgia, and more Kurds than in Syria and Iraq, meant that political problems in these surrounding countries and regions played a role in the development of Turkey's domestic agenda. The direct flight of Bosniaks from the Bosnian war, Kosovars from the Kosovo crisis, Albanians from the Macedonian crisis, Abkhazians from the Abkhazian crisis, Georgians from the problems in Georgia, Chechens from the war in Chechnya, Kurds from

Saddam Hussein's chemical attacks and oppression, and Arabs, Kurds, and Turkmens from Assad's tyranny, to the safe harbor of Turkey, has reawakened connections between this historic legacy and a consciousness of political and cultural belonging. And in terms of its own national order, the most significant challenge Turkey will face in the coming period concerns how the country will be able to establish embracing, inclusive, and constructive relationships between these senses of belonging in the maelstrom of regions shaken by successive earthquakes.

Although the United States lacks a historic heritage of this kind and has a relatively new state tradition, the tension between cultural and political identity consciousness is valid there as well. The fact that American identity has not been indexed to an ethnic, religious, and sectarian reference point in the flow of its direct history such as Russian, German, Turkish, Arab, or Chinese, and its identification simply as the name of a continent, has been and continues to be an advantage in terms of its capacity for inclusiveness. The fact that its shared history of immigration makes it impossible for any ethnic, religious, or sectarian group except for native Americans to claim proprietorship over this vast territory and present other groups as strangers or foreigners, serves to strengthen this inclusive feature.

However, the reawakened exclusionary attitude of the WASP identity, which regards itself as the founder of the state, and, based on that perception, the owners and fulcrum of national order, constitutes the most serious risk to this inclusive capacity today. Exclusionary racist tendencies that trace their roots as far back as the American Civil War have begun to declare their political affiliation as the only legitimate reference point, regarding cultural pluralism as a peril for the future of the United States. Native American, African-American, Jewish, and Catholic identities that were excluded[14] through about two hundred years of struggle appear now to have been replaced by Muslim[15] and Mexican identities. This new exclusionary approach, which defines an American identity theologically legitimized on an Evangelical basis, has led to the creation of a sociocultural atmosphere in which the American political sense of belonging today has been able to change more or less state by state. This new theological definition of identity has the capacity to take even American foreign policy captive,[16] as in the case of Jerusalem being declared the capital of Israel. In this sense, the transition in the Oval Office from Obama to Trump represents not just a change of presidency, but of political culture that directly affects the American sense of belonging. Changes in the consciousness of American political/cultural identity is set to have an impact both on US national order and consequently on the course of international order in the upcoming period.

Europe is also undergoing one of the most complicated processes in terms of the harmonization of political and cultural senses of belonging. In the aftermath of the earthquakes of the past quarter-century and the integration/disintegration state of flux triggered by developments in relation to Brexit, Scotland, and Catalonia, a dynamic process is in play in Europe today in which three options under consideration: (i) the integration of national identities within a unifying superior European identity, (ii) entering a process of disintegration via the substrata of national identities, and (iii) the preservation of the present status of national identities and a definition of the grounds for the internal sense of belonging of each national identity.

The first option, which emerged during the 1990s at a time when a highly optimistic atmosphere was shaping up after the Cold War, created the expectation that an inclusive European identity could be developed. This expectation created such an atmosphere of optimism in the beginning of the 2000s that it appeared to many to herald the birth of a new generation (given the name "Generation E") with a European identity that was set to give rise to a United States of Europe: "Sociologists love to study Generation E, because it represents a new breed of European: a person who considers the entire continent – not just one country or city – to be 'home'."[17]

The most serious challenge in this context has emerged with the issue of whether this new European generation would be geographically, or culturally/religiously, based. Approaches based on a classification drawn up by political movements that reduce the European identity to a Greco-Roman-Christian cultural identity and see themselves as "true Europeans" and those who do not share this identity as "accidental Europeans" in spite of the fact that they themselves have different cultural/religious backgrounds have led to the exclusion of members of Generation E who see themselves as an essential element of the continent.

The ethnic slaughter in the Bosnian war, encouraged by a state of hesitation and unease over the formation of a Muslim majority state in the middle of Europe in the 1990s and far greater resistance to Turkey's accession process compared to other candidates despite the fulfillment of the Copenhagen and Maastricht criteria as confirmed by European institutions in the 2000s, constituted negative tests in terms of the envisioned European political identity's ability to embrace and include a Muslim cultural identity.

With respect to my country's future position in the continent of Europe, a term that gained currency in the negotiations in which I took part at the beginning of the EU–Turkey accession talks very much occupied me not only as a negotiating party but as an academician: *absorption capacity*. This concept was strongly emphasized in the Negotiating Framework set out by the EU on 3 October 2005 and presented us with an extremely ambiguous and subjective benchmark for the negotiations:

> In accordance with the conclusions of the Copenhagen European Council in 1993, the Union's capacity to absorb Turkey, while maintaining the momentum of European integration is an important consideration in the general interest of both the Union and Turkey. The Commission shall monitor this capacity during the negotiations, encompassing the whole range of issues set out in its October 2004 paper on issues arising from Turkey's membership perspective, in order to inform an assessment by the Council as to whether this condition of membership has been met.[18]

This concept was once again stressed in the Presidency Conclusions of the Council of the EU of June 2006 that effectively initiated Turkey's accession negotiations.[19]

Whenever this concept, which contrary to the Copenhagen and Maastricht criteria is totally vague and open to abuse, appeared on the agenda, I struggled to understand where this concept stood in the intellectual world of my interlocutors. Did this concept refer to technical problems in the process of economic integration, or was it paving the way for a cultural exclusion? Frankly speaking, although most of the time the stated reason was the former, it was the latter that lay in the intellectual background. Indeed, in terms of inclusivity, intellectual/mindset absorption capacity remains the fundamental issue facing the EU, regardless of Turkey's accession. Unless this issue is resolved by EU decision-makers and intellectuals, it will be extremely hard to develop an inclusive European identity and to maintain the EU's global power position based on this inclusive identity.

The recent reaction to the influx of refugees and the increasing influence of rising extremist currents in the political arena has increased doubts on the question of the ability of the European political identity to take an inclusive stance towards cultural identities. In addition, Brexit has shown that this test of an inclusionary capacity is not limited to Muslims.

The trend of cultural sub-identities to form their own sense of political belonging, which constitutes the opposite end of the first choice of European identity and escalated with the Catalan and Scottish referenda, has created an atomizing atmosphere of political culture within Europe that is paving the way for a domino effect process whose endpoint is far from certain. The disintegration of an identity of common citizenship into subcultural identities could result in a fragmentation that would shake European integration and even go as far as a transition to a kind of feudalism.

The Catalan referendum contained noteworthy elements with respect to EU and nation-state identities. First of all, the development of the crisis in Spain,[20] which had until recently been seen as one of the most successful examples of federalism, at the same time as Brexit, constituted a serious warning to the EU, which had set out a future of federal unity for itself. The dissolution being experienced in federated nation-states formed a new reality that required consideration for an EU vision that itself foresees a larger-scale federalism. In addition, the rapid growth of public support for independence in the non-separatist Catalan movement based on a federalist concept brought the risk of the rapid loss of the line between federal and separatist tendencies. The fact that this entire process gained pace as a result of the 2008 economic earthquake whose aftershocks were felt in the EU, especially from 2010, is also remarkable in terms of showing the relationship between the sustainability of nation-state structures and the economy. The risk of atomization faced by an EU aiming to achieve unification of the continent of Europe as an economic success story has raised doubts concerning the consciousness of a common identity and common destiny within Europe.

The failure of the first option and the potential uncertainties of the second have led to the third option being seen as an optimal way out. The future of both the entire nation-state experience that was born in Europe as well as that of the experiment in supra-nation-state integration – also developed in Europe – will be determined by what kind of common political future components can be forged from British and

French identities with their colonial imperial past, a German identity that remains a very powerful historic reference point at the center of Europe, a Belgian identity accommodating diverse cultural elements that impact politics even in its capital city, Spanish and Italian identities marked by economic income disparities that divide them into northern and southern regions, a Polish identity that has been under the pressure of German–Russian strategic rivalry throughout history along both banks of the Vistula, and international Scandinavian identities less affected by the ebbs and flows of European history.

The question of how European nation-states are going to be able to contain the clash of political cultures induced by the extreme racist tendencies that have risen to the top of the agenda in the context of the harmonization of cultural and political identities is one that concerns all these options. The answers to this question will not only be determined by the future of national orders in Europe and the common order of the European continent, but also by the way in which the international order will take shape from now on.

To sum up, one of the most critical elements of the sustainability of national orders in times of increasing international uncertainty is the internal harmonization between a consciousness of a shared political identity and cultural identity among the individuals who constitute one of the most critical elements of national order. The unique nature of the historical experience of each country and its specific geopolitical and geocultural environment are challenging this harmony in various ways. The ultimate sustainability of national order will depend on whether these challenges steer towards internal harmonization governed by inclusionary and embracing political methods and approaches. For Europe in particular, but also other places, the pressures and challenges of refugee and migrant flows have been testing harmonization capacities.

The Geographic Element of National Order: Geopolitics

The second significant compatibility issue in terms of the sustainability of national orders is conformity between the nation-state's territorial existence as recognized by international law, and the geopolitical existence comprising its geographic living space. No state in history has ever managed to grasp a conjuncture in which all such contradictions are eliminated. Every state has had various contradictions between their domain of legal sovereignty and their geocultural, geoeconomic, and geopolitical lines. The idea that these issues will evaporate as states' sovereign domains expand is also misconceived, since every expansion of territory or sphere of influence brings its own problems of geopolitical harmony. The crucial point is how the issues that can arise from these contradictions are contained and managed.

Therefore, one of the material bases upon which to evaluate the subject of the sustainability of national orders is an accurate understanding of the contradictions between territorial and geopolitical existence; the other is the ability to manage these contradictions using the correct methods. It is wrong to ignore these contradictions with a utopian approach that assumes the absolute invariability of areas of territorial sovereignty, just as it is to make them into an existential problem. The first will result in being caught unprepared for unexpected crises, the second leads to the emergence of zones of intense geopolitical tension with neighboring countries.

The static bipolar structure of the Cold War harbored within itself a global-scale geopolitical divide.[21] The geopolitical struggle between the Warsaw Pact/USSR in their effort to maintain control over a central land belt in the framework of traditional geopolitical theories and NATO/US efforts to control the seas and waterways surrounding the world's main continental land mass served to conceal the contradictions between nation-states' geopolitical realms of existence with a larger-scale geopolitical commonality. It was a direct reflection of this geopolitical logic that the bipolar struggle during the Cold War era took place principally on the *Rimland* belt, which consists mainly of the Eastern Europe–Balkans–Middle East–South Asia–Southeast Asia–East Asia peninsulas. The wars and tensions that coursed through the Cold War era manifested a reflection of global geopolitics rather than geopolitical struggles between individual nation-states.[22]

Even if the Cold War period appeared static in terms of geopolitical balances, it also witnessed highly dynamic developments with regard to the emergence of new geopolitical maps in nation-state formations. While established nation-states entered a period of geopolitical transformation,[23] ninety-five new nations joined the international community as subjects of international law between 1946 and 1986. Each of these nation-states, which emerged with the dissolution of the colonial empires, faced challenges related to its own geopolitical habitat. The concept of the "Third World" emerged as a result of this geopolitical transformation in the world order.²⁴ These nation-states also formed fascinating geopolitical maps either while emerging within natural geopolitical lines or in terms of the legacy of different colonial empires.

In this respect, for example, the geopolitical map formed by Senegal, which gained its independence from the French colonial empire, and Gambia, which gained its independence from the British colonial empire, reflect the 1889 Anglo-French colonial partition agreement rather than natural geopolitical lines. In such geopolitical conditions, while the continuity of nation-states is achieved when there is a relationship that reflects global geopolitical balances, changes in countries' global polar preferences constitute an existential tension for countries that have unnatural geopolitical maps. A striking example of this phenomenon is the fact that the 1981 Marxist uprising against President Dawda Jawara in Gambia threw Senegal into crisis. The efforts of the leaders of both countries to form the Confederation of Senegambia in the wake of the uprising aimed to overcome this geopolitical artificiality. The decision of Senegalese President Macky Sally and his Gambian counterpart Adama Barrow to set up the Senegalo-Gambian Presidential Council in March 2017 represents a good example of an effort to overcome geopolitical abnormalities handed down from the colonial period while preserving nation-states' existence in international law.²⁵

In summary, the emergence of numerous nation-states during the Cold War period led to tensions that remained until such time as the position of these states in the global geopolitical balance became clear. These tensions, which intensified when legally recognized borders did not conform to geopolitical lines, were brought under control by means of the global geopolitical balance between the two poles. In this sense, global-scale geopolitical stability has granted nation-states microgeopolitical balances. Political elites tried to form the national order of new states within this balance.

However, the fact that the post-Cold War geopolitical earthquake shook national structures at the same time as global geopolitical balances made it harder for national orders to achieve a new equilibrium. In addition, the fact that unlike the other colonial empires Russia, the central country of the ideological Soviet imperial order that dissolved after the end of the Cold War, had direct borders with the newly emerging states had a direct impact on their national orders. Every convulsion in the newly emerging states had an impact on Russia's national order while every change in Russia had an impact on the orders of the new nation-states. The geopolitical tension between de facto borders, ongoing ceasefire-based orders, and legally recognized nation-state borders threatens the internal order of nation-states as well as the nation-state order itself.

With the dismantling of this global geopolitical umbrella at the end of the Cold War,[26] the geopolitical struggle began to spread on a micro-scale to multiple areas of tension sustained by each nation-state for its own survival and existence. The geopolitical earthquake that struck in the immediate wake of the Cold War activated fault lines between the territorial integrity of states on the Balkan–Black Sea–Caspian belt, natural geopolitical areas and the distribution of geocultural demographics. As a case in point, Bosnia-Herzegovina, whose geopolitical grounding within the State of Yugoslavia was anyhow somewhat unnatural and only had a very narrow corridor to the open sea, broke up into two subunits with the further fragmentation of its internal geopolitical ties in the aftermath of a bloody civil war. Tensions between territorial integrity and geopolitical fragmentation also confronted Moldova, Georgia, and Azerbaijan with issues of internal integrity that have lasted for a quarter-century. And finally, the throes of tension between the geopolitical and geodemographic dynamics of the Eurasian steppes and internal territorial integrity began to unfurl in Ukraine.

Another striking example is the fact that the fragmentation undergone first between the colonial empires with Sykes-Picot and then between the nation-states that emerged after the Second World War in Mesopotamia – which has maintained its characteristic as a common geopolitical area from the earliest periods of history to the present day and played a determining role in Akkadian–Sumerian, Assyrian–Babylonian, Greek/Roman–Persian, Byzantine–Sasanian, and Ottoman–Safavid balances – became one of the main focal points of regional problems during and after the Cold War. This fragmentation was accompanied by the issue of the sustainability of these nation-states' borders.

In this sense, each nation-state has faced different challenges in its ability to protect and preserve its borders. For example, the nature of Turkey's borders with Iraq and Syria are associated with two differing challenges. While Turkey's border with Iraq separates natural geopolitical lines passing through extremely high mountain ranges, its border with Syria split up the natural human fabric by virtue of the fact, just to give one example, that it runs along railway lines that pass right through town centers. The fact that the border lines drawn by the 1921 Treaty of Ankara were determined by the course of a railway line that cut through the center of cities and towns meant the fragmentation not only of natural geopolitical structures but of family structures as well. This is why cities and towns along the Turkey–Syria border have names with the same meaning in Turkish and Arabic.[27]

Every crisis in the region profoundly shook the geocultural and geoeconomic makeup of an abnormal geopolitical structure. Countries wishing to preserve their own national orders on this geopolitical foundation had to confront cross-border risks. During the Iran–Iraq War and the subsequent intervention in Iraq, Turkey therefore found itself confronted with the obligation to go behind the mountain range to mount cross-border operations in order to counter a terror threat that had infiltrated across these mountainous zones along the Iraqi border, whose security is extremely difficult to control, and with exceptionally harsh confrontations with regard to terror and refugee issues along the Syrian border that overlaps a web of human fabric.

Kuwait, established in the most strategic geopolitical zone where Mesopotamia opens onto the Gulf of Basra, felt itself under the unremitting pressure of Iraq, which considered itself to have been cut off from the geopolitics of the Gulf of Basra over this area. This clash of geopolitical perceptions, which Saddam Hussein's ambitions turned into an occupation that led to the first widespread war of the post-Cold War era, played havoc not only with the balance between Kuwait and Iraq, but the past quarter-century's balances over the entire region. With the intervention of the international coalition in the framework of UN resolutions, Kuwait reestablished its sovereignty within its internationally recognized borders, while Iraq has effectively lost sovereignty within its own borders and has effectively been divided into three geopolitical zones of control.

Just as it was thought that the previous state of integration would be restored with the 2003 US intervention, this time the Daesh threat emerged as a challenge right along the lines divided by the north–south Sykes-Picot borders in a geopolitical area that split the Iraqi and Syrian states horizontally from east to west along the Mosul–Dayr al-Zawr–Raqqa–Aleppo lines. The efforts first of Daesh and then the PKK/YPG terror groups to fill the vacuum to the east of the Euphrates, caused by the struggle for control between regime forces and the moderate opposition FSA along the Aleppo–Homs–Hama–Damascus–Daraa line that constitutes Syria's geopolitical backbone, led to consequences that threatened the territorial integrity of Turkey, Iraq, and Syria.

Today, as a result of the Arab Spring structural earthquakes in nation-state structures in the Middle East, the Turkey–Syria, Syria–Iraq, Syria–Lebanon, Turkey–Iraq, Iran–Iraq, Egypt–Libya, Libya–Tunisia, and Saudi Arabia–Yemen borders run along fragile lines that are very difficult to control in terms of areas of sovereignty, and the geopolitical foundations of national orders are being shaken. It is not possible to forge the elements of regional order in a state of affairs in which national orders are so fragile.

Similar issues concerning the compatibility between the territorial integrity that has such a direct impact on nation-states' sustainable stability, and geopolitical lines, also apply to other regions. Problem areas such as Bosnia-Herzegovina, Kosovo, Transdniester, Abkhazia, Ukraine, Crimea, and Karabakh all reflect the same discrepancy between nation-states' legally recognized areas of existence and their geopolitical spheres of influence.

Today, the most fundamental question that will influence the sustainable stability of national orders, as well as the reconstruction of regional and global order, concerns the manner in which these contradictions will be resolved. The most essential prerequisite action is to avoid tensions that will further intensify problems in these areas and threaten the security of nation-states as a whole. Efforts to resolve problems by diplomatic means reduce the risks inherent in emotional or epic reactions by bringing a sense of shared rationality into play.

The inclusivity, internal consistency, and interest optimization that we have cited as the principles of a new order serve at least to contain these contradictions. Relations of shared security and economic interdependence to be developed between the nation-states who are parties to these contradictions shall constitute the infrastructure for both national orders and regional order. It should be remembered that every deployment of hard power aimed at overcoming these contradictions in favor of one particular party may also threaten the overall security of the party that seeks to exploit such power. The devastating effects of Saddam Hussein's invasion of Kuwait on Iraq, and the bloody wars in Bosnia and Kosovo initiated by Milošević on Serbia, are there for all to see.

The transformation of the Alsace-Lorraine region, the cause of countless wars that had affected the borders between France and Germany ever since the Treaty of Verdun in 843 divided up the legacy of Charlemagne between the two countries, into a zone of cooperation by means of abolishing the region's status as an area of geopolitical tension under the umbrella of the EU, a policy that has created an area of common interest between them, is a case of successfully overcoming geopolitical contradictions. The replacement of historic claims between the two countries by political reality, and of sentimental heroics with an approach of rational cooperation, played a key role in overcoming geopolitical tensions.

The burgeoning relations between Turkey and Syria between 2003 and 2011 also represent a positive case in point. The fact that the two countries were on opposite sides during the Cold War resulted in relations in the border regions that housed a legacy of human and spatial continuity to follow an extremely harsh course governed by an iron-curtain rationale. This iron curtain led to a process of alienation between human and spatial elements divided by unnatural borders harboring geocultural and geopolitical continuity. This alienation narrowed the area of security, cultural, and economic cooperation. Relations that started to develop rapidly from 2003 laid the grounds for overcoming these geopolitical contradictions as well as geopolitical and geoeconomic ruptures, and the reestablishment of the natural relations along the border that had endured over centuries. The opening of the borders, lifting of visa requirements, mine clearance in border zones, and joint economic development projects in border regions strengthened both states' national orders and minimized the risks stemming from geopolitical contradictions.

However, the bloody and wide-ranging attack against its own people by a Syrian regime in the hands of a sectarian/cultural minority of 12 percent of the country's population after the Arab Spring in 2011, and the mass exodus of much of the population as refugees across the Turkish border, turned a border that in spite of all geopolitical contradictions had finally been turned into a belt of peace into a belt of threats that posed all kinds of security risks to Turkey. The failure of the Syrian regime to manage the gap between its peoples' consciousness of political belonging and sectarian/ethnic belonging (indeed, their provocation of existing divisions), combined with the negative interaction of geopolitical contradictions along the Syria–Iraq line, led to an ever-accelerating snowballing of problems that had a profound impact on both national orders and the regional order.

To sum up, it is extremely difficult to overcome fragilities in nation-states without establishing geopolitical harmony, which is one of the most important prerequisites for the sustainability of national order. This harmony can be achieved through the consolidation of a political consciousness of belonging based on the principle of equal citizenship within nation-states, and the elimination of geopolitical contradictions in border areas by creating common areas of security, economic, and cultural cooperation.

The Legitimacy Element of National Order: The Freedom–Security Balance and Justice

The main element that holds a state together as a political order is not an imposed identity buttressed by components of hard power organized around such an identity. On the contrary, the binding glue is an area of functional legitimacy and associated sovereignty based on an approach that unites cultural pluralism with an identity of equal non-discriminatory citizenship. Functional legitimacy is the legitimacy derived from the functional opportunities and possibilities provided to citizens by the state in question. While these opportunities can bind even very small-scale minorities to that state with a deep-seated sense of belonging, the majority of the masses deprived of these possibilities may be driven to break away from, or even rebel against, this political affiliation.

Functional legitimacy creates a sense of belonging to the extent that the state is able to meet the basic needs of its citizens. In terms of a sense of belonging to the political system, the most fundamental inherent need and expectation of human beings is the preservation and protection of human dignity. In this sense, mankind has worked throughout history to realize two elements to ensure the reflection of human dignity in their lives: security and freedom. Security is the guarantee of a person's existential continuity; freedom, the bestowal of depth and meaning on this existence with human dignity. Where there is no security, freedom cannot find the space to thrive; where there is no freedom, security may enable people's existential continuity but will always remain inadequate to the task of transforming it into a state of dignity through self-respect.

So the answer to the question *"what is the most comprehensive definition of the legitimacy of a state or a political system?"* is clear: a state achieves the most comprehensive basis of legitimacy when it becomes a political order that guarantees the widest area of freedom providing maximum security to every individual through a sense of belonging to that state without restricting their freedom, together with the widest area of freedom without putting their security at risk. Sacrificing freedom for security lays the ground for authoritarian regimes; neglecting security in the name of freedom, for chaotic processes. In this framework, the legitimacy of a state depends on its provision of a balance and harmony between freedom and security.

We have also seen the significance of this balance and harmony in the political practices we have experienced in Turkey. When the AK Party (Justice and Development Party) came to power in Turkey in 2002, the domestic policy dimension of the foreign policy principles we had defined were based on a conceptualization of the freedom–security balance.[28] This is because the authoritarian tendencies that generated military coups and restricted areas of freedom were based on the exigencies of the need for security to enhance their legitimacy. Authoritarian regimes that came to power in the wake of military interventions repeated every ten years prepared the ground for chaos, while chaos prepared the ground for authoritarian regimes. This vicious circle could only be broken by means of a fresh political understanding based on a proper freedom–security balance. In fact, this vicious circle could only be broken through democratization steps that were carried out after a series of arduous processes.

Today, both nation-states and the international system are undergoing crises brought about by fluctuations in the freedom–security balance. For example, Iraq has swung from Saddam Hussein's freedom-destroying understanding of security to a chaotic situation that is unable to meet even the most basic security needs of its citizens.[29] And this time, in order to be saved from this chaotic situation, mechanisms formed on the basis of a hard power-oriented understanding of security that gives prominence to the identities that were crushed by Saddam Hussein have begun to limit the areas of freedom of other identities.

Two possibilities present themselves to citizens who see their freedoms and security, and thereby their existence and dignity, under threat in the midst of a conjuncture in which the nation-state is in such a state of flux: either to take refuge and organize themselves within structures built on sub-identities such as sect, ethnicity, or tribe that will ensure their security, or to flee their country and seek refugee status in countries they believe will be able to ensure their security and freedoms.

Today, we face the chaotic pictures created by both these states of affairs. In countries such as Iraq, Syria, and Yemen, taking refuge in sub-identities has triggered tensions and chaotic developments that go as far as civil wars. For a Syrian who knows that the upper ranks of the Syrian army are almost entirely in the hands of a sectarian sub-identity and that all kinds of violence may be inflicted in order to preserve the privileged status of this sub-identity,[30] and when the Syrian national army has begun to be seen as a sectarian army that is no longer definable as a national body, there is no longer any possibility of the protection of a security order at the national level. A Syrian in this situation either feels the need for another security structure (the FSA) for self-preservation, or looks for ways to flee the country. The former case has led to the disintegration of the national security order, the latter to a chaotic situation in which refugee flows escalate the situation from a national level to take on regional and international dimensions.

All these examples demonstrate the fact that authoritarian regimes that exclude different identities and political approaches, and believe that security can only be achieved by means of hard power elements, lead either to the emergence of oppositional authoritarian tendencies or to reactions that lead to chaos over time. Genuine and lasting security can only be achieved through a sense of belonging that reunites citizens with their own dignity. Authoritarian security rests solely on elements of hard power; democratic security is based on a freedom-oriented approach founded on human dignity, without neglecting the power elements that bring sovereignty to life.

Recent experiences have made it crystal clear that authoritarian tendencies based on heroic identity-based populist rhetoric are insufficient for legitimacy. The fact that individuals who think there are no areas of security and freedom left are driven to escape the domination of this heroic and populist rhetoric and, although their language, religion, and ethnicity – in other words, their identity – is completely different, seek asylum in countries where they believe their freedom and security will be assured, reconfirms the twin pillars of the quest for legitimacy: security and freedom.

The ability of nation-states to form their own internal orders as well as to make constructive contributions to the international order depends on their ability to undergo a restructuring process that addresses both these quests. Every hold-up in this matter will lead to an increase in national, regional, and international disorder and an intensification of the systemic earthquake.

The Economic Component of National Order: Welfare and Income Justice

The economic infrastructure underlying the sustainability of nation-states concerns their ability to fulfill these two fundamental needs. People's ownership of sufficient economic resources to sustain their lives at a minimum level is in fact an existential security requirement. Individuals whose basic needs are not met due to hunger, drought, and insufficient income cannot feel secure and may be driven to take actions to protect their own existence that in turn create risks to security. It should not be forgotten that large-scale migrations, which have led to wars, destruction, demographic changes, and major shifts in order in the past, have been caused by a lack of economic resources triggered by factors such as hunger and drought.

The level of economic prosperity and welfare strengthens people's sense of belonging in terms of realizing the aims for which human beings yearn through their own free will. The fact is that in nation-states with rising *per capita* income and equitable income distribution, the risks of uncertainty and disorder are reduced. By contrast, nation-states undergoing economic recession and unjust income distribution face escalating mass reactions and conditions that render it hard to maintain a state of order.

In this sense, there is a linear, interdependence-based, relationship between national order and the level of economic development. Economic activity and associated levels of economic development increase in well-functioning nation-states, especially with regard to legal safeguards; as the level of economic development rises and citizens take a fair share in this rise, the sustainability of political orders gains strength.

Contrariwise, fragility in the political order and the consequent weakening of legal safeguards leads to a contraction of economic activity as a result of which the reduction in citizens' share of the national income diminishes their sense of trust and attachment to the political order. In a sense, while the consolidation of the bonds between the political order and the level of economic development mediated by legal safeguards reinforces the sustainability of order through mutual inter-action, in the event that this interaction follows a negative course, national order is thrown into a vicious circle. Unless a political ration-ality comes into play to extract national orders from this vicious circle, the road leads first to an intensifying state of crisis, followed after a while by the advent of a process that renders orders fragile, and eventu-ally to their collapse.

In the postwar era, many countries have managed to gain middle-income status,[31] but few have been able to attain the status of high-income economies. Instead many have exhibited a drastic slow-down in growth and productivity, following an initial period of rapid ascent. This is the critical threshold between political order and the economic development trap also referred to as the "middle-income trap":

> Some studies support the existence of a middle-income trap by finding empirical evidence that growth slowdowns are more likely at middle-income levels. An analysis of all growth slow-downs between 1960 and 2005, for example, suggests that they are more likely to occur in middle income countries than in low or high income countries. There is also evidence that rapidly growing economies tend to slow down significantly when they reach middle-income levels, often near per capita income levels of $10.000–$11.000 and $15.000–$16.000 in 2005 PPP adjusted dollars.[32]

While there are severe difficulties in maintaining political order in nation-states below the middle-income level, the interest optimization-oriented legitimacy relationship between citizens and the political order is strengthened in countries reaching the middle-income group. The need for qualitative transformations and structural reforms for sustainable growth is felt after reaching this stage. This need includes not only the technical fields related to the economy but also political and legal fields. Sustainable development achieved in this manner delivers the material dimension of political legitimacy that in turn ensures the sustainability of the national order.

In this context, there is an integrative relationship of comple-mentarity between the need for security and freedom, which makes up the backbone of political legitimacy, and the level of economic develop-ment that constitutes its material manifestation. There is therefore a linear relationship between the middle-income trap in the economic context and the minimum threshold of legitimacy in the political context. Any legitimacy deficit in terms of the security and freedom that constitute the minimum prerequisites of political legitimacy mostly leads to an economic crisis that makes itself evident in budgetary and current account deficits. The negative link between these two deficits, which leads to fragility in the national order, generally emerges in conjunction with a deficit in law and justice in the judicial order.

We may talk about two factors that affect the stability of the political order in the middle-income group: fair income distribution that spreads rising incomes to the masses, and the motivation for structural reform that will facilitate a transition from the middle- to the upper-income group. When both of these conditions are met, the economic-political basis of the national order is reinforced by overcoming the middle-income trap. However, the fulfillment of both these conditions depends on the strengthening of a field of security and freedom guaranteed by legal safeguards.

In the event that a contrary approach is adopted, the middle-income trap has an impact that tends to fracture the national order. Although situations in which economic rationality recedes, legal safeguards, especially property law, are weakened, growing national revenue is concentrated in the hands of a narrow elite instead of reaching the masses by means of a fair distribution of income, transparency is disregarded so that this concentration of wealth is not subject to legal sanction, and the informal economy masks real economic values, may give the appearance of a state of political order realized by a narrow elite in the short term, such a situation cannot sustain a genuine national order.

It follows that there is a dual-option future for countries in the middle-income group. The first option is the consolidation of a national order in the eyes of the general public that strengthens economic security through legal transparency and adapts to dynamic economic-political conditions by means of structural reforms that expand the fields of freedom in economic activities, thereby ensuring the fair distribution of growing revenues. This option engenders a rationalization of the political field as well as increasing productivity and efficiency in the economic field, and lifts the country to a higher-income group that further strengthens the stability of the national order.

The second option presents itself precisely at this critical crossroads. By reaching the middle-income group and satisfying the national order's central actors with rising incomes, steering the country to a *rentier* economy in the hands of a limited economic elite based on the distribution of this revenue through public authorities and causing the decline of economic productivity propped up by exclusionary populism can only satisfy the mass of people not through rising economic prosperity but through the resources of the public purse. Such conditions will in time force countries, especially those without commodity revenues and whose economies fail to make productive use of their human resources, into a vicious circle that can lead over time to their regression to the lower levels of the middle-income group, and even to their decline towards the lower-income group.

The first option can be brought to life via a principle of inclusiveness that encompasses all sectors of society, both politically and economically, within a transparent order. Autocratic orders and concentrations of power based on oligarchic structures in which certain economic segments exclude the wider community by means of an inequitable distribution of income, backed by a legal order that has eliminated the principle of transparency, lead in time to the narrowing of areas of freedom and security and weaken the basis of political legitimacy.

The enlightening comparative analysis between North and South Korea entitled "the economics of the 38th parallel" in Daron Acemoglu and James Robinson's work *Why Nations Fall* reveals the different outcomes of two different nation-state structures and economic institutionalizations established by one nation with the same sociocultural codes and historical background. As this analysis clearly shows, the key factor that determines nation-states' economic performances is whether they have "extractive" or "inclusive" economic institutions.[33]

It should be recalled that all these options and economic-political preferences are navigated within the context of an international economic-political order. Neoliberal economic policies widely adopted in the post-Cold War era have served to strengthen the economies of individual nation-states in periods of economic expansion and growing prosperity; yet in periods of economic recession and deteriorating income distribution, they have become a source of disorder and chaos. The main reason for this is that these policies lack the means to ensure economic security and regulate income distribution at times of crisis.

The political turbulence experienced by a number of nation-states in the aftermath of the latest economic crisis is a result of this economic-political interaction. Increasing income inequality during periods of economic crisis and recession, and the divergence of standards of living between communities living side by side, have had a profound impact on the internal order of nation-states. Above all, income disparities within the same region such as the Middle East have reached a point where the region has morphed into two separate worlds in which the gap has become more or less unbridgeable, threatening the very sustainability of the existing, fragile, order.

The aftershocks of the global economic earthquake were accompanied by new approaches on the control powers of nation-states over the economy. The protectionism and policies of keeping national economic areas under control that has grown in recent years and become a global trend during the Trump administration has opened up to debate the "internalization of production finance and other economic resources is unquestionably eroding the capacity of the state to control its own economic future"[34] assumption that gained general recognition in the post-Cold War period. Whether the efforts to increase the control over national economies by means of nation-states' protectionist policies is a temporary and conjectural reaction in the wake of the global earthquake or a more enduring trend will be seen after the impact of these policies on the cumulative performance of the world economy.

Our post-Cold War experiences have shown us that extreme globalization approaches based on a "state of denial"[35] concept that assumes that the nation-state came to an end with the development of global and regional economies,[36] as well as modernist/nationalist approaches that ignore the interdependence and transnational structures between national economies, lack the ability either to deal with actual realities or to develop holistic solutions within the molds they have created. A consistent, coherent, and inclusive relationship model between national, regional, and international structures of political economy needs to be developed in order to bring the aftershocks of the global economic earthquake under control and establish sound contacts between national, regional, and global orders. In any case, the two most critical elements in efforts to restore national orders shall continue to be productivity-based prosperity and equitable income distribution.

In summary, the sustainability of interacting national economic-political orders as well as the international economic-political order depends on the same prerequisite conditions: (i) an inclusive economic-political approach that provides a level of income to enable each individual to live in a state of human dignity; (ii) a transparent and predictable legal framework that constitutes the safeguard for economic activities; (iii) dynamic structural reform programs that adapt to changing production-consumption mechanisms and new technologies; (iv) a multidimensional and creative educational paradigm open to all segments of society based on the principle of an inclusive equality of opportunity designed to improve the quality of the human resources that constitutes the key factor in economic success; and (v) an understanding of fair income distribution that includes every segment of society.

The Organic Element of National Order: Institutionalization and Structural Harmony

Another of the most fundamental issues facing national orders today concerns the state's internal structural harmony and the institutionalization of public order. In the end, the nature of the state, which is the organized manifestation of public order, requires that this order is protected and made sustainable. Any structure that loses this quality also loses its claim to be a state. As Ernest Gellner underlines, "culture and social organization are universal and perennial. States and nationalisms are not."[37]

In the modern era, in Weberian terms, this functional state of order, considered to have been put into practice through a rational bureaucracy, is also significant in terms of furnishing the infrastructure that enables the realization of objectives we have already emphasized such as security, freedom, and economic welfare. State orders operated through strict rules and a central bureaucracy narrow the public sphere shaped by the free will of civil society, while states lacking central functionality and the power to protect public order lose the features of national order.[38]

In terms of the institutional future of national orders today, we may speak of five challenges that manifest themselves in different ways in different countries. The main headings of these challenges are: the total collapse of the institutional structure of the state; the fragmentation of institutional integrity; the inability of the institutional bureaucracy to renew itself through the ossification of autocratic tendencies;

discordance between elected populist administrations and the bureaucracy; and the revolutionary effect of technology in transforming the mechanisms of governance.

The first challenge is the fragility that confronts nation-states, the fundamental pillars of whose state institutional structures have collapsed in the wake of the post-Cold War geopolitical and security earthquakes. The most striking examples of this are Iraq and Afghanistan, where such institutional structures have completely collapsed in the aftermath of foreign interventions. State structures already weakened by prolonged wars and embargoes have been crippled by the latest interventions. It is hard to claim that the new bureaucratic institutionalization attempted in these countries over the last fifteen years has created a national order. The processes initiated by state institutions to purge the Taliban in Afghanistan and the Ba'ath in Iraq have gone far beyond these goals, severely weakening the state's functional capacity to sustain national order and destroying any internal structural integrity that lent functionality to state institutions. The enfeeblement of the state in these countries is not only limited to their national territory but also poses a risk to the national orders of surrounding countries. The fact that nation-building and state-building processes are not issues of engineering, but of complex social texture and historic formation, was clearly and particularly demonstrated by Bremer's ham-fisted liquidation of the state and bureaucracy in Iraq. Just as one could hardly expect a snake to survive by skinning it on the basis that snakes do survive by shedding their own skin, it is inconceivable to expect states to perform the same function after the liquidation of their institutions on the supposed basis that they are in need of institutional renewal.

No power in history, including the colonial states, has ever dismantled the local institutions of a country it has occupied with such an utter sense of recklessness and disregard. While a rational approach requires the reform of established state institutions, the liquidation of these institutions, especially the army, destroyed the accumulation of experience and institutional continuity of the nation-state and initiated a period of chaos in which the basic needs of citizens, especially for security, could not and cannot be met within the national order. The fact that about ten years after the new army had been established they abandoned Mosul without putting up any resistance to Daesh groups entering the city, and that the reclamation of Mosul required the formation of irregular militia forces known as the Popular Mobilization Forces (*Al-Hashd Al-Sha'bī*) beyond the scope of the regular national army shows that reinstitutionalization cannot be carried out at the same rapid pace as the elimination of an existing institutional continuity.

Secondly, the emergence of parallel de facto institutional structures that have no organic integrity within the boundaries of the nation-state leads to the institutional fragmentation of the national order in these countries. The territorial and institutional fragmentation experienced in the post-Cold War era in Georgia, Moldova, and Azerbaijan after the geopolitical earthquake, and in countries such as Syria, Libya, and Yemen after the structural earthquake in the wake of the Arab Spring, rendered it impossible for these countries to establish a single institutional structure to ensure the continuity of order within their recognized national boundaries. The latest striking instance of this institutional anomaly arising as a result of internal conflicts forming de facto areas of domination has been witnessed in Ukraine. The bureaucratic institutions that had been organs of the same state before these conflicts, broke off from the organic structural whole and acquired parallel functionalities in the de facto areas of sovereignty that emerged during the conflicts. This led the institutional backbone of national order to disintegrate.

A notable example in this sense is presented by the experience of how the existence of bureaucratic structures with virtually no organic connection within the same nation-state boundaries gained legitimacy with the signing of the Dayton Agreement in Bosnia-Herzegovina. Privileges granted to the Republika Srpska within the boundaries of the Bosnia-Herzegovinian State in the agreement signed in order to end the conflicts made it impossible to form a national army, an essential element of national order, or a national security system. In addition, the same agreement's establishment of layered bureaucratic mechanisms based on highly complex configurations within the scope of the federation obstructed the formation of an efficient and productive public administrative bureaucracy.

This fragmentation, observed at every stage in institutions that constitute the organic and functional backbone of national orders and the cornerstone of efforts to establish order, is a reflection of the systemic earthquake on different geographies. It is only possible for nation-states to form a national order to overcome this systemic earthquake through peace processes that resolve this institutional fragmentation.

The third challenge comprises issues of continuity and consistency in countries where contradictions between governments that have stormed to power on the winds of an ascendant extreme populist trend, and the entrenched establishment and bureaucracy, have had an impact on the institutional functioning of national order. The presence of leaders who do not confine themselves and the authority they deploy to any institutional custom or established rule and whose actions are based solely on the daily populist reaction to their decisions, and the tensions generated between these leaders and the established bureaucracy, which sees the continuity of any leader as being dependent on certain institutional processes, constitutes one of the most important challenges facing democratic systems today. While the established bureaucracy's bypassing of an elected leader or government in the decision-making process constitutes a serious issue of democratic legitimacy, the fact that elected populist leaders or governments make daily decisions in total disregard of the institutional experience of the state also brings with it problems of continuity, consistency, and functionality in the running of the state. Over time, the distrust that populist leaders feel towards established institutional bureaucracies leads to the operation of decision-making processes around the leader by a narrow staff appointed on the basis of nepotism rather than competence. This shakes the institutional continuity and structural harmony between institutions that constitutes one of the most important characteristics of the state, ultimately rendering its institutions dysfunctional.

The most striking manifestation of this challenge today is that of President Trump, with the turbulent and tense experience between the presidency and the established US bureaucracy in the first year of his administration. The President's taking of sudden and reflex decisions without feeling any need to gain an institutional perspective even on the most intricate and sensitive issues in US politics, combined with the rapid turnover of public officials, starting with his National Security Advisor, continuing with a host of others (most lately his top economic advisor, Secretary of State, once again his National Security Advisor, and his Secretary for Defense), and petulant stances such as sending messages to his own Secretary of State and Attorney General over social media, has awoken profound doubts concerning the institutional continuity and predictable rationality of the national order. The letter of resignation of Secretary of Defense James Mattis submitted to President Trump and circulated in the press on 20 December 2018 is a striking reflection of this institutional crisis: "We must do everything we can to advance an international order that is most conducive to our security, prosperity and values and we are strengthened in this effort by solidarity of our alliances. Because you have the right to have a Secretary of Defense whose views are better aligned with yours on these and other subjects, I believe it is right for me to step down from my position."[39]

In the event that this trend becomes a general pattern in which the mindset of the state is reshaped with the election of a new type of populist leader every four years will mean that the predictability that constitutes the most important indication of the existence of order shall cease to exist. Most worryingly of all, the integration of the exclusionary extreme racist tendencies of this populist trend into the administration and governance could be accompanied by the corrosion of shared social values, and the replacement of the rationality inherent in institutional continuity and accumulated experience by micro-level, personal and emotional reactions. One of the key tests facing democratic societies today concerns the establishment of new meaningful relationships between the democratic legitimacy bestowed by elections and the institutional continuity that reflects a shared accumulation of experience. It should not be forgotten that, like democracy, the sustenance and survival of all political systems can be maintained through an institutional culture and functionality.[40] Today we are facing a political and sociocultural reality that differs from that of the 1990s when the post-Cold War global *resurgence of democracy* hypothesis gained wide currency.[41]

It is clear that this trend for change, which has entered the mainstream in democratic countries, is set to present the theory and practice of democracy with new challenges and elements. After all, the historical development of democracy has not been a single, one-dimensional model.[42] And today, the relationship between world order and models of democracy shall also be determined by the interaction between different implementations of democracy in different countries within this global trend. As David Held writes, "the meaning of democracy, and of the model of democratic autonomy in particular, has to be rethought in relation to a series of overlapping local, regional and global structures and processes."[43]

Unlike the previous three, the fourth challenge concerns the institutional ossification of an established bureaucracy run with harsh, inward-looking rules. Although such an ossification, which serves to integrate autocratic regimes and narrows civil society's areas of influence and oversight, may give the impression of a consolidation of national orders and an increased level of predictability in the short term, it leads in time to problems of harmony and compatibility in rapidly changing conditions due to the absence of institutional renewal and a living space for original ideas and approaches. We are well advised to recall how socialist systems, regarded at one time as the most predictable and disciplined systems in history, and which fully embodied bureaucratic continuity and sovereignty, collapsed with unforeseen rapidity due to these compatibility issues.

This trend, manifested most strikingly in the examples of Russia and China, has also brought the validity of liberal/democratic values after the Cold War to be brought into question. The rise of political currents far from these values in the traditional democracies of the United States and Europe, seen as the victors of the Cold War, has given birth to a new phenomenon defined as autocratic populism. The discipline and rigid continuity of autocracy, and the unpredictability inherent in populism, also show how the internal contradictions of autocratic populism can have a radical impact on national orders. Above all, the embellishment of this kind of autocratic populism with an exclusionary ideology and the propagation of a pre-Second World War psychology, this time by means of far more sophisticated mass communications technology, could bring humankind face to face either with an apocalyptic scenario of chaos that many racist leaders see as inevitable, or a control mechanism that even George Orwell could never have imagined.

The fifth challenge concerns the impact on national orders of the technological revolution, which has the capacity to add considerable momentum to all these challenges. The astonishing pace of this revolution has transformed the ability of nation-states to establish and sustain order in both positive and negative directions. This impact has characteristics that know no bounds. The power of communication and the accessibility attained by this technological revolution may facilitate the increasingly orderly functioning of state institutions; on the other hand, it can lead to a state of affairs in which a single hacker can disable the conventional functions of the same institutions by means of a cyberattack. The chaos that a rapid collapse in the computerized system today could cause in a state institution is equivalent to the simultaneous destruction of all branches of the same institution in a war. And in the event that such a collapse was to last for a number of days, the consequences could have a profound impact on the course of public order.

Furthermore, the capacity of technological and control capacities to be concentrated in the hands of bureaucratic powers increases their ability to orient themselves towards becoming autocratic structures. The capacity to reach even the details of citizens' private lives, and control all kinds of information flows, incorporates certain characteristics and features that could increase the risks of autocratic populism, layer by layer. Given the evident fact that Goebbels's propaganda techniques, which lacked any of these technological capacities, turned people into robots, the potential risks of the exploitation of this growth in technological capacity so as to shape the will of individual human beings is profoundly alarming. In reference to the manner in which the Nazi system relied on the mechanics of national order and how this caused a state of chaos on a global scale, the important thing is not only the mechanical orderliness that destroys the human will of a national order. The important thing is for the national order to be a voluntary and organic element of the overall order on regional and global scales.

To summarize, a five-pillared restructuring process is now needed in order for nation-states to achieve internal order against the successive earthquakes and challenges that have arisen after the Cold War, and to become constructive elements of the international order: (i) a redefinition of citizenship-based identity in such a way as to be able to include cultural sub-identities and embrace common values and pluralism; (ii) the overcoming of contradictions between national boundaries and natural geopolitical lines by means that promote geo-cultural inclusiveness and economic interdependence; (iii) the creation of an area of political legitimacy that achieves the freedom–security balance that constitutes the most fundamental ontological need of individual citizens; (iv) achieving a state of harmony and compatibility between competitive free-market mechanisms that provide economic efficiency and productivity and a fair income distribution guaranteeing everyone a minimum level of economic security; and (v) the preservation and protection of national orders' internal state of harmony by means of establishing a balance between institutional continuity and renewal.

7 INCLUSIVE REGIONAL GOVERNANCE: FROM REGIONAL COLD WARS TO REGIONAL ORDERS

Forming a line of linkage and transition between national orders and the international order, regional structures influence, and are influenced by, these orders. Regional structures that accommodate subcomponents of geopolitical, geoeconomic, and geocultural lines are sometimes unifying, sometimes divisive, but always dynamic in terms of their order-forming mission. While this dynamism plays a seminal role in the formation of order when appraised with an inclusive approach, it can also lay the ground for regional chaos in conditions of exclusionary polarization. The course of history thus ebbs and flows dynamically between regional orders with an inclusive capacity relying on the political will and intentions of political actors in the region, and exclusionary regional hot and cold wars.

When geopolitical complementarity, geoeconomic transitivity, and geocultural interaction are evaluated around an awareness and consciousness of a shared destiny, exceptional opportunities are presented for regional stability and the creation of an area of prosperity and welfare. Such a consciousness of shared destiny may be expected to guide regional actors towards a win–win option through the principle of interest-optimization.

Political rationality requires regional actors to come together in a common effort to overcome risk-laden geopolitical fragilities, develop a cooperative understanding to maximize the benefits of regional geoeconomic transitivity, and cherish geocultural interaction as a civilizational treasure. Such an approach ensures the formation of a regional order's common ground and will, enabling the region in question to achieve stability and prosperity.

Conversely, if each actor starts acting on the basis of their own particular interests and priorities rather than regional-scale common values and interests, the infrastructural components of regional order begin to fracture. Struggles for domination along fragile geopolitical belts fragment common geoeconomic basins, turning the geocultural riches of diversity into elements of cultural conflict. Crisis management can be implemented in the event that the tensions emanating from any of these elements is contained, but if all three of them spring into action at the same time, inciting one another, conflicts intensify and risks spread rapidly throughout the region. The disintegration of Mesopotamian geopolitics that shattered Iraq, the geoeconomic fragmentation arising from the struggle for control over energy lines, and finally the domino-effect triggering of ethnicity and sectarian-based geocultural tensions in all structures in the region, constitute striking instances of this phenomenon.

Today, the evident tendency towards the disablement and disintegration of intermediate regional structures represents a significant underlying factor in the most fragile areas of international order. The end of the Cold War actually created a positive environment to enable the reduction of regional tensions, the rise of regionalism,[1] and the establishment of regional order, because it also had a disintegrative impact on the subregional elements inherent in the Cold War's global-scale, ideological polarization. The ideologically-based regime polarization within countries (such as East and West Germany, North and South Yemen, North and South Korea), as well as on a regional basis in Eastern Europe, the Balkans, the Middle East, South Asia, Southeast Asia, East Asia, sub-Saharan Africa, and Latin America, morphed into regional-scale geopolitical tensions, geoeconomic fragmentation, and geocultural conflicts. The Iron Curtain drawn across Eastern Europe and the Balkans, the Korean and Vietnam wars, ongoing tensions between neighbors more or less throughout the Middle East, and Israel–Arab conflicts, together with wars and interventions over spheres of influence in Africa and Latin America that divided countries as well as bringing them into conflict with one another, arose more from the ruthless exploitation of global bipolar rivalry than from regional tension.

Cold War balances made it necessary for nation-states to enter into a strategic alliance with one or other of the global poles, and settle all other relations within this framework. This state of affairs resulted in the restriction of regional actors' areas of maneuver, as well as the weakening of bilateral economic relations and cultural networks even between neighboring countries. Intertwined, centuries-old regional relationships and interactions were thus severely disrupted.

The dissolution of the Cold War bipolar structure paved the way for the re-emergence of natural geopolitical, geoeconomic, and geocultural lines of interaction in regional spaces; the flow of events began to be shaped through their own distinctive dialectic. This situation empowered regional players to determine their own positions, as well as expanding their zones of tactical maneuver. While situations in which driving-force actors managed to reconcile their differences steered this natural state of affairs towards efforts to establish regional order, in areas of conflict between leading regional players, global tensions infiltrated and intensified local tensions. For example, while Central and Eastern Europe were unified through the opportunities afforded by the EU, the Balkans and the Caucasus entered a process of fragmentation in their lower-level units and structures. Unable to transform the Cold War's structural legacy, the Middle East then faced the ravaging effects of regional tensions and polarizations.

On the other hand, transformational changes in international organizations such as the African Union and Association of Southeast Asian Nations (ASEAN), which have undergone processes of self-renewal to incorporate all relevant actors and been able to calm regional crises, are positive examples of efforts to establish regional order. Founded in 1963, the Organization of African Unity played a positive role in the Algeria/Morocco (1963–1964) and Kenya/Somalia (1965–1967) crises during the Cold War, and has come a long way since becoming the African Union in 2002 in terms of resolving continental problems, fulfilling peacekeeping missions, expanding economic interaction, and forming common political structures. This meant the African Union's transition from a stage of reactive anticolonialism to a constructive, proactive stage. This transformation was also clarified with a newly defined vision:

> The vision of the African Union is that of: An integrated, prosperous and peaceful Africa, driven by its own citizens and

representing a dynamic force in global arena. This vision of a new, forward looking, dynamic and integrated Africa will be fully realized through relentless struggle on several fronts and as a long-term endeavor. The African Union has shifted focus from supporting liberation movements in the erstwhile African territories under colonialism and Apartheid, as envisaged by the OAU since 1963 and the Constitutive Act, to an organization spear-heading Africa's development and integration.[2]

Similarly, ASEAN has contributed to the creation of a common platform in a region that suffered grievously from the Vietnam and Cambodian wars during the Cold War, and to resolving problems through dialogue. The establishment of the ASEAN Charter and the adoption of the ASEAN Security Community, the ASEAN Economic Community, and the ASEAN Socio-Cultural Community at the "One Vision, One Identity, One Community"-themed eleventh ASEAN summit held in Kuala Lumpur in 2005, constituted the main pillars of the Association's restructuring process. The fact that the ASEAN Charter, agreed on the fortieth anniversary of the organization's founding, foresaw not just a regular cooperation but a regional order was clear even in its first two clauses: "1. To maintain and enhance peace and stability and further strengthen peace-oriented values in the region: 2. To enhance regional resilience by promoting greater political, security, economic and socio-cultural cooperation."[3]

In spite of all these positive efforts, regional structures now being shaken by successive quakes have become even more fragile as a result of the impact of the systemic earthquake. Developments in the Middle East during the post-Cold War era hold significant clues in terms of grasping the challenges of establishing a new international order in a regional framework.

Events unraveling in the Middle East region represent conspicuous examples of fragility in the context of crises that are intensifying at all dimensions – local, national, regional, and global. While national crises rapidly take on regional features with geopolitical, geoeconomic, and geocultural interactions, every tension and divergence of preferences between global actors also drives the region into a spiral of crises. These national and international-scale pressures are leading to the breakdown of the regional links in the local–national–regional–global relations pyramid, which lacks the capacity to absorb them internally.

Weaknesses and fragmentation caused by an environment of insecurity and uncertainty, especially those accompanying the Arab Spring, have increasingly neutralized such structures as the Arab League, the OIC, and the GCC, demolishing common platforms able to bring together actors in the region.

In this context, the scope of the Gulf crisis that broke out in June 2017 exceeds the scale of four regional countries' disagreements with Qatar; rather, it is a reflection of the fact that the order of the region is becoming increasingly atomized.[4] The risk of polarization, tension, and fragmentation in the geography of the GCC, which is generally regarded as a success story that has managed to create internal autonomous mechanisms, reflects a much more profound regional and global problem in the international order and is, in a sense, symptomatic of a period and process of systemic crisis.

Regional Initiatives: Lessons and Challenges

Today, the most critical link in the effort to create a new international order is the consolidation and restructuring of regional structures that bridge national and international order. In this sense, the development of regional initiatives to consolidate regional order and contain potential crises is of great significance not only in terms of regional, but also global, peace. While achievements in this field serve the cause of steering the course of history towards a new order, obstructive regional efforts are activating chaotic processes that transcend the regional scale.

In this context, three regional initiatives with which I was personally involved contain highly instructive lessons for future initiatives of a similar kind; (i) Regional Initiative/the Platform for Iraqi Neighbors (2003–2008), (ii) the Syria–Israel Peace Talks (2008), and (iii) the Tehran agreement on Iran's nuclear program (2010).

Regional Initiative/The Platform for Iraqi Neighbors

The *Platform for Iraqi Neighbors* established under Turkey's leadership in Istanbul on 23 January 2003 immediately prior to the Iraq War and which convened regularly until 2008, played a key role in containing the regional tensions and conflicts that gave rise to the spread of the Iraqi crisis. Following its inaugural prewar meeting, which achieved a consensus on the territorial integrity and political unity of Iraq, the foreign ministers of Iraq's neighboring countries convened under the umbrella of this platform five times within a year after the war. The common principles emphasized at these meetings prevented the war from taking a different course based on the rivalries between neighboring countries at a critical period. This platform has subsequently met nine times with Iraqi participation, and three times in an expanded format with the participation of the P5, G8, EU, Arab League, OIC, GCC, and concerned regional countries.[5]

This platform, which brought together neighbors and regional countries with widely differing regional policies and perceptions of strategic interests, was effective in bringing their positions on the future of Iraq into closer alignment, ensuring the containment of potential tensions through face to face contacts, and resulted in the issuing of joint statements at each meeting that reinforced the common ground between these countries. Formed before the Iraq War, the *Platform for Iraqi Neighbors* was regarded with suspicion by the United States, which perceived it as an effort to obstruct US intervention, and was thus deprived of international support. These meetings, in which Iraq participated in the postwar period and continued with the participation of UN and P5 countries as observers in subsequent years, were terminated in 2008 at the request of the United States, based on their hypothesis that Iraq no longer had any need for such a platform.

Syria–Israel Peace Talks

Looking back over the past, I vividly recall another regional initiative that could have changed the course of history in the Middle East – namely, the 2008 indirect peace talks between Syria and Israel through Turkey's mediation, which rapidly achieved significant progress. This process, initiated through the will manifested in talks between Prime Minister Erdoğan of Turkey, Syrian President Assad, and Prime Minister Olmert of Israel and then run by a delegation under my chairmanship, was announced on 21 May 2008 simultaneously in three capitals:

> Syria and Israel have started indirect peace talks, under the auspices of Turkey. The two sides stated their intention to conduct these talks in good faith and with an open mind. They

decided to pursue the dialogue between them in a serious and
continuous way, in order to achieve the goal of comprehensive
peace in accordance with the Madrid Conference terms of
reference for peace. Both sides thanked the Prime Minister of
Turkey, Recep Tayyip Erdoğan, and Turkey, for their role in
this process and their generous hospitality.[6]

This process covered a great deal of ground in five rounds of talks
between the months of May and December of that year. Had this
process – which was brought to an end by Israel's bloody attack on
Gaza at the end of 2008 in the very week when the final text that would
have initiated direct talks had been completed with the exception of
small disagreements over one or two words – succeeded, regional
balances today would be on a dramatically different track. Israel's
violation of the "preservation of calm in Gaza and Lebanon" principle
that we had presented to the parties as a prerequisite to the process
represented not only the loss of a historic opportunity. A significant
foundation on which to orient the regional changes that would later
begin with the Arab Spring was also lost.

    This critical process was never achieved with the UN or global
power backing at any stage. Nonetheless, if our call in the first hours of
the Gaza attack, addressed particularly to Israel, to cease the attacks
and return to the process had received the decisive support of the UN,
especially the P5 countries, heavy civilian massacres would have been
prevented, Turkey–Israel relations would not have come under such
strain, and Syria's engagement with the international community would
have been achieved.

    However, the reservations of the Bush administration, which
distanced itself from an initiative that it saw as an effort to legitimize
the Syrian government, and the fact that certain other countries were
troubled that such a momentous process had been realized through the
good offices and influence of a regional country like Turkey, made UN
support for a successfully operating initiative impossible. The election
victory of President Obama, who had defended multilateralism and peace
initiatives during his election campaign, and the possibility that he would
take ownership of this process, mobilized the hawks in Israel, provoking
them to an attack that sabotaged the process in the period immediately
before the transition to a new administration in Washington. The sabo-
taging of a process by Israel through the massive attack against Gaza on

27 December 2008 that had been agreed between Erdoğan and Olmert on 22 December 2008, and that was undergoing the necessary finishing touches for direct talks to start a week later, occurred in this international context. The ending of this process meant that while Israel entered a trend of domestic political radicalization, Syria was forced to face the negative conditions of ongoing international isolation in the tense environment induced by the Arab Spring.

The Iran Nuclear Program and the Tehran Agreement

The Tehran Agreement on the Iranian nuclear program signed on 17 May 2010 as a result of the negotiations initiated through the mediation of Turkey and Brazil met a similar fate. These negotiations were based on a consensus reached between President Obama, President Lula, and Prime Minister Erdoğan in the nuclear summit in Washington held on 12–13 April 2010 and a letter from President Obama to Prime Minister Erdoğan and President Lula on 20 April describing possible compromises with Iran: "There is a potentially important compromise that has already been offered. Last November, the IAEA [International Atomic Energy Agency] conveyed to Iran our offer to allow Iran to ship its 1,200 kg of LEU to a third country – specifically Turkey – at the outset of the process to be held 'in escrow' as a guarantee during the fuel production process that Iran would get back its uranium if we failed to deliver the fuel."[7]

We intensified diplomatic contacts in the wake of finalization of the general framework of negotiations. I flew to Tehran as soon as I received indications that Iran had accepted this general framework in a telephone conversation with Iranian Foreign Minister Manouchehr Mottaki on 15 May and we, together with the Brazilian Foreign Minister Celso Amorim, drew up an agreement text at the end of eighteen grueling hours of negotiations with the Iranian side on 16 May. According to the terms of the agreement, 120 kilograms of fuel required by the Iranian Research Reactor would be supplied by the Vienna Group (the United States, Russia, France, and the IAEA) in return for Iran's delivery of around 1,200 kilograms of low-enriched uranium in its possession to Turkey. In addition, Iran would confirm its commitment to the NPT and guarantee its cooperation with the IAEA.

When we signed the text at a ceremony attended by Prime Minister Erdoğan, President Lula, and President Ahmadinejad on the morning of 17 May, there was no doubt in our minds that we had taken a significant step for regional and global peace and order, not least because the agreement contained the principal elements of the negotiating framework set out in President Obama's letter on behalf of the P5+1: "5. Based on the above, in order to facilitate the nuclear cooperation mentioned above, the Islamic Republic of Iran agrees to deposit 1200 kg LEU in Turkey. While in Turkey this LEU will continue to be the property of Iran. Iran and the IAEA may station observers to monitor the safekeeping of the LEU in Turkey."[8] The text, which was presented to the UN and the IAEA on the same day, was generally greeted positively except by the P5+1.

Instead of welcoming this agreement, achieved at an early phase in the nuclear enrichment program and at a highly auspicious regional conjuncture, it failed to gain the acceptance of the P5+1 group, in particular the United States, which had in fact encouraged Turkey and Brazil in their pursuit of this process. In spite of the agreement, the UNSC P5 members agreed to a resolution intensifying sanctions against Iran shortly later, with Brazil and Turkey voting against the resolution. Inasmuch as they laid bare the perpetuation of Cold War conditions in the global order, these developments created a sense of profound disappointment.[9] They say a good deed never goes unpunished, and here a negotiation process that deserved praise was indeed punished. An agreement was signed on 14 July 2015 to resolve this issue, at a much later stage in the nuclear enrichment program and under highly inauspicious regional conditions. It was duly hailed as a historic accomplishment.

As a mediator since the beginning of the negotiating period, I have always asked myself why the Tehran agreement was not accepted, and how history might have followed a different course in the region had it been. The contents of the agreement were sufficient to meet demands: the delivery of materials to advance Iran's enrichment program to Turkey restricted the potential to develop nuclear weapons and paved the way for negotiations on the next phase of the process. Moreover, IAEA experts welcomed developments during and after the process leading up to the negotiations.

After the passage of eight long years since then, it needs to be stated with the utmost sincerity and frankness that the reason for the rejection of the agreement was not its contents, but its methodology and actors. The P5, regarding itself as holding a monopoly on problem-resolution and having turned this perception into a rule, interpreted the resolution of a prominent international issue by two ascendant regional powers as a threat to the status quo. Their unease that any repetition of such an example would undermine this unspoken rule of the status quo overrode the prospect of resolving a regional and global problem. Yet Turkey and Brazil were both non-permanent members of the UNSC at that time, and this achievement could have been entirely attributed to the UNSC. Or, the P5+1 comprising the P5 plus Germany could have been turned into the P5+3 with the participation of Turkey and Brazil, who were anyhow UNSC members. And yet, and yet ... the psychology of arrogance arising from a privileged status drove rational diplomacy off the road.

Lessons for Future Regional Initiatives

My purpose in alluding to processes in which I was personally involved is not to bring back memories of certain disappointments that we experienced in crisis resolution processes affecting the international order. One cannot turn back the course of history, but it is possible to draw lessons and to shape the future in the light of these lessons by recalling them. So many more examples could be cited. But just for a moment, let us indulge the thought underlying this question *"If these three cases alone had succeeded with sufficient international support, what impact would they have had on regional and global developments?"* In my view, an assessment of the negative consequences that have accrued from the failure of these three regional initiatives as a result of inadequate international support may be of benefit in terms of developing a clearer vision of the contribution that could be made by the establishment of a sound mechanism between global and regional structures in general, the UN system, and regional initiatives in particular.

If the *Regional Initiative/Platform for Iraqi Neighbors*, which the Bush administration proved unable to endorse from the outset and then wanted to terminate on the alleged basis that it damaged the sovereignty of the Iraqi government, had continued under the aegis of the UN, the domino-effect proliferation of numerous Iraq-centered crises could have been prevented; there would have been a far higher possibility of containing the risks brought by the regional rivalries that began with the Iraq crisis and then spread to other areas; the impact of ethnic and sectarian conflicts reflecting the rivalry between various countries would have been diminished; and it would have been possible to create a far more coordinated and wider regional front against Daesh. Most importantly, it would have facilitated the formation of more inclusive governments in elections that were held after the US withdrawal, and the backing of neighboring countries for these governments. Overall, it would have increased the positive contributions of neighboring countries to the restructuring of Iraq.

As was argued at the time, this platform was not an enterprise to construct some kind of tutelage over Iraq, but the product of an effort to stabilize the region through Iraq. This objective of regional order was clearly mentioned in the joint declaration of the first meeting held in Istanbul on 23 January 2003 before the war: "We agree that this initiative in Istanbul by the regional countries is a process that has as its immediate objective the peaceful solution of the crisis in Iraq. Moreover, this initiative will continue until issues in our region are resolved, as well as ensuring peace, security and prosperity for all."[10] However, the reservations of global powers that regional initiatives would narrow their field of action prevented these kinds of success stories from establishing a pattern. After this platform was brought to an end, it proved impossible to create a second platform to deal with problems between Saudi Arabia and Iran, or between Turkey and Egypt, on the same basis. Over time, the lack of face-to-face dialogue has fed mutual suspicions as countries have drifted away from interest-optimization and been driven to a zero-sum environment of competition and rivalry. As a result of this drift, lose–lose scenarios are the only ones left standing today.

On the other hand, had the Syrian–Israeli peace process continued and the foundations of peace been laid, the occupation of the Golan Heights would have ended, the tensions that have destabilized Lebanon reduced, and peace efforts leading to a Palestinian State gained momentum.

In fact, two arguments that we developed as mediators before the parties covered a vision of regional order and the areas of risk that threatened this vision. After emphasizing in separate discussions with each side that "in the event of the achievement of peace between the two parties someone living in Damascus will be able to travel unimpeded to Jerusalem and a resident of Tel Aviv will be able to travel unimpeded through Syria to Turkey," we stated throughout the discussions that a conclusive end to tensions in Lebanon and Gaza was a prerequisite to the realization of this vision. The calm that prevailed in Lebanon and Gaza during the negotiations showed how positive initiatives played a significant role in reducing regional tensions.

Above all, if this process had been completed before the Arab Spring in, say, 2008 or 2009, the course of the Arab Spring and the fate of Syria would have followed a different course; Israel's internal balances, which came under the influence of extreme anti-peace elements immediately after the end of this process, would have shaped up in a different manner; and these circumstances would have created an environment more conducive to dialogue. In addition, the engagement of Syria in the international community and the lifting of the restrictions imposed on that country would have prepared the ground for the minimization of the impact of a Cold War culture based on embargoes and isolation policies in the region.

The fact that an agreement on Iran's nuclear program occurred after the invasion of Iraq and just before the Arab Spring could have had a profound impact on many factors, from the nuclear threat to regional balances. The engagement of Syria and Iran with the international community would have accelerated the process of transforming the region's economic-political infrastructure, and the economic interdependence relations that would have developed upon the ending of their isolation would have contributed to regional peace and a stable order.

None of this happened and, as we said, there's no going back on history. Yet these examples give us important lessons with respect to regional and global order. The lesson that regional actors should take is that initiatives aiming to ensure that intraregional dynamics are activated in a positive direction comprise the key factor in the achievement of regional order. In particular, as with the *Platform for Iraqi Neighbors* case, when these initiatives acquire an inclusive and embracing trait that brings all concerned parties into the process, they make a major contribution in terms of averting potential crises and creating a new order of stability. The shared benefits of coming together on platforms in this manner always outweighs the dubious benefits of acting individually, or within groupings formed against one another. Processes that involve *all* players may function slowly, but they prevent the emergence of crises stemming from diverging interests and help to create the psychological and procedural infrastructure to achieve the emergence of a sustainable order.

And from the perspective of global actors, it is not possible to contain regional crises or to establish a new regional order by means of processes and methods in which regional players are driven out or ignored with a view to preserving the international power status quo. Trying to block the positive roles that rising regional players can assume rather than benefiting from the opportunities they can generate will only lead to lost opportunities as well as triggering chaotic regional processes. Efforts to establish regional order may bear fruit through patiently run, step-by-step processes in which all actors play an active role at different stages.

As we shall discuss in more detail in a subsequent section on global order, the lesson that regional actors and international organizations, especially the UN, should draw from all these cases is the fact that regional engagement is the most effective instrument for building an order of peace and stability. One of the most important and practical prerequisites of global order and stability is the creation of inclusive, consistent, and functional bridges between UN mechanisms, especially the UN Security Council, and regional actors, structures, and initiatives.

Regional Order and the Principal Elements of Stability

In the wake of all the bitter experiences the region has suffered, all political leaders, elites, and intellectuals who hold positions of responsibility in the region face a critical dilemma of options: to construct a new regional order that will provide security and prosperity for the people of the region, or to trigger and provoke a regional Cold War accompanied by a series of hot wars, whose impacts will last for decades or even centuries. While the first option requires patience, reason, intelligence, and a consciousness of an inclusive shared destiny, the second would be based on an irrational, senseless, and confrontational division of destinies based on exclusionary "heroics," fear, ambition, and impulse.

In point of fact, in Turkey, we had already acknowledged this duality of options when we proposed the principal bases of a new regional order in the aftermath of the Iraq and Lebanon wars. In my address as a guest speaker at the 132nd Foreign Ministers Council of the Arab League on 9 September 2009 as the Foreign Minister of Turkey, I defined the four principal pillars of a possible new regional order as follows:[11] (i) the principle of "security for all," which should be applicable to all states and societies as well as to all communities and individuals in the region; (ii) the prioritization of high-level political dialogue as the main mechanism for the peaceful settlement of regional disputes, avoiding the use of force and the escalation of tensions; (iii) creating economic interdependency between the countries and peoples of the region as a means to lay the groundwork for a peaceful regional order; (iv) embracing cultural pluralism and coexistence as a shared value in order to protect and cherish ethnic, sectarian, and religious diversity and the diverse compositions of our cities, societies, and countries.

About a year after setting out this framework of principles, the Arab Spring that sparked off in Tunisia at the end of 2010 and then spread to Egypt, Libya, Syria, and Yemen brought with it fresh opportunities in this search for regional order, as well as serious risks and challenges. During the first phase of this process, between the end of 2010 and the summer of 2013, there was a period in which the masses, especially groups led by young people, were watching events in a spirit of self-confidence and optimistic anticipation for the future. Indeed, the acquisition of political structures in the region with high levels of legitimacy and transparency based on the consent and will of the people would have meant the end of the autocratic structures and polarizations in the region that were remnants of the Cold War, signposting the dawn of an era more open to dialogue, with greater security, freedom, and participation. Moreover, the opening of the region both within itself and to the wider world would have meant an increase in economic and cultural vitality and diversity, which might have laid the groundwork for the development of a pluralistic sociocultural structure supplemented by freedom and economic interdependence and freedoms capable of delivering shared prosperity, welfare, and productivity.

In brief, an atmosphere was created in which it would have been possible to develop the philosophical and practical grounds for a new regional order able to overcome both the uncertainties of the post-Cold War era and the paradoxical and restrictive conditions of the Cold War. For these reasons, demands for a new regional order based on a consciousness of shared destinies, shared security, a shared economy, and a shared culture that would protect and transcend political borders at the same time, were spreading. This picture was especially thrilling for young people rebelling against a century-old psychopolitical legacy that destroyed political, economic, and cultural self-confidence.

However, as we mentioned in the previous section, after the developments of the summer of 2013, this optimistic exhilaration began to take on a rather pessimistic psychology fed by an environment of chaotic uncertainty. In the wake of the emergence of Daesh as an organization committed to the evisceration of all human values; the Egyptian coup and the failure of the democratic transformation process in a country that constitutes the political and intellectual center of the Arab world; and the absence of any sanctions against the Syrian regime in the wake of their UN-acknowledged use of chemical weapons, an egocentric competitive environment in which every group and actor promoted their own short-term security and interests took the place of a vision of a new regional order based on human dignity and shared human values.

In this chaotic picture, reaching a new state of order in a region caught in a pincer between Cold War-remnant autocratic regimes trying to return to the pre-2010 status quo and terror organizations keen to intensify this chaotic situation as well as propagate it globally necessitates a new paradigm on a groundwork of principles agreed upon by regional and global actors. In spite of the new conditions and challenges accompanying the Arab Spring, I believe that such a paradigm of regional order fundamentally depends on the same methods and methodology of principles.

Shared Destiny/Common Security

Today, the most important psychological prerequisite for building a new order in the region is the ability to recreate a consciousness and awareness of a shared destiny, which has almost entirely disappeared. No ethnic or sectarian group, country, or actor has the slightest possibility of discussing the need for regional order on a rational basis in a psychological environment in which their destiny is treated separately from that of others. It is only possible to implement the concept of shared security that constitutes the backbone of regional order through the development of a consciousness of shared destiny.

As well as the idealist basis of the "zero problems with neighbors" principle that, as the Turkish government, we declared in 2002,[12] it was also directed at changing Turkey's introverted perspective towards its neighboring regions as well as developing and spreading a new understanding of regional order based on a general consciousness of shared destiny. This principle, which we implemented in a highly comprehensive and successful manner until the regional earthquake triggered by the Arab Spring, was of its essence the psychological basis of a strategy to prevent intraregional alienation and isolation. The perception inherited from the Cold War that Turkey was surrounded only by enemies was giving rise to a psychological environment of suspicion and tension that obstructed the formation of any kind of regional order. Those of us with some knowledge of the nature of history and international relations naturally appreciated the impossibility of "zeroing" all problems with neighbors, but psychological shock treatment was needed to create a new national and regional security paradigm. We saw and put into practice the "zero problems with neighbors" principle as the symbolic key to such shock treatment.

And as it turned out, the tense and turbulent relations we had had for various reasons throughout the Cold War with countries such as the USSR/Russia, Greece, Syria, Iran, Iraq, Egypt, and Serbia were improved and settled within a new framework; relations were developed with countries undergoing processes of political transformation in the post-Cold War era such as Bulgaria, Romania, Macedonia, Georgia, Moldova, and Ukraine; relations with countries with which we enjoyed deep cultural connections such as Azerbaijan, Bosnia-Herzegovina, Albania, and Kosovo were expanded; the protocols signed with Armenia in 2009 after comprehensive negotiations paved the way for improved relations with that country[13] and an agreement of comprehensive settlement had been signed on Cyprus which would have led to normalization of relations with the Greek Cypriot administration if it had not been rejected by the Greek Cypriot side in the referendum held on 24 April 2004.

Furthermore, in order to minimize problems in the context of a "common security understanding," crisis-resolution and security initiatives were developed between different Iraqi groups during Sunni participation in the December 2005 elections, between Lebanese groups during their 2008 presidential crisis, between different groups in the name of national reconciliation after the civil war in Kyrgyzstan in 2010, and with Palestinian groups at different times; efforts were also made to establish subregional security structures in order to reduce tensions between neighboring countries with the tripartite Turkey–Iraq–Syria and Turkey–Afghanistan–Pakistan mechanisms set up in 2009.

The impact of this principle opened the way for certain neighboring countries to develop new approaches using similar formulae, and gave rise to a general easing in the environment, especially in the Balkans and the Middle East. This environment, which was serving to enrich networks of regional relationships, was shaken by countries' internal structural crises, especially in the aftermath of the Arab Spring, and led to the birth of a security environment that prioritized each country's own concerns for survival. Such concerns drove countries away from any strategic regional vision towards defensive conjunctural power struggles. An environment in which everyone has become everyone else's security rival has shattered neighborly relations and profoundly shaken any consciousness of shared destiny.

The most important factor ensuring the positive maintenance of relations between neighboring countries, which constitute the essential foundation of any sustainable regional order, is that the identity of one's interlocutor is clear and that a relationship of trust is established with this counterpart. The notion that the "zero problems with neighbors" principle has been totally invalidated, especially with regard to Syria, is a fallacy. Post-Arab Spring situations in which this principle has been rendered ineffective – as in the case of Syria – have come about because, to coin an expression, the counterpart was no longer a counterpart. The fact that the government of Syria is in a state of war with its own people, and its complete loss of control of the borders between our countries, means that they can no longer be characterized as a problem-solving interlocutor.

Today, the key issue in the formation of the security mainstays of regional order concerns the question of who the interlocutors and partners in such an order might be. With reference to the same striking example of Syria, eight years ago, Turkey's ability to establish a common security zone along the Syrian border required only an agreement with the central government in Damascus. Now, apart from having to reach agreement with the United States, Russia, and Iran for the same objective, non-state actors also need to be brought under control.

In the meantime, this chaotic state of affairs has destroyed the sense of shared security of different ethnic and sectarian groups living side by side even in neighboring villages, as well as leading to the domino-effect proliferation of localized security risks to global centers such as Paris, London, Istanbul, and New York. Just as the consciousness of shared destiny was dealt a severe blow in local communities, the global community now faces the same security risks as a component of shared destiny. This clearly shows the decisive position of regional order betwixt local, national, and global orders.

The security dimension of regional order has therefore taken on a highly complex guise in which global, regional, national, and local actors all perform at the same time. Overcoming this multi-tier security problem depends on the creation of a new security framework where all parties not involved in terrorism and international war crimes are able to take part. And such an outcome can only be achieved if the principles of inclusiveness, internal consistency, and integrity we discussed in the previous section are applied without discrimination.

In this context, a sustainable regional order in which everyone feels secure cannot be established without developing a regional security understanding based on common principles and consistent criteria that include and embrace all sides. First and foremost, it must be recognized that a sustainable sense of common security can never be realized through a zero-sum game approach. For example, no regional security can be built on the reality of an Israel whose security is entirely guaranteed and a Palestine whose security is entirely disregarded. And the privileged status of one country or another with respect to international conventions on weapons of mass destruction, as in the case of Israel's stance on the Nuclear NPT and CWC runs in direct contradiction to any concept of lasting and sustainable regional order.

Likewise, defining the phenomenon of terrorism that regional or global actors see as a common threat and reconciling the classification of terrorist groups applicable to each side also constitutes one of the key conditions for the shaping of a common security paradigm. In this context, one needs to avoid the two extreme approaches of hyperbole and understatement. One of these extremes is that preferred by autocratic administrations in the wake of the Arab Spring, who view all kinds of different approaches and civil opposition as terrorist groups even if they do not resort to violence. Such an approach has led to the elimination of civil counterparts and resulted in obstacles to processes of social dialogue that are of particular necessity during critical periods. A state of affairs in which the processes of civil dialogue through which legitimate opposition is able to express itself have been blocked has only brought the reality of ever-escalating terror. For example, in the Geneva negotiations on the Syrian crisis in the summer of 2012, the Syrian government defined the national opposition as a terrorist group and prevented it from proceeding, laying the ground for the emergence of a group like Daesh, the most brutal terrorist group the region has ever seen, and a state of chaos in the security of the entire region, indeed the global arena.

The other extreme is a state of affairs in which every actor ignores the concerns of others on the basis of liquidating the terrorist group they regard as a threat to themselves, even exploiting and establishing contacts with terrorist groups seen as a threat by others. The US arming of the PYD-YPG, the Syrian wing of the PKK that constitutes the most perilous terror threat against Turkey, at the same time as the United States was struggling against Daesh in an international coalition of which Turkey was a part, represents one of the most vivid examples of this contradictory stance. The fact that the PKK is officially recognized as a terror group by the US demonstrates the extent that contradictions in principles have reached on this matter.

Divergent approaches to the definition of terror organizations are now leading to the proliferation of the phenomenon of proxy wars,[14] the most severe security risk for the region, and the expansion of the spheres of influence of non-state actors deployed in such wars. In cases of interstate tensions, there is always the chance of negotiation, even in the most challenging conditions, because it is obvious who the interlocutors are. Yet proxy-war scenarios give rise to outcomes that make it impossible to identify the counterparts and procedures required to manage security provision negotiations. While they offer some actors a measure of tactical success, proxy-war methods lead to a state of affairs that absolutely prohibits the establishment of any enduring order. Today, the rapid emergence of the region from this proxy-war psychology and the establishment of direct relations of mutual trust between legitimate actors is one of the most critical prerequisites for efforts to create regional order.

High-Level Political Dialogue

When we consider the issue of the successful implementation of continental and regional order, the most significant contributory factor in such achievements is the development and institutionalization of direct, high-level relations. To give a noteworthy example, had the mechanisms and summits that allowed leaders to come together on a regular basis not existed, the substructure that enabled the development of the EU as an institutional means to continental peace and unification could never have been created. A generation of leaders who had lived through the agonies of the Second World War in various countries saw that the common living space of the European continent could become a zone of peace and stability not through hegemonic wars, but direct dialogue and cooperation based on a consciousness of shared destiny. Ever since then, the EU's successful performance as an integration project has depended not on the total absence of crises, but mechanisms for direct dialogue in crisis-resolution processes.

The occurrence of crises in every era of history and every corner of the earth is a natural phenomenon. Even human beings themselves first encounter life through birth pangs. Crises are a natural consequence and inevitable feature of nature and life. The existence of an order is not about the absence of crises but the way in which they are managed and the capacity of the order to regulate itself. The most effective means by which any order can reorganize itself in the face of new challenges are mechanisms for high-level dialogue operated with a political will based on mutual trust between actors. These dialogue mechanisms lay the groundwork for the development of a dual effect comprising a common vision of regional order and an ability to manage any crises that may emerge, two capacities that complement one another.

The underlying reason for the ever-deepening crises in the Middle East today is the lack of high-level political dialogue. Groupings between countries in the region that gained independence after the Second World War were generally based on reactionary antagonisms. The wave of Arab nationalism that arose in the wake of the Egyptian revolution in the 1950s under the leadership of Gamal Abdel Nasser gave rise to reactionary associations of traditional dynastic orders troubled by these developments. The 1950s and 1960s were deeply scarred by these divisions. And no confidence or trust building political dialogue could be fostered between the parties in that period.

The Camp David Accords subsequently signed by Egypt[15] then led to the emergence of a Rejectionist Front, this time in opposition to the accords. This development, which led to the exclusion of Egypt from regional processes, made it impossible to set the groundwork for an inclusive regional dialogue. The Iranian Revolution brought about a counter-front motivated by the urge to counter the revolution's sphere of influence and the division of the region along the lines of armed conflict in the Iran–Iraq War. The rupturing of both Egypt and Iran from the regional dialogue processes in the 1980s meant that the region entered the post-Cold War era in a state of unpreparedness in terms of internal dialogue. The invasion of another Arab country, Kuwait, by Saddam Hussein, who came to prominence in this period of conflict claiming to be the guardian of the Arab world against Iran, was accompanied by a state of instability that marked the first decade of the post-Cold War era. As Egypt returned to the system in the 1990s, this time Iraq remained entirely aloof from the grounds of dialogue and began to undergo a process of disintegration that would in turn have its own domino effect. The security earthquake of 9/11 and the US interventions in Afghanistan and Iraq triggered ethnic and sectarian divisions and spread the breakdown of dialogue directly to subordinate elements of society.

In brief, the anyhow inadequate grounds for dialogue during and after the Cold War have been further shaken by nation-state fragilities and the regional-scale polarizations caused by the Arab Spring. These fragilities and polarizations destroy any possibilities of regional dialogue and lead to the rapid escalation of even small-scale crises into regional crises that are not subject to preventive dialogues when they first begin.

This picture requires the establishment of a platform for inter-linked, multi-tiered dialogue for a sustainable regional order. First, and as we discussed in the previous chapter, it is imperative that international and local dialogue platforms be strengthened in order to overcome this fragility in nation-states, and to enable nation-state authorities to become effective actors in a genuine regional dialogue. It is very hard for leaders and governments that lack solid social support in their own country to be partners in a sustainable regional order.

The second tier constitutes bilateral dialogue between country leaders and their governments, which forms the key building block of any regional order. Well-prepared regular bilateral high-level contacts are the most important means of building trust. Above all, institutionalized bilateral relations not only help to prevent crises but also constitute the substructure for the adoption of regional order as a strategic vision. In this context, High Level Strategic Cooperation Council Mechanisms[16] and High Level Cooperation Council Mechanisms[17] in the format of annual joint cabinet meetings co-chaired by country leaders that we initiated in Turkey with Iraq and Syria in 2009 and subsequently established with neighboring countries such as Russia,

Greece, Iran, Egypt, Bulgaria, and Azerbaijan had a highly positive impact and generated a serious motivation in bilateral relations. These council meetings, which continued to a large extent with other countries after Egypt and Syria dropped out in the wake of the turbulence induced by the Arab Spring, strengthened the sustainability of relations by institutionalizing bilateral relations.

The lack of high-level dual-tiered dialogue is among the most important causes of regional instability and uncertainty today. Breakdowns in bilateral dialogue between countries, especially important regional powers such as Turkey, Egypt, Iran, and Saudi Arabia, give rise to consequences that impact the whole region; issues of trust and confidence arising from these breakdowns are then reflected throughout the region.

The third tier comprises dialogue mechanisms in the subregional structures that represent the intermediate pillars of regional order. For example, the creation of intermediate-scale dialogue mechanisms in subregional basins such as the Gulf, North Africa, Mesopotamia, the Horn of Africa, and the Eastern Mediterranean, which in themselves foster integrity and interdependence, are influential in maintaining the regional order.

The experience of the tripartite mechanisms we developed had a notably positive impact in terms of overcoming regional fragilities. To give a particular case in point, the Turkey–Syria–Iraq tripartite security and intelligence mechanism we formed at the Foreign Ministers level in order to normalize relations between Iraq and Syria, which had escalated to the point of conflict as a result of the terror attacks that had taken place in Iraq in 2009, achieved a restoration in mutual trust between the two countries. Similarly, the tripartite Turkey–Afghanistan–Pakistan mechanism established in 2008 that met annually at leaders' level until 2014 following preparatory work by intelligence-diplomacy-security units had a significant function in this sense as a constructive mechanism for high-level dialogue. A similar mechanism established between Turkey, Bosnia-Herzegovina, and Serbia in 2009 set an important and successful example with regard to stability, confidence, and lasting peace in the Balkans. The ideas that lay the ground for this initiative were "ensuring the territorial integrity, sovereignty and the internationally recognized borders of Bosnia and Herzegovina, normalization of relations between Bosnia and Herzegovina and Serbia and contributing to strengthening of regional cooperation and good neighborly relations between the countries so that mutual understanding and trust again prevails in the Balkans."[18]

The profound structural earthquake caused by the Arab Spring has narrowed the areas of influence of such mechanisms and brought about severe weaknesses in previously functioning subregional synergies and collaborations, especially in the Gulf region. The restoration of the functionality of these kinds of initiatives is important in terms of creating a regional atmosphere conducive to containing crises and taking more wide-ranging visionary steps.

The fourth tier concerns the regional-scale institutional structures that constitute an important vehicle for high-level dialogue between actors. Today, the institutional platforms that empower high-level dialogues are being extensively eroded. In fact, efforts to create order-forming elements in the post-Cold War era did yield certain positive developments. Exemplary institutional initiatives include the implementation by the GCC, set up in the prevailing conditions of the Cold War in 1981, of the GCC Common Market on 1 January 2008; the transformation of the OIC from the Organization of Islamic Conference into the Organization of Islamic Cooperation and its structuralization following a process of reform in the 2000s; the development by the Arab League of new models of cooperation such as the Turkey–Arab Forum with a non-member neighboring country like Turkey; and the expansion of the fields of activities of the Economic Cooperation Organization (ECO) as an organization linking the Middle East with Central Asia.

In addition, efforts have been made through regional platforms such as the ongoing Afghanistan focused "Friendship and Cooperation in the Heart of Asia: Istanbul Process" established in 2010. This was an attempt to move from crisis-resolution to a vision of regional order in a geography where several nation-states have very diverse conflicting views and interests:

> In the region that surrounds Afghanistan we aim to weave a rich, positive, and progressive mosaic of initiatives and efforts that each shoulders a part of the common task to ensure peace, stability and prosperity. The bonds between us constitute a strong basis to establish a consensus underwriting a code of conduct that is based on fundamental principles of good neighborly relations. Our solidarity today with Afghanistan will be a

facilitator and a test for the irrevocable establishment of timeless friendship and cooperation in our region.[19]

Yet today, all these structures are in a state of serious stagnation, dysfunction, and even disintegration. Finally, the crisis within the GCC is ringing alarm bells concerning the regional order's institutional infrastructure. The cracks that have appeared in the GCC, undoubtedly the most successful cooperation and integration project in the history of the region, and its choice of insecurity over an understanding of shared security, an absence of dialogue instead of high-level dialogue, and embargoes instead of economic interdependence, constitutes a striking example of a structural cycle of crisis experienced at the regional level.

Economic Interdependence

Economic interdependence is one of the most important means of bringing neighboring countries closer together and making their regional order sustainable. From imperial antiquity to the present day, no means of creating and maintaining any order has been more effective than shared interests. For example, the common parameter of the imperial orders established on the Silk Road, which cuts through Eurasia from east to west, has been the safe passage of the trade caravans that comprised the common interest of everyone and every society along this route. The caravans were seen as the infrastructural components for common interests; common interests were seen as the infrastructural components of a sustainable order. This necessity, which makes societies and geographies interdependent, shows that interest optimizing win–win situations are only ever possible through an agreed common order. The Silk Road, in this sense, "was the entire local political-economic-cultural system of Central Eurasia, in which commerce, whether internal or external, was very highly valued and energetically pursued."[20]

Today too, the most efficient and most peaceful means of establishing and institutionalizing regional regimes, and making them sustainable, is economic interdependence. The new opportunities brought by globalization have diversified the tools of this interdependence and expanded its scope to an extraordinary scale. Transregional, transcontinental, and transoceanic trade and transport corridors replacing caravan routes; energy lines that add a new dimension to geopolitics via geoeconomics; customs unions that integrate production–consumption mechanisms; and technological communication networks that are progressively becoming more strategic in nature have created areas of common interest and competition that transcend national boundaries. Situations in which these interdependencies are regarded only as areas of rivalry lead to tension and disorder, while those seen as areas of common interest serve to reinforce elements of regional, continental, and global-scale order.

The transition on the continent of Europe, the cause and scene for massive and devastating wars of hegemonic rivalries over centuries, from a sector-scale iron and steel community based on economic interdependence, then to a large-scale customs union, and finally a currency union, enabled a European order initially limited to Western Europe to encompass the continent as a whole at a later stage. Despite the destructive impacts of the recent global economic earthquake and Brexit, the main factor behind the sustainability of this order is the belief that the common interest in economic interdependence overrides any interest that might be served by disorder and any state-by-state benefits that disintegration might bring. This economic interdependency was reinforced by security cooperation via NATO during Cold War in the face of a perceived Soviet threat. So, the success story of the EU has been a result of the combined impact of shared destiny of security and common interest of economic interdependency.

In this context, initiatives such as ASEAN, North American Free Trade Agreement (NAFTA), Asia-Pacific Economic Cooperation (APEC), Economic Community of West African States (ECOWAS), GCC, and ECO have also contributed to creating an area of common interest at regional levels by means of fostering economic interdependence on various scales. While the energy lines operating between Russia and Europe have strengthened Eurasian-scale interdependence in the post-Cold War era, the Blue Stream project between Russia and Turkey has served to bind these two countries, which have a history of rivalry over this line, closer together. Likewise, the BTC (Baku–Tbilisi–Ceyhan) project has brought the Caucasus closer to the Eastern Mediterranean. Still under construction, TANAP (the trans-Anatolian gas pipeline) is set to bring the Caspian basin and the Balkans together around a shared interest. If successful, the *Belt and Road Initiative* recently developed by China and aimed at reestablishing the Silk Road by contemporary means, could also provide the infrastructure for the creation of interregional and intercontinental orders transcending countries.

The main obstacle to the formation of a regional order infrastructure in the Middle East, which has the most deeply rooted agricultural areas, trade corridors, and shared economic basins in history, and has consolidated this feature in the modern period with the richest natural resources on the face of the earth, is that all this potential has proved impossible to activate on the basis of a rationale of common interests based on economic interdependence. The separation of geo-economically integrated basins through the Sykes-Picot Agreement's drawing of lines in the sand as entirely artificial borders;[21] the economic-political integration of countries separated from each other one by one, with colonial economies; the divergence of interests caused by the exponential growth in the income gap between countries rich in resources and those rich in population; the focus of natural resource-rich countries on particular extra-regional income instruments rather than areas of employment-generating production at home; the envisioning of energy lines that could unite the countries through which they pass towards the goal of a common order as a field of rivalry rather than an area of common interest; and, most significantly, the failure to develop a common political will and economic rationale to overcome all these negativities has prevented the introduction of the idea of a regional order based on interdependence.

Yet on the contrary, the region's extraordinary natural resources and geoeconomic riches are being exploited with such a degree of irrationality that it actually escalates interest rivalries, rather than creating an area of shared interests. The existence of oil and natural gas in the region has been the leading cause of intraregional tensions and extraterritorial interventions in the modern era. The fact that extraordinary reserves bestowed by these riches are spent not by way of increasing the quality of life and the standard of living of the people of the region, but in armaments associated with intraregional rivalries, actually represents the continuation of colonial economic relations in terms of the resources transferred to the international arms industry.

Like nature, geopolitics abhors a vacuum. The lack of any regional order with the capacity to balance regional geopolitics, create interconnections that will lead to win–win regional geoeconomic outcomes, and safeguard geocultural wealth does not preserve the status quo, but only replaces the status quo with chaos. Indeed, the chaotic situation of recent times has significantly weakened existing areas of common economic interest. Today, the environment of tension and conflict that is deteriorating every passing day has made the development of a coolheaded rational psychology to activate an understanding of shared economic interests impossible. Actors who conceive of themselves as being in the throes of an existential struggle for survival see the undertaking of efforts for economic interdependence as futile, or at least ill-timed. Yet one of the leading factors to ensure geopolitical survival is economic interdependence, which forms the rational basis of a sustainable regional order.

The big picture of the Middle East is one in which the replacement of the concept of rational cooperation by a culture of irrational conflict and revenge has made it impossible to nurture the idea of shared ideals and shared interests in a region dominated by shared risks and threats. The last striking example of such a case is the *Levant Union* project through implementing visa-free travel and free trade planned between the Levant Quartet of Turkey, Lebanon, Syria, and Jordan based on agreement establishing a High Level Quartet Cooperation Mechanism signed on 10 June 2010[22] just prior to the earthquake triggered by the Arab Spring. After the demise of this peace project as a result of developments in Syria – a project based on regional economic interdependence whose subcommittees had already started work following Foreign Minister-level meetings between the quartet with a view to the ultimate inclusion of Iraq – tension, terror, and chaos took command over this same line. The very word Levant, considered an appropriate sobriquet for an area of common economic interests, was then used by the terror organization Daesh/ISIL (L for Levant) to denote a belt of terror.

The disintegration of the GCC, a successful model not only in the region but also on the global scale, is a striking and cautionary example of how the loss of common economic perspectives can leave geopolitical tensions in its wake. The occurrence of a rupture that has moved the Gulf away from an understanding of regional economic unity as far as embargoes and the closure of transportation corridors is an irrational manifestation of the transition from a win–win to a lose–lose logic.

The transition from geoeconomic fragmentation to an understanding of order based on economic interdependence can also be brought about through internally consistent steps taken at different levels. At the first level, one needs to focus on projects that expand areas of common economic interest, especially between neighboring countries, and on transport and energy corridors that link countries through free-trade and visa-free measures. A good case in point is the Kirkuk–Yumurtalik pipeline's strengthening of ties between Iraq and Turkey from the 1970s to the present day. Free-trade agreements and visa-free practices developed over the past decade have also had an impact in increasing countries' mutual interests. The continuation of Turkish investments in the organized industrial zone established in Cairo by Turkey in the Mubarak era even in spite of political crises between the two countries reveals the resilience of economic interdependence against political tensions, once that interdependence has been formed.

The second layer consists of subregional economic interdependence areas created by a group of at least three countries. The formation of such areas is significant in terms of laying the infrastructural basis for larger-scale regional economic cooperation. A noteworthy and positive example has been developed between Turkey, Azerbaijan, and Georgia. The common economic interests and interdependence formed between these three countries began with an oil pipeline (BTC) and continued with a joint Baku–Tblisi–Kars railway project (BTK). The construction of the TANAP natural gas pipeline is currently under way. Overcoming the dispute within the GCC, with its background of achievement in the Middle East, the increased activation of ECO, which connects the Middle East to Central Asia, and the formation of subregional areas of economic cooperation in conjunction with geoeconomic, logistic, and energy corridors in regions that have constituted common economic basins throughout history (albeit within the borders of different countries with the creation of nation-states over time) such as Mesopotamia, the Levant/Eastern Mediterranean, the North African Maghreb, the Nile basin, and Aden/the Horn of Africa, may create the infrastructure for a regional order as well as ensuring the economic development of individual countries.

The third layer involves the formation of an area of economic cooperation encompassing the entire region in such a way that such a structure, one of the three pillars of a lasting and sustainable regional order, can rise up on the success achieved by the previous layers. It will be extremely hard to establish a sustainable regional order without the development of an understanding of economic cooperation that facilitates connections between production and consumption regions, ensures the coming together of human resources and natural resources at an optimal level, accelerates the transfer of energy resources within the region and to other regions, lays the ground for technology transfer through joint projects, and reduces intraregional income gaps.

These kinds of economic cooperation perspectives, which may look like mere pipedreams especially in the context of the chaotic conditions currently prevailing in the Middle East remain the only option by which everyone has something to gain through a win–win understanding in the long term. Overcoming the Cold War rationale in which only one country or group of countries could win also depends on this perspective. Any idea of regional domination is entirely bereft of both rationality and applicability. Eventually, the countries of the region will arrive at an understanding of economic cooperation that will achieve interest optimization. The important thing is for rationality to conquer perceptions of polarization and hegemonic impulses, and for this current process to be overcome without further suffering.

Cultural Pluralism and Coexistence

The cultural pluralism and coexistence that is so important in terms of the sense of a common belonging that underlies nation-states' internal orders, applies to regional orders to an even higher degree. There is not a single region in the world that only accommodates a single ethnic or sectarian identity. Even in Scandinavia, which is more homogeneous due to its distance from the main migration routes, there are communities that cut horizontally through parts of the region, especially, for example, the indigenous Sami/Lapp peoples.

Traditionally, land or sea transport corridors and migration routes, and regions hosting intercontinental transit routes, have an extremely complicated structure due to the intense ethnocultural interaction they have undergone throughout their histories.[23] The regions where this complex geocultural structure intersects with changeable geopolitical and multifaceted lines constitute areas where it is extremely difficult to establish a sustainable order.

Periods in which the international conjuncture undergoes change that causes the disintegration of large-scale structures activate the cultural fault lines on these regional belts, and problems of order trickle down to small-scale areas. For example, it is clear that ethnic/ cultural differences, which were not recognized or given prominence in the USSR, a great modern imperial order, gave rise to problematic issues of order in the post-Soviet period in the Caucasus, right down to the micro-zone level. The area of regional disorder that arose with tensions between local identities in the Caspian–Caucasus–Black Sea corridor, where the richest linguistic, ethnic, and religious diversity of history in the Eurasian context are evident on the north–south and east–west transit routes, remains one of the most striking examples of the inter-action between geopolitics and geoculture. The geocultural turbulence set off by the global geopolitical earthquake in such a narrow regional corridor gave birth to a regional environment that triggered various conflicts. Conflicts that started with ethnic-religious tensions brought about by geocultural turbulence could only be stopped by means of extremely fragile, temporary ceasefires. For a sustainable order in the Caucasus, there is a need for a shared living space and a multicultural consciousness based on taking possession of the region to assuage this geocultural turbulence.

The Balkans and Eastern Europe geocultural belt, which had found its own internal balances on different bases within large-scale political systems such as the Ottoman State, the Austro-Hungarian Empire, and the Soviet/Warsaw Pact, was also activated by the geopol-itical earthquake that accompanied the end of the Cold War. This geocultural turmoil, which caused immeasurable suffering and human devastation, especially in Srebrenica, brought with it tensions that cas-caded down to the micro-scale. The painful experiences of the 1990s in this belt on the Mediterranean–Black Sea–Baltic line taught us one fact: the most essential element for regional order is a regional ownership based on a sense of cultural belonging.[24] In these regions, it is very difficult to put in place a stable geopolitical order and achieve a sustain-able order without a geocultural rapprochement at local, national and regional levels.

In Southeast Asia, which has a highly complex cultural identity map due to the interaction of Indian, Chinese, and Islamic civilizational legacies and its location astride global-scale sea routes, there was an interaction between geopolitical, geoeconomic, and geocultural lines beneath tensions that had taken on an ideological guise during the Cold War. The recent transformation of the tragedy of the Rohingya Muslims, who have recently suffered one of the greatest crimes against humanity in history, into a regional problem transcending the borders of Myanmar from Bangladesh to Indonesia, also represents a striking indication of how national structures that lose the capacity to be inclusive can become the source of regional problems. In summary, ethnic-religious-sectarian tensions that cannot be resolved *in situ* in the framework of the principle of inclusiveness soon bring geocultural turmoil to a much wider area, threatening the stability of regional orders.

Perhaps the most striking, most comprehensive, and most tension-ridden experience of how problems arising from the intersection of geocultural, geoeconomic, and geopolitical lines can play havoc with regional order is what is occurring in the Middle East today. About a century after the dissolution of the Ottoman order, which granted autonomy to cultural identities in the region through the *millet* system for four centuries, contradictions between the horizontally rupturing geocultural lines of nation-state structures with new identity definitions emerging as a result of the nation-building experience of different nation-state structures were masked by Cold War static polarization and the control of autocratic regimes. The process that shook territorial structures with geocultural and geopolitical tensions that started in the post-Cold War era – with Saddam Hussein's invasion of Kuwait and the initial weakening of the central Iraqi state structure after the intervention that ended this adventure and restored the status quo – gained momentum with its complete disintegration in the second and more extensive intervention after 9/11, then turned into a structural earthquake that had a profound impact on the entire region after the Arab Spring.

The structural earthquake and turbulence in the aftermath of the Arab Spring clearly exposed the difference between the "top down" identity definitions of the central elites of nation-states, and the natural horizontal nature of the variety of identities stemming from the region's historic legacy. Shiite, Turkmen, and Kurdish identities excluded by a Ba'ath ideology that defended a monolithic Arab nationalism in Iraq during the Saddam Hussein era, and the trauma experienced by Sunni, Kurdish, and Turkmen identities at the hands of the regime based on the same monolithic Ba'ath ideology in Syria, has made the Iraq–Syria line an area of ethnic-sectarian conflict and chaos today. The concept of political order after the Iraq War that this time excluded Iraqi Sunnis has created conditions not only in Iraq but also in the region that are triggering sectarian abuse.

In all of these ethnic and sectarian tensions that shake the foundations of regional order, tensions in both directions have the potential to coexist within the local–national–regional pyramid. Local cultural tensions are rapidly transforming into national cultural tensions, and the monolithic identities that remain the preferred option at the national level are intensifying regional polarizations. And this time, once cultural identity tensions have reached a regional level, their concurrent reflections at the local level intensify when the dynamics of conflict are added to the mix.

The intensification of areas of tension in the context of cultural identity brings with it a destructive effect that leads to the purging of history as well as the human and social fabric. The destruction of ancient sites, churches, and mosques regarded as heretical by Daesh in the regions under their control reveals the fact that once started, ideological/ethnic/sectarian annihilation knows no bounds and leads to a fanatical devastation that seeps down to the micro-scale. When viewed in the context of human devastation, ethnic massacres and forced exiles carried out in order to control strategic areas and corridors under a single ethnic and sectarian group destroy the long-established local human factor, which constitutes the main element of any regional order. References to cities as being Shiite, Sunni, Arab, Kurdish, and Turkmen are an indication of how the social fabric of city traditions, which is fundamentally based on cultural diversity, is being destroyed.

One of the most important requirements for the formation of sustainable regional order today is the provision of an environment of stability that will protect the cultural heritage that has been a part of the living experience of every cultural community for centuries over the geocultural belts that have come to be inhabited by different ethnic, religious, and sectarian communities. Embarking from the smallest local units, the preservation of coexisting cultures gradually reduces the fragility in geocultural belts and opens up an environment of consensus at national and regional levels. Today, the region's most essential requirement from the geocultural perspective is that every ethnic, religious, or sectarian group should not close itself off for its own security, but open up to other groups and establish an environment of cultural security and dialogue. In whatever country, and whatever their sense of belonging to ethnic and sectarian groups, what statesmen need to do to achieve this goal is not to exploit them in the form of a populist exclusionary discourse, however much that may gain favor within their own base, but to develop an inclusive and embracing political discourse and methodology that will gain the respect of apparently opposing groups.

Is an Action Plan for Regional Order in the Middle East Possible?

It may appear unrealistic to talk about a new regional order in the Middle East, where local tensions are rising, national structures are in danger of disintegration, and regional organizations are at risk of becoming inoperable. However, as in Europe after the Second World War, the formation of enduring order often takes place just when conflicts have proliferated and the parties have been left exhausted by these conflicts. The issue is to initiate discussions about the infrastructure for such an order before an even more comprehensive environment of conflict emerges.

Today, the establishment of a new regional framework in response to the problems that are intensifying in the region and not only penetrating other regions but also the global arena, requires a highly patient, rational, consistent, and inclusive international process. The necessary course of action in this context can be gathered under six headings:

First, infrastructure work for a Helsinki process-like initiative that contributed to stability in Europe under Cold War conditions should be initiated on the basis of the absolute inviolability of borders in order to ensure the continuity of their existing international legal status and to prevent adventurist tendencies that may pose a security risk. In this context, channels of dialogue between countries should be kept open to be able to contain interstate tensions, and to limit the impact of non-state actors, while communication between security bodies should not be cut even during the most intense moments of crisis.

Secondly, and in conjunction with political processes that will take place with the participation of all concerned parties, multilateral initiatives should be focused on resolving political problems in countries such as Syria, Libya, and Yemen, where different countries have different approaches to the question of legitimate interlocutors due to the continuation of civil war conditions. In this regard, a *modus vivendi* should be settled between the parties, and regional and global actors should suspend their claims until the formation of a legitimate counterpart who has gained the recognition of all concerned parties in these countries. The militia structures whose support by various parties leads to proxy wars must be disbanded in conjunction with the assumption of duties in political processes by all parties who have not been involved in war crimes and terror activities, while security at the regional level is ensured by well-defined national security units.

Thirdly, a new set of principles and criteria concerning weapons of mass destruction and terrorist threats should be established to embrace all actors in the region, who will form the basis of regional order. International organizations should play a facilitating and encouraging role in this process. Global actors should avoid exclusionary and polarizing rhetoric and interventionist policies that will only pave the way for a regional Cold War psychology.

Fourthly, in order for the region, which has been so severely impacted by the devastation that has occurred from the First Gulf War after the end of the Cold War to the present day, to stand on its feet economically, an international economic rehabilitation program should be implemented and the conditions leading to mass refugee movements should be addressed and corrected. Projects to revitalize national economies and develop areas of regional cooperation should adopt an approach that prioritizes rational common interests in areas of regional and global rivalry, especially in the transfer of natural resources to the global economy.

Fifthly, a large-scale regional consensus should be drawn up to overcome the current state of affairs in which geocultural fragmentation has profoundly shaken regional geopolitics, and to rebuild the cultural pillar of a prospective regional order. The principal elements of such a consensus, which would set out the principles with which all actors in the region and relevant global actors should comply, may be defined as follows: (i) no ethnic or sectarian community should be granted special protection or patronage against any other ethnic or sectarian group; (ii) the adoption of a common stance against all efforts to distort the cultural demographic map, and the establishment of the cooperation necessary for all parties to return to their original homes from where they were driven by conflicts; (iii) the formation of platforms to ensure intensive dialogue and positive interaction between ethnic, religious, and sectarian communities; (iv) the establishment of a regional UNESCO body, or a subunit of UNESCO, and the creation of an international fund for the preservation of all historical cultural heritage and treasures, without regard to the religious, sectarian, or ethnic group to which it belongs.

Sixthly, regional organizations should be restructured and consolidated to include relevant actors, and mechanisms should be created to provide effective interregional cooperation with international organizations and afford opportunities for common intervention in crisis areas. In this framework, structural arrangements that will enable regional organizations and actors to play a more formal and effective role in the UN system will encourage outcomes that enable them to conduct effective crisis management. For example, the participation of the African Union and concerned countries on issues related to the African continent; the OIC on issues related to the Muslim World; and regional organizations such as the Arab League, the GCC, and the Economic Cooperation Organization, and relevant regional powers on issues related to the Middle East will facilitate the achievement of results through greater sharing of responsibility.

In short, if we fail to develop a visionary approach based on a long-term shared destiny, common values, and a consciousness of common interests instead of short-term conjunctural and personality-based reactionary approaches in the Middle East today, it will prove impossible to prevent this region from shedding further blood in internal conflicts long into the future. So this is the phenomenon we have called a *systemic earthquake* – the precise cause and consequence of such an environment. Our approach to regional problems and our quest for solutions must therefore transcend the problem-based conjunctural context. Otherwise, every issue will become the trigger for new, more wide-ranging, problems.

Such a climate of uncertainty and conflict, open to any kind of provocation, can activate any number of fragile and lawless balance of power systemic situations on a global and regional scale, and eventually trigger widespread tensions, conflicts, and wars that spill over from the regional to the global level. It may be easy to trigger a war with invasions, occupations, ultimatums, heroic tirades, and expectations of victory, but it is impossible to predict the consequences of such wars. It is easy to find some justification or fabrication for wars that were supposed to end easily, such as Saddam Hussein's occupation of Kuwait, or Bush's invasions of Iraq and Afghanistan, but it is not so easy to end a war even on much more genuine and powerful justifications. This kind of approach, which adopts short-term populist methods, causes an equal and opposite reaction and leads to a period of uncertainty induced by interminable struggles for revenge based on implacable feelings that deploy similar methods.

Today, all political actors, faith leaders, and intellectuals in the region, regardless of their particular viewpoints, are facing a common test of responsibility. To cite an example from the history of Europe, it is in their hands whether to bequeath future generations a bloody future like the prolonged wars of religion and ideology that lasted from the Thirty Years War to the Cold War, or to initiate a period of new political and intellectual enlightenment and economic vitality in a spirit of mutual respect in the Middle East. Let us not forget: either all of us shall continue to experience and witness a further series of catastrophes, or we shall build a future together. All political actors in the region are faced with the responsibility to set all past obstacles to one side and remove the roadblocks to this common future by taking serious stock of the situation and carrying out a process of self-criticism. We have an obligation to focus not on past conflicts, but on the difficulties we shall face in the future and the shared future we must attain by overcoming these difficulties.

8 INCLUSIVE GLOBAL GOVERNANCE: A NEW PARADIGM OF GLOBAL ORDER

The systemic crisis we face today imposes the need for a new paradigm of global order and governance that takes into account the dynamics brought by globalization. The various components of the current international order handed down from the twentieth century and grounded on the philosophical and institutional structures of pre-globalization modernity are struggling to manage the rapid dynamics of a globalization-fueled oceanic wave and to contain the associated risks.

First and foremost, the fate of mankind as a whole now faces a series of very large-scale threats. These threats require an endeavor beyond just optimizing nation-states' self-interests, because they are of their nature *transnational* not *international*. Issues such as climate change, environmental problems, cybercrime, the proliferation of weapons of mass destruction, and terror have now reached a scale that presents a threat to everyone, everywhere, and are becoming increasingly difficult to resolve purely through interstate relations based on "territorial sovereignty and hegemonic geopolitics."[1] There is a clear need for a comprehensive new system of values in which states and concerned international civil society can participate to address these threats to humanity's shared destiny, together with conventions based on such a system.[2]

Secondly, the remarkable communication opportunities afforded by globalization have revolutionized conventional diplomatic techniques on which the international order depends.[3] Instantaneously transmittable messages have dynamized diplomacy, which used to operate on the basis of telegraphed instructions. Smart mobile technology has made everywhere a diplomatic bureau and every message a diplomatic communication. As someone with experience of trying to manage a number of crises by means of direct messaging with my counterparts as Foreign Minister and Prime Minister, I have come to appreciate the possibilities of this technological revolution in diplomacy. Yet we have also experienced many cases of their misuse in the emergence and spread of crises.

Today, the fact that US diplomacy is being followed via President Trump's twitter feed rather than the concerned Secretaries and diplomats represents a striking example of the extent and scope of the impact of this revolution of digital diplomacy defined broadly as "the use of social media for diplomatic purposes."[4] The fact that a single tweet can ignite an instantaneous crisis or economic fluctuation has led to a shaking of confidence in the existing order and the escalation of uncertainty-based reactionary responses. This has led to the phenomenon of international order losing its structural character, and a pattern of behavior marked by individual and unilateral actions.

Thirdly, the progressively intensifying relations between societies and individuals in different corners of the world have surpassed the speed and intensity of relations between states. The capacity now exists for instant communications on every scale between the citizens of states that do not even have diplomatic relations with each other. In an era when the speed of individuals' communications has overtaken that of official diplomacy, it is hard to maintain a conventional diplomacy-based perception of order.

All these new elements ushered in by globalization are leading to a paradigmatic change in the concept of interstate structural order. If a global order is to be established, it can no longer be achieved by means of a central military, economic, and political controlling power as was the case in ancient imperial orders, nor solely on the basis of the balance of power and international organizations on which the experiences of modernity have been based. A concept of *inclusive global governance* that takes all these actors into account needs to be established on sound foundations. This global governance requires a three-legged restructuring of the political, economic, and cultural global orders.

Global Political Order

In the immediate wake of the Cold War at the beginning of the 1990s there was an overwhelming expectation that a new global order would be realized under the leadership of the United States as the absolute victor of the Cold War through the application of its de facto power. The conceptual reference of this expectation was the "New World Order" motto, and its first real-world manifestation was the broad US-led coalition formed in the first Gulf War. To adapt a saying from the order of ancient Rome, "all roads were leading to Washington." American exceptionalism in post-Cold War era was part and parcel of this international atmosphere.[5]

This concept of global order, which effectively meant bestowing modern international methods on the ancient imperial tradition of unipolar order,[6] materialized (albeit using different tools and styles) in the interventions of Bill Clinton in Kosovo and George W. Bush in Iraq. In the framework of a humanitarian intervention conceptualization in line with his Democrat affiliation, Clinton's Kosovo operation was conducted as a NATO-based coalition of the willing within a semi-multilateral structure. The second Bush administration's unilateral Iraq operation clearly showed the limitations and shortfalls of a unipolar, military power-oriented method of establishing order based on the rhetoric of security. This unilateralism was the peak of American exceptionalism based on "a belief by national policy makers and legislators that they have other options for pursuing their nation's interest and that acting through multilateral institutions is only an option, not an obligation."[7]

In this atmosphere, the Obama administration strove for the multilateral resolution of every crisis that posed a clear threat to the existing order, including the crisis over the use of chemical weapons in Syria, by turning G20 summits after the global economic crisis into annual platforms for the discussion not only of economic but international issues in general, and bringing such issues to the attention of domestic and international platforms. Interpreting this as weakness of will, other power centers concentrated on maximizing their own interests and we began to see the emergence of powers challenging the unipolar understanding of order.

The failures of the new world order under US leadership brought uncertainties as well as quests for an alternative Rome. At the same time, the ineffectiveness of the UN system encouraged the emergence of crisis and region-based power centers and an environment of disorderly and lawless competition within them. More often than not, these power centers went on to establish new de facto orders in certain areas through unilateral interventions. Russia's unilateral annexation of Crimea and its interventions in Ukraine and Syria based on mutually contradictory arguments represent striking examples. However, the limited nature of these players' capacities either singlehandedly or by forming new coalitions to form a balance of power and meet the consequent economic costs also prevented the emergence of centers with the capacity to establish an alternative order.

The Uncertainty of Multiple Balances of Power

Today, there is in fact no single global-scale balance of power, but rather a picture of chaotic uncertainty based on crisis and multiple regional balances of power. A number of players of varying influence in the Middle East, East Asia, Eastern Europe, the Caucasus, sub-Saharan Africa, and Latin America are in the process of forming regional balances of power. For example, China, the leading player in the balance of power with regard to issues in East Asia such as North Korea and the Spratly Islands, remains a decisive player in the context of its stance posited on its UNSC veto card regarding issues in other regions. By contrast, Russia, striving to boost its influence with every crisis along the Cold War's famed *Rimland* belt stretching from Eastern Europe through the Black Sea and Central Asia down to East Asia and become the lead actor in regional balances of power, has a more limited role in Latin America and sub-Saharan Africa. Likewise, countries such as Turkey, Iran, Saudi Arabia, and Egypt may have the capacity to affect regional balances of power as the leading players in every Middle East issue, but their influence in regions beyond their own neighborhood is much more restricted.

In the uncertainty borne of the absence of any power to manage a common set of values and mechanisms, all these subsystems based on regional-scale balances of power are leading to a rise in the level of uncertainty. The United States, which claimed such a role in the immediate post-Cold War period, cannot even play the regulating role in the balance of power that Britain fulfilled in the nineteenth century and behaves as just another player in the regional balance of power in every problem area. This approach, which hampers the development of a global-scale, integrative strategy, gives rise to even greater levels of confusion when combined with Trump's impulsive micro-reactions.

The UN system is also affected by all these fragmentary regional balances of power as it becomes a technocratic mechanism without the tools or indeed the will to mobilize the shared values that enabled its establishment in the first place. International problems are now resolved (or not) according to the course of balances of power in the field rather than on the UN platform. The development of a field of gravity by the Astana Process run by countries with influence in the area – Russia, Turkey, and Iran – is a notable case in point. An international organization whose representation and willpower have been weakened will inevitably become irrelevant in time. The fate of the League of Nations should provide a salutary lesson.

Thus, like a ship adrift in turbulent waters without a captain, the global political order has lost its bearings and its steering. Sailors fore, aft, and amidships want the ship to be steered according to the areas of command applying in their particular section of the vessel. This renders its course uncertain; as they realize this, actors struggle to take positions to save themselves in the event the ship goes down. This psychological state has now turned into a vicious circle. Uncertainty over the course leads to unilateral moves, unilateral moves led to uncertainty over the course. This vicious circle accelerates the rhythm of this procession of crises as its impact grows ever stronger and deeper. Unless it is stopped in its tracks, this vicious circle stumbling from efforts to establish global and regional dominance to global and regional chaos will continue day by day to increase the possibility of a devastating global war that would threaten the future of the human race on a much bigger scale of destruction than the previous historic experiences of world wars.

In summary, there is no possibility of getting the global political order on track in the midst of a systemic earthquake through unilateral interventions and regional-scale balances of power. We must learn the lessons of past experience; yet the new tools and factors brought by globalization require a new system and taxonomy of order. What is needed is a transition from a unipolar, unilateral concept of governance to an inclusive and overarching paradigm of governance through representative power and influence.

I take the view that a staged transition within the context of the main elements of a global order of governance and a workable action plan such as this can serve to create the framework we envisage. Psychologically and intellectually preparing a roadmap for this framework may serve to lay the groundwork for discussions and exchanges of ideas to overcome future uncertainties.

An Urgent Action Plan: Shock Therapy for the International System

First of all, there is an urgent need for shock treatment to dispel the psychology of uncertainty in the short term. This can be achieved through the use of existing conventions and mechanisms by means of a widely supported binding joint declaration. The modus operandi could be a joint declaration defined by a UN Security Council resolution approved by the P5 countries as a global document, in consultation with the UN General Assembly. It could consist of the following clauses:

i *The principle of the immutability of UN-recognized nation-state borders and the resolution of current border disputes through peaceful diplomatic channels as of the date of the declaration*: a principle of this kind halts adventurist tendencies aimed at changing borders and prevents frozen crises becoming hot conflicts. It should also be recorded within the framework of this principle that border changes made without the agreement of the concerned parties shall not be recognized by the UN.

ii *Preparation of an action plan first to limit and then to eradicate all weapons of mass destruction with the capacity to escalate an environment of global crisis and threaten humankind as a whole*: the announcement of a common sanction to be imposed against the threat or use of weapons of mass destruction in this framework, by whomever and from wherever they emanate, will serve to deter fresh crises.

iii *An undertaking to oppose all terrorist groups threatening the global community as a whole without regard to their ethnicity, religion, and sect, on a common front*: in this framework, a common stance will be demonstrated against the use of these groups in proxy wars in countries and regions undergoing political crises; giving voice to this stance may stop the destabilizing impact of non-state actors.

iv *A review and update of international laws and conventions inherited from the Cold War era, including areas such as climate change and cybercrime that threaten the future of humankind as a whole*: such a redefinition will serve to increase the decisive influence of the core values upon which the international system is based and ensure that it is able to control the process and risk by which the system is de-"value"d.

v *The preparation of a comprehensive action plan for humanitarian aid, including the rehabilitation of civilians affected by post-Cold War crises, particularly of refugees, and the formation of a dedicated international fund for their repatriation*: such a rehabilitation process will stabilize the progressively accelerating rate of uncontrolled mass migration of people arising from economic and political crises now being experienced on this earth.

vi *The establishment of a council of wise men composed of general secretaries, statesmen, and thinkers, mainly from the UN and other international organizations, with a view to restructuring the international order formed under the UN umbrella after the Second World War in such a way as to reconcile it with post-Cold War era conditions, and the holding of this restructuring process to a schedule*: such a process will of itself also lead to the transition from the current mood of pessimism stemming from the uncertainty that currently holds sway over the international community, to an environment of rational discussion.

vii *The appointment by the UN of an authorized body to control and manage any crises that might emerge during this period and spread by domino effect and, if and when necessary, the strengthening of this body with a peacekeeping mission*: even if they cannot be resolved, keeping crises with a tendency to escalate at any moment and in any place under control is an essential prerequisite for the success of this reevaluation process, because climates of crisis will bring new power rivalries and uncertainties.

By dissolving the rapidly evolving environment of pessimism in the international community, gaining time for rational negotiations, marginalizing irrational actors and reactions that feed on an atmosphere of international uncertainty, and redefining the counterparts involved in prevailing issues as well as methods of resolution, a declaration of this kind, to be issued by the UN General Assembly and Security Council on the basis of international consensus, will be significant in terms of motivating decision-makers and opinion leaders to contribute to the formation of a new international order.

This declaration, to be promulgated in the short term as a matter of urgency, must not remain a mere piece of paper but rather it must be activated to restructure the international system towards the goal of inclusive global governance in the medium term. Such a mission requires an intellectual, legal, and structural transformation. One of the principal reasons for today's systemic earthquake is the logjam created by the failure to enact UN reform in spite of its constant presence on the international agenda. Dealing with the fault lines underlying this earthquake without clearing this logjam will be well-nigh impossible.

The UN Reform Process: Methodological Dilemmas

In this context, the most critical issue remains that of UN reform, the political framework of which was drawn up after prolonged debate at the 2005 World Summit. The fact that virtually no progress has been made up to now is a leading factor in the increased level of insecurity in the international system. Longer-term realization of this reform remains beyond reach in the absence of a sincere and realistic discussion of the causes of failure. As an academician and politician who has had the privilege of participating in various capacities in almost all the work of the UN General Assembly over the past fifteen years as well as closely following the views of country representatives with different interests, I have come to the opinion that four main factors underlie the inability to enact reform.

The first concerns the reform process's methodology. This methodology, which seems technical but is in fact entirely political, has been tied to a series of steps that render internal change impossible. The resistance mechanism observed in nation-state constitutions whose self-imposed rules make change impossible are also valid in the case of the UN Charter. According to the current charter, any change to the structure of the UN Security Council can only be implemented by amending the Charter itself. Article 108 defines how this can be accomplished: "*Amendments to the present Charter shall come into force for all Members of the United Nations when they have been adopted by a vote of two-thirds of the members of the General Assembly and ratified in accordance with their respective constitutional processes by two-thirds of the Members of the United Nations, including all the permanent members of the Security Council.*"[8]

In and of itself, the fact that any reform is subject to the approval of the permanent members of the UNSC, who may use their privileged position in the current UN system to maximize their national self-interest, constitutes the greatest procedural barrier to change, because these countries do not see the UN reform process as an opportunity for the creation of a new international order but as a risk factor to their own privileged position. In this context, it is hardly surprising that permanent members with widely divergent interests share a common platform on the question of resisting reform.

While this state of affairs is open to criticism in terms of idealist values, it is an entirely comprehensible reaction in terms of *realpolitik*, because no country wants to lose its privileged status. Yet these countries need to read the decline in the UN's performance and effectiveness in recent years accurately. The UN is progressively moving away from its positive mission as the founder of international order and its role is being debased to that of a braking mechanism against any process that might affect permanent members' own national interests. If this continues, the UN will turn into an increasingly irrelevant organization alienated from developments in the field. Having a privileged position of power within such an organization will become more and more devoid of meaning, at least for peace and security functions.

The second factor is that UN reform has not been seen as part of a comprehensive reform of the international order; on the contrary, it has been reduced to the issue of reforming the UN Security Council. This has served to dislodge the reform process from being a necessity that concerns the entire international community and turned it into a power struggle, especially with regard to the veto power. Countries like the G4 (Brazil, Germany, India, and Japan)[9] are involved in a struggle to gain permanent membership while those seeing no chance of attaining such status oppose the expansion of this category. The justified demands of the African continent, widely seen as a victim of the UN system, have become a tactical trump card exploited by parties to this struggle. The UN Security Council permanent membership structure and representative capacity is truly very far from being any kind of reflection of today's balances of power. And the debasement of the issue to a question of which country should obtain a new privileged status has blocked the development of a comprehensive reform process.

The third factor is that the imposition of particular conditions by some P5 member countries has turned the reform process from being a time-limited mission into an open-ended mental exercise. And in spite of the intensification of crises during this period, the failure to bind the reform process to any kind of schedule has cast a long shadow over the seriousness of the entire process. Like all routine international processes, UN reform has turned into a recurring agenda item in a succession of technical meetings.

The fourth factor is P5 members' reluctance especially on the issue of Security Council reform, and the role their tacit alliances to conserve the status quo play in depriving such a difficult process of political will. This has made the expectation and process of change more important than change itself; a routine and technocratic process recognized as unachievable from the outset has turned into a merry-go-round diplomatic exercise whose perpetuation is useful to all. Discourse and rhetoric have thus prevailed over the will actually to change the status quo.

The Possibility of a Result-Oriented UN Reform Process

So how can a genuine reform process be achieved? First of all, there is a need for a thorough reassessment of the UN reform process in the light of the experiences of the past quarter-century in terms of its principles, methodology, and implementation processes. A reevaluation unaffected by political and conjunctural concerns is key to identifying bottlenecks in the UN reform process and developing a method capable of delivering results.

Preparatory work for this process may be conducted by working groups focusing on three main axes: (i) a group consisting mainly of intellectuals and academicians who will concentrate on the intellectual and philosophical groundwork of the new international order taking account of the transformation's historical context; (ii) a group consisting of international legal experts and representatives who have served on international organizations who will address the need to update the international legal acquis or consider what items are required to draw up a new one; and finally (iii) a working group of statespersons and politicians who have played a role in international crisis management to address structural and institutional transformation.

The most fundamental principle with respect to the legitimacy of the entire process should be the inclusion in these working groups of representatives from all elements of the world community and cultural and civilizational basins, as well as groups from all continents and regions at different levels of development. For the proposed institutional reforms to be realized, work that is going to be carried out must be based on the idealist foundation of *inclusiveness* and *integrity* and the realist framework of *interest optimization* and *implementation of power*.

Secondly, a common international will needs to be shown by extracting the reform process from the field of tactical maneuvering and lifting roadblocks based on P5/the rest, status quo/change or center/periphery dichotomies. Unfortunately, unlike outrageous rhetoric, it is difficult to talk about the existence of a common will of this kind today. This is precisely the point at which the difference between the rationale of global governance and that of the balance of power emerges. Great powers that approach the question of the international order from a balance of power rationale are focused on achieving an outcome that will strengthen their position in that balance, whereas had they adopted the principle of global governance the process could have shifted from being an area of tactical maneuver and turned into a strategic process of establishing order.

Thirdly, a participatory and results-oriented method must be adopted for a genuine, comprehensive reform process, and this method linked to a reasonable but not open-ended schedule. Flexibility needs to be brought to the reform process' self-immobilizing decision-making, and the UN General Assembly should have an increased role in order to encourage comprehensive participation in the final round of the process. Binding the final stage of an international structural reform that sees 193 member states as equal to the decision of just five countries reflects a logic that holds the citizens of those five countries superior to those of 188 and divides humanity into two ranks in a manner that defies the equality-based philosophy of the first sentence of the preamble to the *Declaration of Human Rights* that constitutes the UN system's principal founding reference text: "Whereas recognition of the inherent dignity and of the equal and inalienable rights of all members of the human family is the foundation of freedom, justice and peace in the world."[10]

Fourthly, the reform process must be absolved from any impasse arising from debate over which power is to be a permanent member, and based on common principles applicable to all. Representation and participation principles should be reconsidered within a rationale of inclusivity and the question of how these principles are reflected in the UN structure must be based on objective criteria. The equitable reflection in the UN structure as a whole, especially the

UN Security Council, of balances of power, population distribution, cultural and civilizational basins, continents and regions, and different categories of economic development shall serve not only to legitimize this global body but boost the possibility of resolutions being effectively implemented.

Fifthly, the relationship between the UN Security Council and the UN General Assembly should be redefined as one of the most critical areas of the UN's institutional restructuring process. Such a redefinition is the only way to prevent the entire reform process from gridlock over the issue of UN Security Council membership. The maintenance of the current kind of relations between these two main structures without change will make it extremely difficult either to overcome blockages in the reform process or to argue convincingly for the prospects of a new participatory order.

In this context, the gulf in the decision-making process between the authority of the UN Security Council, which holds all operational decision-making authority, and the UN General Assembly, which is prominent for its symbolic and comprehensive representation, must be narrowed, because the differences in alignment between the UN General Assembly, which represents the global conscience of humanity, and the UN's organ of authority, namely the Security Council, only serve to widen the chasm between that global conscience and the will of the UN. For example, the failure in spite of all relevant UN resolutions to present to the Security Council UN resolutions on the membership status of the Palestinian State, recognized by an overwhelming majority in the UN General Assembly as having the status of a non-member state, on account of one permanent member's veto, represents a significant and striking case of the inability to turn the global conscience into an implementable resolution. The General Assembly resolution on Jerusalem on 21 December 2017 to ask nations not to establish diplomatic mission in the historic city of Jerusalem by a crushing (128:9) majority[11] in the face of all the objections and arm-twisting of the United States has again conspicuously exposed the gap between the global conscience and the unilateral exertion of power.

The distribution of authority between the two bodies needs to be redefined based on issues and proportions; the exemption from veto of resolutions carried by a certain proportion of the General Assembly should be adopted as a matter of principle. The rare cases in UN history in which the "Uniting for Peace" Resolution 377a[12] has been implemented may shine a light on future steps.

Sixthly, intermediate mechanisms should be set up in which regional organizations and powers can engage with the concerned authorities in parallel to formal Security Council meetings, or come to decisions jointly with the Security Council, regardless of the subject. The fact that countries paying the price for global crises are out of the loop while, as a result, countries taking final decisions about these crises see negotiations as cards in their own internal bargaining processes, is an unsustainable state of affairs.

In this context, structural arrangements providing a more formal and effective role for regional organizations and players within the UN system will help to ensure sound crisis management. For example, the involvement of regional organizations and directly concerned regional powers such as the African Union in matters concerning Africa, the OIC in issues of concern to the Islamic world, the Arab League, GCC for Middle East issues, and ASEAN for those related to Southeast Asia, will facilitate resolution by boosting participation and accountability.

The most fundamental lesson that international actors, including the UN, other international organizations and global players, should draw from their experience in different regions over the past quarter-century is that regional engagement is the most effective means of establishing peace and stability. Excluding regional engagement in order to maintain a grip on a monopoly of international power and seeking solutions only in diplomatic maneuvers carried out in New York or the P5 capitals instead of in the field is not the way to achieve lasting peace.

For these reasons, an approach that encourages regional engagements with the UN should be adopted, and issue-focused, result-oriented mechanisms developed that also involve concerned regional players between the UN General Assembly and the Security Council. Intermediate mechanisms such as UNSC + Regional Actors or P5 + Regional Actors have a significant contribution to make in terms of alleviating suddenly escalating crises and bringing them under control, as well as activating elements that support the formation of international order. Since regional crises now have such a tendency to become global crises, we now find ourselves at a critical juncture in which the need for precisely such mechanisms is keenly felt.

Seventhly, international problems' increasingly transnational nature should give ever greater weight to mechanisms and processes involving non-state actors and civil society groups taking into consideration the strength of interaction brought by developments in communication technology and the ever-spreading impact of non-state actors. For example, identity conflicts stemming from growing sectarian and ethnic tensions, escalating xenophobia, and Islamophobia can only possibly be resolved as problems transcending national boundaries by transnational means and mechanisms. These problems arise not from interstate relations but from elements that slice societies down the middle,[13] making it necessary to resolve them through intensive interaction between communities rather than through formal diplomatic negotiations.

In this context I can cite the example of two initiatives from my own experience: the Alliance of Civilizations and Friends of Mediation initiatives we developed in Turkey, in conjunction with Spain and Finland respectively. The former, started in 2005 at a time when the "clash of civilizations" atmosphere was on the rise in the wake of 9/11, was first recognized for its work in a UN resolution co-sponsored by 96 members and adopted by the General Assembly on 10 November 2009[14] and in a second resolution of 6 July 2015 co-sponsored by 101 members.[15] With its Group of Friends comprising 146 members including UN member states and international organizations as of January 2018, and the involvement of national and international civil society and private sector representatives, this initiative has taken the form of an organization that embraces the whole of human society. The *Friends of Mediation* that we founded with Finland on 24 September 2010 currently consists of forty-seven UN member states and seven regional and international organizations, with the draft it tabled at the sixty-fifth session of the General Assembly subsequently becoming an official UN resolution on strengthening the role of mediation.[16] The initiative has also pioneered a number of efforts to develop a transnational consciousness for mediation and peace initiatives. Today, there is a keenly perceived need for interventions able to appeal to the whole of humanity and all layers of societies in almost every area, and in that context to encourage nation-states with respect to the creation of a more peaceful atmosphere as well.

All these complex elements of debate demonstrate the existence of serious intellectual, political, legal, and institutional barriers to reforms addressing the ongoing systemic earthquake in the global political order as a UN-centered phenomenon. This process, which appears now to have reached a dead end, can only be successful with good will and strong resolve. After all, the world has already gone through the agonies of an international state of affairs in which the dominant structure of international order loses its meaning in the League of Nations saga. It is our hope that this time, and based on the shared intelligence of humanity, a new global political order can be achieved not in the wake of a world war, but without further prevarication in a way that prevents the outbreak of a devastating conflict of that kind.

The Global Economic Order

Throughout history there has been a direct relationship between political and economic orders. Chaotic developments are inevitable without the co-presence of a political order that ensures people's ontological security together with an economic order providing a continuity of material existence. The durability and rise of political orders depend on the economic order's capacity to create and develop resources. An increase in this capacity leads to the rise of political orders while the downscaling of resources heralds their decline and fall.

Pre-modern political orders in history relied on geographically continuous dominions that delivered the transfer of economic resources. The fact that all roads led to Rome in the Roman order signified a corridor and dominion that enabled the orderly flow of economic resources to the capital. The common denominator of the multi-tradition, multifaith imperial orders established along the Silk Road over the centuries was their effective command of the economic resource-transfer corridor that cuts right across Eurasia. Until the impact of modernity, which in the nineteenth century propounded a new economic model, the political orders of the Chinese in the East and the Ottomans in the West also formed economic orders based on the control and transfer of commodities/economic resources made possible essentially by their command of geographic continuity.

This ancient concept of economic-political order underwent a radical change with the increase in scale instigated by the new production techniques of the industrial revolution. This increase in scale heralded a new economic-political order compatible with the raw-material resources required for production as well as new supply-and-demand balances the market required for the supply of manufactured goods. The ancient market concept gave way to market mechanisms, economic-political order based on geographic continuity to a colonial order based on the command of overseas territories.

At the same time, this increase in scale brought with it a concept of international economic order that saw the entire world as a zone of economic competition. The colonial empires, which created their own dominions by destroying ancient economic-political orders, initiated an intense struggle not only for their own commodity needs but also for international command of raw materials and markets. British, French, German, Spanish, Dutch, and Portuguese colonial rivalry also gave rise to a Eurocentric international economic-political structure regulated in the capitals of Europe. This served to alienate the economies in regions linked to different colonial empires from each other while ushering in market and currency-based transcontinental economic orders.

The post-Second World War dissolution of colonial empires shook this concept of economic-political order; this time it was accompanied by a US-centered international order around the Bretton Woods system institutionalized by the World Bank, GATT, and the IMF. The socialist concept of economic-political order, also based on modernist assumptions but with a different ideological foundation and vision of production-consumption relations, emerged as an alternative to its capitalist rival.

In this sense the Cold War was not only a struggle between two ideological fronts but also two divergent models of economic order that promised humankind global-scale prosperity and happiness. This economic-political struggle, based on socialist and neoliberal economic paradigms, was in fact the practical reflection of two different theoretical assumptions.

The socialist economic model assumes that monopoly ownership of the means of production by the state, which represents the collective will of society, will eliminate internal contradictions by getting rid of social differences so that individuals with a common interest and consciousness of society will be able to develop and benefit equally from the development of a space of common prosperity and happiness. This approach, asserting that the production–consumption balance emanating from socialist equality would optimally benefit society by doing away with the exploitation of labor inherent in competition and private-sector profiteering, formed a serious gravitational field

of idealistic and ethical attraction during the early stages of the implementation of socialist practices. However, the internal contradictions
brought about by the relegation of the production motive, the loss of
efficiency caused by this demotivation, and the beginning of a distinctive
class of technocrats to manage gigantic production–consumption mechanisms led to this economic model losing its attraction from the 1970s
onwards and the progressive marginalization of socialist economies in
areas of global competition. The economic contraction caused by this
crisis within the socialist model led to the end of the global bipolarity-
based Cold War without the two poles coming to blows together with
the collapse of the Warsaw Pact that had acted as the platform from
which the socialist model was promulgated.

On the Cold War's other front, the productivity of competition
represented by the capitalist global economic model and driven by
impulses innate to human nature was to achieve a form of economic
development in which all could take a share; the liberal-capitalist
approach that advocated the need for a global economic order based
on free-market and free-trade conditions underwent a neoliberal process
of renewal that led to its victory in the economic-political struggle at the
end of the 1980s. In a sense, the nature of competitive efficiency prevailed over the theoretical precepts of egalitarian allocation.

The 1990s was a period when economic expectations on a
global scale rose in tandem with the motivation and market expansion
this victory brought, and the unchallenged expansion of this model.
However, the quarter-century since the end of the Cold War has witnessed the emergence of serious question marks over the global economic order formed by this model, and its sustainability.

In particular, the 2008 global economic crisis brought with it a
three-tiered challenge to the model's sustainability and global applicability. The fact that the crisis began in the Cold War victor states'
inner stratum, principally the United States, exposed weaknesses in
the model's own internal logic and financial architecture. The intense
economic crisis in countries that might be seen as the model's peripheral
states specializing in particular sectors of the economic order such as
Greece, Portugal, and Ireland has shown that significant difficulties are
also being experienced on the lines linking the model's national
economies.

Yet the most serious challenges to the model's capacity to form
a global economic order lie in third-tier geographic territories beyond

its sphere of application. At least in the past twenty-five years, expect-ations that competitive productivity and free-market mechanisms would over time create a global zone of prosperity have not been reflected in practice. As income inequality in the global economy has grown exponentially, refugee-flows fleeing economic hardship and political instability have triggered perhaps the most widespread migrations of the modern era. At least as of today, it is hard to claim that the neoliberal economic model that brought an end to the Cold War has exhibited the same success in building a new global economic order.

The existence or success of a new global economic order should not be seen through cumulative figures for the world economy, which hardly seem encouraging, but from the realities of practical life. I have had the opportunity to observe the wide gaps caused by global-scale injustices and inequalities during official visits to a number of African, Asian, and small island states. But two of my trips in particular showed me that in terms of economic levels, paradise and doomsday coexist; these were my trips to Somalia in August 2011, and Myanmar/Rakhine State exactly one year later. In the Somalia trip, together with then Prime Minister Erdoğan, our wives and numerous ministers, business-people, intellectuals, and representatives of the arts, we witnessed a catastrophe beyond imagination. The tragedy of drought and hunger, along with the civil war, seemed to have taken all life hostage; babies dying of thirst in front of our eyes, patients being "treated" in condi-tions no hospital would attempt, their skin hanging off their bones from malnutrition and hunger, piles of rubbish infesting the roads, and ruins that could no longer be called shelters let alone homes.

At that moment my mind's eye flashed to the luxurious hos-pitals in the brightly lit cities of the economically developed world, with food being thrown away because no one could consume it. As the government of Turkey we expended tremendous efforts to lighten the terrible burden of that tragedy with the decisions we took that day; we cleaned up the roads with the help of Turkish municipalities, rehabilitated hospitals, and dispatched food and medical aid with our doctors, healthcare teams, and the air bridge we set up.

In August 2012 we observed a similar or even more horrifying state of affairs in Rakhine State, which is back on the international agenda today. What made it more horrifying was that people wracked with hunger in the inconceivably awful conditions of refugee camps were at the same time being subject to attacks on a scale that can safely be called ethnic cleansing. The image of what we saw remains forever engraved in our minds and souls. Once again, we organized aid campaigns, but these measures could only alleviate, not cure.

To complement and follow up on these observations, we hosted the UN LDC Summit in Istanbul on 9–13 May 2011; I also attended numerous meetings as Foreign Minister of the LDC coordinator country. The Istanbul Action Plan agreed at the Istanbul summit attended by 8,931 participants from forty-eight LDCs with a combined population of 900 million people, including thirty-six heads of state and government, ninety-six ministers, and the heads of sixty-six international organizations,[17] which provided a road map for the LDCs for the next ten years, set out a clear objective in terms of global governance: "The international economic system and architecture should be inclusive and responsive to the special development needs of least developed countries, ensuring their effective participation, voice and representation at all levels."[18]

After this summit we made strenuous efforts to close the gap between LDCs and developed countries for a fairer global economic order. Finally, we strove to show the reality of the world that existed beneath the global economy's radar to the central countries of the global economy by organizing an LDC meeting prior to the G20 summit we hosted in 2015 and presenting a report to the G20. And as the report set out, "Turkey has made inclusiveness a key theme of its G20 Presidency."[19] In this framework, in spite of the fact that the Antalya Action Plan adopted by the G20 summit hosted by Turkey on 16 November 2015 stated that "Internationally, recognizing that the G20 serves as the premier forum for global economic cooperation, we sought to increase outreach efforts towards low income and developing countries (LIDCs) and to improve the ways we support their development efforts,"[20] it proved impossible to take serious steps towards creating an architecture for a global economic system by bringing together the world's richest and poorest country groups such as the G8/LDC and G20/LDC mechanisms. On the contrary, recent years' trend towards ever-growing protectionism and introversion brings with it the risk of further widening the gap between these groups of countries.

The call "for a more fundamental transformation of the relations between rich and poor, powerful and powerless, men and women, the elites and those without resources, the dominant and the marginalised" and the plea "for this conference to mark a turning point towards a more just, more equitable and more sustainable world"[21] made at the May 2011 summit by the Istanbul Civil Society Forum attended by international civil society and opinion leaders, remains valid. As Jeffrey D. Sachs clearly underlines, "a mass public movement aimed at an Enlightened Globalization ... would insist that the United States and other rich countries honor their commitments to help the poor escape from poverty, as well as honor to limit environmental degradation including human-made climate change and the loss of biodiversity."[22]

The conclusion I have reached after all these experiences is that humanitarian aid campaigns are a human obligation and an urgent necessity for bandaging the wounds; but the ultimate cure cannot come solely from humanitarian aid but from a new global economic order schema. It should never be forgotten that every economic fluctuation will trigger global-scale migrations and uncertainties unless the necessary structural measures are taken in line with a new global economic order rationale with the capacity to reconcile productivity and efficiency with equitable income distribution.

Yes, the neoliberal economic model demonstrated the economic-political dynamism to win and bring an end to the Cold War, but it has not been able to posit this within a new economic order schema. The ability to develop such a schema in a period when technological interaction is unsettling living standards could also be successful within the logic of global governance. In this context, steps need to be taken on all three tiers.

The fundamental requirement in the first tier, comprising the central countries of global economics-politics, is the formation of a new economic order architecture to provide institutionalized coordination. The goal of establishing a new financial architecture, which has been much emphasized in the wake of the crisis, should be expanded both institutionally and in scope to bring together all economic decision-making mechanisms. The most appropriate platform for institutionalized coordination of this kind remains the G20. The post-global crisis elevation of G20 meetings to the level of annual leaders' summits is a correct step, but does not go far enough. Despite resistance from some countries, the increasing institutionalization of the G20 is a necessity for global coordination and governance. The prevention of any future crisis will not be achieved on the basis of flexible or inconsistent platforms. In addition, as we have emphasized before, international economic institutions, especially the IMF and World Bank, should be restructured to take account of changed post-Cold War economic balances of power; no player with the capacity to influence global economic fluctuations should be excluded from this system's operating and decision-making mechanisms. This inclusiveness and internalization should not only apply to member nation-states but to various socioeconomic strata, as well as representatives of the private sector. The transnationalism we regard as essential for the global political order is even more essential for economic structures, because the size of many international companies is now set to exceed the GDP of some G20 states.

Developing a special model of governance for countries and groups of countries that make up the periphery of this central economic-political stratum is of great importance in diminishing the domino effect of economic crises and ensuring a proper balance between productivity and equitable income distribution on a global scale. The sustainable economic stability of this intermediate economic group will also have a key function in ensuring that the economic order can absorb global fluctuations without them blowing up into crises and that the economic order can be made permanent within the right productivity/income distribution balance.

Finally, the most comprehensive arrangements must be finalized with respect to the third tier comprising a wide geographical area outside existing global economic-political dynamics that remains vulnerable to all kinds of crisis, scarcity, drought, and famine. Ensuring that these communities participate equitably in the global economic order will contribute to the increase in global growth by increasing the world's total production-consumption potential, as well as leading to a reduction of migration flows to reasonable levels by ensuring a certain level of economic wellbeing. The creation of a special fund for this purpose and under the aegis of the World Bank or a separate structure would be constructive. A similar mechanism should be established for the problems associated with the prospect of growing numbers of climate migrants escaping from drought and flood conditions. The cost of such a fund would obviously be far less than the cost of systemic earthquakes that might result from global imbalances. Otherwise, we should be aware that today's economic-political burdens have already exceeded the institutional capacity to produce solutions.

In summary, while pre-modern economic-political orders in history relied on a concept of domination that envisioned the transfer of commodities on the basis of geographic continuity, the modern economic-political order is based on market mechanisms that have no need for geographic continuity to achieve a balance of supply and demand. In the global economy, opportunities afforded by technological developments have activated a highly dynamic and hard-to-control process in which anywhere with a mobile telephone or a laptop becomes a part of the field of economic activity and the economic-political order. This requires a new understanding of economic-political order based on processes that transcend space, rather than markets concentrated on certain centers. In ancient orders, directing and taking the pulse of economic flows was just a matter of keeping an eye on the flow of caravans along trade routes like the Silk Road. Yet in the modern era, keeping tabs on movements and trends in economically ascendant markets like Amsterdam, Frankfurt, London, Paris, New York, and Tokyo has become the absolute prerequisite to understanding and managing any crisis in the international economy or the state of order.

As for today, economic crises or processes that are determining the state of order are forming everywhere, all the time. With Bitcoin heralding the demise of the monopoly on printing money, which had been seen as a nation-state prerogative, the transition from a location and political authority-centered economy to a decentralized economy based on processual dynamics appears to be accelerating. The replacement of conventional market players by non-conventional actors who are hard to define let alone control is increasing the need for an inclusive economic-political order. As we specified while discussing the global economic earthquake, the speed and interactivity of international economic relations today necessitates a new method of governance that includes states, international organizations, companies, and potential non-conventional newcomers, rather than a single-centered approach to governance.

The Global Cultural Order

When Huntington wrote his article "The Clash of Civilizations?" in 1993, he was aiming to present an explanatory framework for conflicts along a Eurasian *Rimland* belt being rocked by a geopolitical earthquake, and propose a suitable strategy to the US administration. Fukuyama's "End of History" hypothesis that declared an end to clashes and the start of a period of enduring peace was shaken when clashes spread out along the *Rimland* belt, finally reaching the point of collapse with the large-scale ethnic carnage that unfurled in Bosnia. There was a perceived need to determine the new actors in international clashes, conflicts, and crises. And the guilty party behind the human tragedy arising from the weaknesses of international institutions and the great powers was indeed determined: Civilizations.

In point of fact, Huntington's article was, however unintentionally, exposing the limits modernity had reached. With its progressive concept of history based on the assumption that humankind has been flowing towards a monocultural future (i.e. a single civilization) along a single stream transcending cultural differences, modernity has asserted the arrival at various times of the end of religion, metaphysics, civilizations, ideologies, and finally of history itself. The article, which I criticized at the time for its selective use of historical fact for strategic purposes,[23] also drew attention to an important point in its oblique exposition of the return of different civilizations and cultures to the stage of history.

However, what should be strongly disputed here is the presentation of this return as an element of risk and threat, and indeed the near demonization of certain civilizations. This approach, in which civilizations are evaluated within generalized and conflicting categories while ignoring the intracivilizational rivalries that have led to major wars, offered a pretext to political actors keen to shed their own responsibilities, while also laying the ground for an extremely negative perception around the concept of "civilization" – or at least non-Western civilizations. This perception has led to the presentation of different civilizational legacies and their interactions as an element of chaos. Placing the very concept of civilization on such a grotesquely negative and chaotic theoretical basis has also given rise to outcomes that incite civilizations' extreme elements.

Contrary to this hypothesis, civilizations have in fact risen throughout history from foundations that have shaped philosophical awakenings and new cosmopolitan social orders. All the ancient civilizational legacies are remembered through the orders of the city centers that accommodated this fundamental characteristic. How could we make sense of Greek civilization and Athens without the Greek system of thought crowned by Plato and Aristotle and without the order of the Greek city state; Persian civilization and Persepolis without Zoroastrianism and the Persian order; the Alexandrian order and Alexandrian

cities that paved the way for the first interaction between great civilizations without that pivotal era's intellectual revival; the civilizational
accretions of South and Southeast Asia and Pataliputra without the
Buddha's enlightenment and the Mauryan order; Chinese civilization
and Xi'an without Confucian virtue and ethics; Islamic civilization and
Baghdad without the egalitarian *Tawhid* concept of the oneness of God
and the melting-pot concept of order it brought; and how could we then
make sense of the Ottoman order, the final traditional order that rose
up from this ancient civilizational legacy, and Istanbul?

First of all, one should not forget that civilizations are the
product not of short-term conjunctural developments, but long-term,
highly complex historic processes. And their entry onto the stage of
history, their rise and fall, and their withdrawal from history are not the
result of mere periodic developments. Civilizations that have emerged
within a dynamic process in history and sometimes endured as a result
of mental, social, economic, and political transformation that goes
from a redefinition of man's self-perception to the formation of a world
order, are shaped by six fundamental structural parameters: (i) ontological redefinition of the self-perception (*Selbstverständnis*) of individual human beings; (ii) epistemological reformulation of human
knowledge; (iii) axiological reevaluation of human norms; (iv) reconstruction of time-consciousness and historical imagination; (v) reshaping of space, particularly in the form of restructuring the city as a
reflection of the "being–knowledge–value" paradigm; and (vi) reestablishment of a world order as a new way of administering political and
economic affairs.[24]

These all-embracing and multidimensional qualities of civilizations reveal that once they enter the stage of history, they are able to
sustain themselves by rebounding from every challenge they encounter.
In this context there have been three approaches on the question of how
civilizations might influence globalization, a phenomenon that cuts
across different societies and cultural basins.

The first approach is based on a one-way progressive understanding that human history, especially of modernity, flows towards a
single stream in which pre-modern civilizations and cultural entities
shall be liquidated, upon which understanding it follows that
globalization shall accelerate this liquidation process. The prognosis
that humankind will turn into a global village, and a monolithic global
culture will arise as priorities, behavioral patterns, and cultural

preferences become increasingly standardized, naturally assumes the disappearance of authentic and local elements of civilization.[25]

This is in fact a reprise of the Eurocentric approach inherited from modernity that Toynbee described as the "egocentric illusion." When a narrative of human history based on the assumption that it starts in Europe and flows directly to Europe becomes a universal educational paradigm, it ends up driving out other civilizational legacies from history and ignoring the existential dynamics of living civilizations.

A personal experience of mine at the start of the 1990s, when the concept of globalization was beginning to gain wide currency, made a profound impression on me in terms of enabling me to see how a Eurocentric concept of history that had taken on the attributes of a universal paradigm impacted local civilizational consciousness. In the summer of 1990, I went to Malaysia as a lecturer. Upon my arrival in Kuala Lumpur one Saturday I was told my classes would start that Monday. One of them was "The History of Political Thought." Accordingly, I entered the classroom bearing a classical textbook in the field, to suggest to my students as a basic resource. As I went in, I felt a sense of shock at the profound contradiction between the dominant educational paradigm and the accumulated legacy of humanity. My class of about forty students resembled a little United Nations. As well as locals of Malay, Chinese, and Indian origin, there were students from a number of African countries, from countries running along a belt from Afghanistan to Algeria, even from Latin America. After listening to them one by one, I put the textbook[26] to one side and told them I would compile a reading list specially for them, because were I to use a book that explained the history of political thought on Greek → Roman → Christian Middle Ages → Reformation/Renaissance → Modernity lines, I would effectively be telling these students of mine from diverse civilizational basins "Your forefathers' civilizational basins produced no political thought; they do not exist as subjects in history, and neither do you." Chinese and Indian political histories preceded ancient Greece by hundreds of years, and Islamic political thought constituted the most effective bridge between ancient thought and modernity; yet there was hardly a single thinker from these civilizational legacies in the book. In the space of a week I compiled a new reading list that stretched from Confucius to Indian texts and from there to a comparison of medieval Christian thought with the accumulation of

Islamic thought via ancient Greece and Rome; discussed the transition from Ibn Bājja, Ibn Rushd, and Ibn Khaldūn to Reformation thought; compared Kinalizāde 'Alī and Machiavelli who wrote books giving advice to their sultan and prince in the East and the West in the sixteenth century; and then moved on to a consideration of the main streams of modern political thought and a treatment of the encounters of leading figures of different civilizational legacies, principally Gandhi, Muhammad Iqbal, and Mandela, with modernity. It was then that I had the opportunity directly to experience the profound differentiation between a monolithic civilizational hegemonic approach and a pluralist concept of civilizational interaction, and to see that this differentiation would be further intensified by the tools conveyed by globalization.

There has been a serious change of perception concerning civilizations and cultural pluralism in the period from the final years of the Cold War when the first stages of transition from modernity to globalization occurred, to the present day. No one remains convinced that different civilizations will disappear over time as a result of globalization. On the contrary, it is an acknowledged reality that globalization has caused localized civilizational legacies to spread to different geographic areas and led to the emergence of space-transcendent civilizational interactions. Today, the cosmopolitan character of cities seen as global centers such as New York, London, Paris, Singapore, Istanbul, and Shanghai, where the heirs to various civilizational legacies live side by side, is manifesting itself much more conspicuously.

In the second approach, civilizations begin to be viewed as opposing forces in chaos scenarios based on the hypothesis that identity conflicts stemming from the cultural differences created by diverse civilizations represent a risk to the international order. First deployed in the Bosnian war, this argument began to be seen as convenient for other crisis areas as well. The impact of this confrontational approach to civilizational identities has become particularly evident in the racist anti-refugee tendencies observed in Western countries in recent years. This approach has led to sweeping judgments and selective perceptions about civilizations as well as masking intracivilizational differences and closing intercivilizational channels of communication.

Developments over the past quarter-century reveal how invalid both these approaches are in terms of forming a new order. The claim that civilizations will be liquidated over time has lost all touch with reality, while the possible consequences of approaches that interpret civilizations in a confrontational context have been agonizingly evident. Developments have exposed the fact that the impact of globalization on civilizations will fade over time and that expectations of the formation of a monolithic human culture will fail to materialize. Moreover, it is obvious that such a process of standardization would sterilize a developing human experience nourished by the accumulated history and accretions of different civilizations. What has emerged is that civilizations continue to thrive, but that establishing a new global order is impossible on the basis of the pessimistic mindset and chaotic polarization of a cultural cold-war psychology borne of a confrontational approach that sees them as a chaos-inducing rather than an order-forming factor.

There is now a clear need for a fresh approach that assesses civilizations as elements with the capacity to establish a new order. This alternative approach should aim to restructure the global cultural order that constitutes the third leg of the global order, in support of its political and economic counterparts. A global cultural order structure in which all civilizational components believe their cultural identities will be included and their authenticity honorably preserved is more important than ever before for overall world peace.

Today we are living in an entanglement with two intensely dynamic processes that seem to contradict one another: the rise of a monolithic global culture accelerated by technological tools that hugely expand space-transcendent communications as a reflection of the dynamic interaction between homogenization and hegemonization;[27] and the boisterous return to the stage of history of traditional worldviews, values, institutions, and structures both in their traditional areas and in the centers of global Western cities. This apparently contradictory situation is actually a productive paradox brought about by the interaction between civilizations.

If this productive paradox can be turned into an inclusive and pluralist global cultural order, we may witness the most wide-ranging and productive intercivilizational interactions human history has ever seen. If not, an attitude that polarizes and excludes different civilizational legacies may lead to global sociocultural chaos not only on the geographic belts where civilizations meet as suggested by the "Clash of Civilizations" hypothesis, but in every district and on every street of the cosmopolitan cities where communities from different civilizations live side by side. The extraordinary communications possibilities afforded by globalization can rapidly transform micro-scale cultural tensions into global disorder. It is an unavoidable fact that every spark of tension in Western capitals where Daesh sympathizers and racist neo-Nazis live side by side has the capacity to trigger global cultural chaos. In this sense, small quakes on a micro-cultural scale are activating the fault lines of a large systemic earthquake.

The intense and widespread interaction between different civilizations needs to be extricated from being a source of chaos and evaluated on a platform that establishes order and enriches the accumulated civilizational legacy of humankind. In this context a certain responsibility accrues to thinkers, intellectuals, faith leaders, policy-makers, and political leaders from every civilizational strand.

First and foremost, we need a "mindset revolution" to deliver an inclusive interpretation of civilization that sees different civilizations as diverse reflections of a shared human history and conscience in order to establish a global order's cultural leg. For this mindset revolution, the paradigm based on Eurocentric, orientalist, and egocentric approaches that repeatedly produces cultural monopolies through its tendency to see the history of civilizations within a center–periphery dialectic needs to be discarded. In this regard, we may reference Kuhn's theoretical framework[28] in stating that we first need to change the textbooks that ensure the repeated reproduction of this paradigm in the form of a universally valid understanding of history.

The adoption and dissemination of an inclusive consciousness of history that embraces and encompasses humanity as a whole instead of this paradigm will form the substructure of a new mindset. A new mental paradigm that includes all civilizational and cultural legacies as honorable elements in a shared human history, replaces the confrontational rhetoric based on the *clash* of civilizations concept with an *interaction* of civilizations conceptualization, and invests new generations with the idea that we are walking from a common human past enriched by the legacy of different civilizations into a common future, once again with the contribution of different civilizational legacies, will bring with it a global cultural order worthy of human dignity. This mindset revolution will serve not only to avert tensions between civilizations but must also take place between different cultural groups with the same civilizational background.

In order for such a revolution to work in practice, a tripartite interaction is required between communities with different identity affiliations, thinkers/opinion leaders representing different civilizational legacies, and the political leaders who will direct the implementation of all kinds of new order. Interaction between communities with different civilizational affiliations based on direct human relations remains the most effective way of eradicating stereotypical prejudices. In a globalized world, one cannot foster healthy communication and interaction channels between communities with different civilizational affiliations without efforts to break down prejudices that can spread rapidly in the virtual environment.

Interaction between thinkers, intellectuals, faith leaders, and artists – in other words, opinion leaders – is essential in terms of transmitting this revolution to new generations. The most effective countermeasure against confrontational, provocative rhetoric that spreads rapidly especially in the virtual world and quickly turns people into opposing camps is the creation of civil platforms on which different civilizational affiliations are represented. The proliferation of platforms that defend human dignity and global justice against persecution and oppression and represent the conscience of any civilization regardless of civilizational background would lead to the formation of a global-scale environment of security and trust, as well as pressuring political groups and individuals who are developing confrontational populist rhetoric for short-term political benefit. In this sense, the reaction of opinion leaders and communities from every religion and civilizational affiliation in the wake of Trump's travel bans directed against the citizens of certain Muslim countries are exemplary. Just as these civil platforms can be realized bilaterally in areas where there is an elevated risk of confrontational provocation, they may also develop into more multilateral or global initiatives.

The point these tiers can directly and rapidly impact is the issue of what is going to unfurl at the level of political and state leaders. Today, the most significant obstacles to a peaceful global cultural order are populist political leaders and groups who try to boost their political power by nurturing stereotypes prevalent in the virtual environment. Leaders and politicians who advocate intercivilizational interactions in opposition to this exclusive populist political culture must stand up and express their political will in a spirit of solidarity. The Alliance of Civilizations initiated by Spain and Turkey in 2005, the success of which led to its adoption as an official UN initiative (UNAOC), is a good case in point. However, it is disheartening that it has lost the momentum of its early years just when such efforts should be assuming a greater role. The revitalization of this and similar initiatives with the participation of political leaders will lay the groundwork for the dissolution of the global community's psychology of pessimism and bring a new paradigm of global cultural order to the international agenda.

Whatever our cultural or civilizational affiliations, we need to remember this fact: a peaceful global order that secures the future of humankind can only be established on the basis of inclusive, pluralist intercivilizational interaction, not monopolistic civilizational hegemony. And the truth that history teaches us is also clear: those who exclude "other" human legacies in one era of history are themselves doomed to exclusion in the next.

NOTES

Introduction

1 "But apart from illusions due to the world-wide success of the Western civilization in the material sphere, the misconception of 'the unity of history' – involving the assumption that there is only one river of civilization, our own, and that all others are either tributary to it or else lost in the desert sands – may be traced to three roots: *the egocentric illusion*, the illusion of the 'unchanging East', and the illusion of the progress as a movement that proceeds in a straight line." Toynbee, *A Study of History*, vol. 1, 55.
2 "Liberal democracy may constitute the 'end point of mankind's ideological evolution' and 'the final form of human government' and as such constituted 'the end of history.'" Fukuyama, *The End of History and the Last Man*, xi. Also see Fukuyama, "The End of History?"
3 George H. W. Bush's "Address to the General Assembly of the UN," 1 October 1990.
4 For a more detailed methodological explanation relating to process analysis, see Davutoğlu, *Stratejik Derinlik*, 1–11.

1 Traditional, Modern, and Global "World Orders"

1 For an analysis of the historical relation between cities and civilizational orders, see Davutoğlu, *Medeniyetler ve Şehirler* (English edition is forthcoming).
2 This term has been invented by Karl Jaspers (as *Achsenzeit* in German) in his book *Vom Ursprung und Ziel der Geschichte* (in English: *The Origin and Goal of History*).
3 For a collection of articles on the historical impact of this awakening in the axial age, see Bellah and Joas, eds., *The Axial Age and Its Consequences*; also see Armstrong, *The Great Transformation*.
4 "The Achaemenid rulers controlled a territory stretching from the Hellespont to north-west India, including Egypt (most of the time) extending into Central Asia up to the frontiers of modern Kazakhstan for over two hundred years." For a comprehensive analysis of the Achaemenid imperial order, see Kuhrt, *The Persian Empire*, 1.

5 "Confucius placed the *raison d'étre* of government, whatever its origin and form, at establishing and maintaining a well-structured political and social order for a state. (p. 97) ... To further increase the mystique and mysterious power of the ruler, Han Fei then utilized Taoist ideas of *tao* (the primordial truth and force for all), *wu-wei* (nonaction), and *ching* (quietness or stillness to imply and manifest sternness and perceptiveness). (p. 112)" For the Confucian and Taoist intellectual background of the Han Wu-Ti's new empire and ideological foundations of Han expansion, see Chang, *The Rise of the Chinese Empire*, vol. I, 96–134.

6 For a historical analysis of this order and its background based on Asoka's policy of *dhamma*, see Thapar, *Asoka and the Decline of the Mauryas*.

7 P. M. Fraser's in-depth critical analysis of the cities of Alexander the Great provides an alternative approach. See Fraser, *Cities of Alexander the Great*.

8 For a recent comprehensive and systematic analysis of the Roman Order, see Gargola, *The Shape of the Roman Order*.

9 James Bryce's comment on the authenticity of the letter referring to the feelings and ideas of the age is striking as the continuation of the Roman tradition: "It is not necessary to prove this letter to have been the composition of Frederick or his ministers. If it be (as it doubtless is) contemporary, it is equally to the feelings and ideas of the age." Bryce, *The Holy Roman Empire*, 184.

10 Reston, *Defenders of Faith: Charles V, Suleyman the Magnificent and the Battle for Europe*.

11 For a comparative analysis of the impact of this *Weltanschauung* on political thought and imagination from the perspective of the justification of sociopolitical system, legitimation of political authority, power theories and pluralism, and the political unit and universal political system, see Davutoğlu, *Alternative Paradigms*.

12 Hodgson, *Rewriting World History*, 171.

13 Bennison, "Muslim Universalism and Western Globalization," 74.

14 For an analysis of this golden age of Baghdad-centric order, see Bennison, *The Great Caliphs*.

15 Starr, *Lost Enlightenment*.

16 For different political, economic, cultural and institutional aspects of this order see İnalcık, *The Ottoman Empire*; İnalcık and Quataert, eds., *An Economic and Social History of the Ottoman Empire*; and İnalcık, *Essays in Ottoman History*.

17 For the impact of cultural interaction and syncretism in the process of the formation of the Ottoman State, see Kafadar, *Between Two Worlds*.

18 Davutoğlu, "Tarih İdraki Oluşumunda Metodolojinin Rolü."

19 Pamuk, "Institutional Change and the Longevity of the Ottoman Empire."

20 Agoston, "A Flexible Empire."

21 For a comparative analysis of the Ottoman order from the perspective of longevity, see Barkey, *Empire of Difference*.

22 O'Brien, *Alexander the Great*, 112.

23 Toynbee, "The Ottoman Empire's Place in World History," 15.

24 Parsons, *The Rule of Empires*, 24.

25 Anthony Pagden uses this title to show how the rulers of the colonial empire adapted the claim of the Roman Emperor Antoninus to be "*dominus totius orbis*; Lord of all the World." Pagden, *Lords of All the World*.

26 "Suleyman the Magnificent signed himself ruler of the thirty-seven kingdoms, lord of the realms of the Romans, and the Persians and the Arabs, hero of all that is, pride of the arena of earth and time! Of the Mediterranean and the Black Sea; Of the glorified Kaaba and the illuminated Madina, the noble Jerusalem and the throne of Egypt, that rarity of the age." Goodwin, *Lords of Horizons*, 81.

27 Cox, "Towards a Post Hegemonic Conceptualization of World Order."

28 Ibid., 132.

29 As Henry Kissinger stresses, "The genius of this system, and the reason it spread across the world, was that its provisions were procedural, not substantive." Kissinger, *World Order*, 27.

30 Benno Teschke argues in his challenging work against conventional assumptions regarding the Westphalian Peace that "1648, far from signalling a breakthrough to modern inter-state relations, was the culmination of the epoch of absolutist state formation; it marked the recognition and regulation of the international – or to be more precise, inter-dynastic – relations of the absolutist and dynastic polities." Teschke, *The Myth of 1648*, 3.

31 For an analysis of the battles from the Thirty Years War to the end of the Napoleonic Wars and their impact on the military structures and policy objectives of states, see Weigley, *The Age of Battles*.

32 See Vick, *The Congress of Vienna*.

33 Although the concept of the "balance of power" system has been used for the European order in the nineteenth century, balance of power was a phenomenon of interstate relations in different historical contexts and in various civilizational basins. For a collection of articles on historical examples of "balance of power," see Kaufmann, Little, and Wohlforth, eds., *Balance of Power in World History*.

34 The origins of this colonial expansion go back to the sixteenth and seventeenth centuries. See Beer, *The Origins of the British Colonial System*.

35 Stevens and Westcott, *A History of Sea Power*, 271.

36 McNeill, *The Rise of the West*, 726–27.

37 "The war also led to a vast expansion of foreign capital investment in the Ottoman Empire, and with it an increase in Turkey's financial dependence on western banks and governments (foreign loans to finance the war and Tanzimat reforms spiralled from about £5 million in 1855 to a staggering £200 million by 1877)." Figes, *Crimea: The Last Crusade*, 427.

38 Aksakal, *The Ottoman Road to War in 1914*, 57.

39 Toynbee, "The Ottoman Empire's Place in World History," 18.

40 For example, Mahan, *The Influence of Sea Power upon History* and *The Interest of America in Sea Power*; Ratzel, "The Territorial Growth of States"; Ratzel, "Studien über politische Räume"; Mackinder, *Britain and British Seas* and "The Geographical Pivot of History"; Kjellén, *Der Staat als Lebensform*.

41 For an exemplary analysis of peace and order in this period before the arrival of the colonial powers see Akarlı, *The Long Peace*.

42 For a comparative analysis see Davutoğlu, *Medeniyetler ve Şehirler*, 107–17.

43 For a prewar (1913) comparative panorama in important centers ranging from the modern colonial capitals of Europe to the capitals of Asia, from traditional African cities to newly ascendant American cities, from the new players on the stage of world politics in Latin America to Australia, see Emmerson, *1913: The World before the Great War*.

44 See MacMillan, *The War That Ended Peace*.

45 Hobsbawm, *The Age of Extremes*.

46 Wilson, "President Wilson's Message to Congress, January 8, 1918." The formation of such an international institution was mentioned before "in President Wilson's peace proposal of December 18, 1916 in which he suggests 'the formation of a League of Nations to insure peace and justice throughout the world'." Moore, *The Principles of American Diplomacy*, 441–42.

47 "There are three kinds of perfect society, great, medium and small. The great is the union of all the societies in the inhabitable World . . . the excellent universal state will

arise only when all the nations in it co-operate for the purpose of reaching felicity." Al-Farabi, *Al Farabi on the Perfect State*, 229–31.

48 "For the sake of its own security, each nation can and should demand that the others enter into a contract resembling the civil one and guaranteeing the rights of each. This would be a federation of nations, but it must not be a nation of consisting of nations." Kant, "To Perpetual Peace," 115.

49 "One thing, he believed, might save the whole structure – the covenant of the League. The effort to save the League became a matter of the most desperate psychological urgency for him. His plans had been hamstrung, his hopes abandoned one after another, until nothing but the League was left." Hofstadter, *The American Political Tradition*, 361–62.

50 Carr, *The Twenty Years Crisis*, 207.

51 Ibid., 208.

52 For a collection of articles on the policies of great powers and regional responses in the Middle East during the systemic crisis of the interwar era, see Dann, ed., *The Great Powers in the Middle East*.

53 For a comparative analysis, see Davutoğlu, "Globalization and the Crisis of Individual and Civilizational Consciousness."

54 Williams, *Failed Imagination?*, 285.

55 "The first goal of this book is to help clarify the form of what is being called the global economy and to show how the rush toward globalization is likely to affect our lives. The second goal is to suggest that the process must be brought to a halt as soon as possible, and reversed." Mander and Goldsmith, eds., *The Case against the Global Economy*, 3. See this title also for a collection of articles against the global economy.

56 "The Global Shopping Mall is a planetary supermarket with a dazzling spread of things to eat, drink, wear and enjoy. We will explore the rise of global advertising, distribution, and marketing and examine their impacts. Dreams of affluent living are communicated to the farthest reaches of the globe, but only a minority of the people in the world can afford to shop at the Mall." Barnet, *Global Imperial Corporations*, 16.

57 "From 1982 to 1990, CNN ran at pretty much the same pace, kept the same schedule and hung around a 7 rating. Then came the glory: first quarter 1991, the Gulf War. During the first two weeks of the conflict, CNN averaged 4 rating points. During the first quarter, January through March, CNN averaged 1,637,000 viewers every fifteen minutes. Maybe the best quarter any cable network ever had." Schonfeld, *Me and Ted against the World*, 304.

58 Fukuyama, "The End of History?"; Fukuyama, *The End of History and the Last Man*.

59 Huntington, "The Clash of Civilizations?"; Huntington, *The Clash of Civilizations and the Remaking of World Order*.

60 Davutoğlu, "Civilizational Transformation and Political Consequences"; Davutoğlu, *Civilizational Transformation and the Muslim World*.

61 In subsequent publications Francis Fukuyama felt the need to make major revisions to his hypothesis that liberal values and institutions had brought about the end of history. In his latest work, *Identity: The Demand for Dignity and the Politics of Resentment*, he acknowledges that the momentum towards a liberal world order has reversed: "Beginning in the mid-2000s, the momentum toward an increasingly open and liberal world order began to falter, then went into reverse." (pp. 4–5) In a sense this recognition confirms the fact that history has not ended and has entered a new flow process.

62 Said, "The Clash of Definitions," 68.

63 Davutoğlu, "The Clash of Interests."
64 Ibid., 109.
65 Ibid., 127.
66 Said, "The Clash of Definitions," 69.
67 Davutoğlu, *Civilizational Transformation*, 8.

2 The Roots of World (Dis)Order: Geopolitical, Security, Economic, and Structural Earthquakes in the Post-Cold War Era

1 Conventional geopolitics was essentially based on power rivalries and balances between Eurasia-centered geopolitical land power and naval power around this land mass. For the theoretical basis of this approach in terms of land power, see Mackinder, "The Geopolitical Pivot of History," 421–42; and Mackinder, "The Round World and the Winning of the Peace." In terms of sea power see Mahan, *The Influence of Sea Power upon History: 1660–1783*; Mahan, *The Influence of Sea Power upon the French Revolution and Empire: 1793–1812*; Mahan, *The Interest of America in Sea Power: Present and Future*; Mahan, *The Problem of Asia and Its Effect upon International Politics*; and Mahan, *Letters and Papers of Alfred Thayer Mahan*.

2 Spykman, *The Geography of the Peace*, 43; and Spykman, *America's Strategy in World Politics*.

3 The LICs on this line in which the United States was directly or indirectly involved provide clues to geopolitical balance in the Cold War period: USSR 1946, 1948, 1956, 1961, 1968; Greece 1946–1949; Palestine 1948; Iran 1951–1953; Lebanon 1958; Philippines 1942–1945, 1946–1955, 1984, 1985–1986; Burma 1945; China 1945–1949, 1953–1979; Indochina 1946–1954; North Korea 1953; Vietnam 1955–1965; Laos 1955–1965; Thailand 1965–1985; Jordan 1970; Iraq 1972–1975; OPEC 1974–1975; Cyprus 1974; Mayaguez 1975; Cambodia 1975; Iran 1979; Syria 1979; Afghanistan 1980; Lebanon 1982–1984; Persian Gulf 1987–1988. Details of these LICs can be found in Collins, *America's Small Wars*.

4 Mikhail Gorbachev's approach shook the foundations of ideological tension-based geopolitical bipolarity which had its origins in dialectical materialism, and contained signs of a fresh dynamism as well as hopes for a new order: "Ideological differences should not be transferred to the sphere of interstate relations, nor should foreign policy be subordinate to them, for ideologies may be poles apart, whereas the interest of survival and prevention of war stand universal and supreme ... I believe that more and more people will come to realize that true RESTRUCTURING in the broad sense of the word, the integrity of the World will be enhanced." Gorbachev, *Perestroika*, 143, 254.

5 For an assessment of this economic-political change from a NATO perspective, see Sandler and Hartley, *The Political Economy of NATO*.

6 Cohen, "Geopolitics in the New World Era," 15.

7 For the neo-con's perception and interpretation of the quest for power and legitimacy induced by the security trauma that emerged from the 9/11 attacks, see Fukuyama, *After the Neo-cons*, 191.

8 "While the United States will constantly strive to enlist the support of the international community, we will not hesitate to act alone, if necessary, to exercise our right of self-defense by acting preemptively against such terrorists, to prevent them from doing harm against our people and our country." See "The National Security Strategy of the United States of America," 6.

9 For the intellectual origins of the Bush Doctrine, see Smith, *A Pact with the Devil*, 25–53.
10 "The Chilcot Report" ("The Report of the Iraq Inquiry") published on 6 July 2016, and reactions to it, remain a striking example of this criticism and self-criticism.
11 The Ten principles of the Washington Consensus described by John Williamson in 1989 are as follows: (i) low government borrowing; (ii) diversion of public spending from subsidies to important long term growth; (iii) implementing tax reform policies; (iv) selecting interest rates that are determined by the market; (v) encouraging competitive exchange rates through freely-floating currency exchange; (vi) adoption of free trade policies; (vii) relaxing rules on foreign direct investment; (viii) the privatization of state enterprises; (ix) the eradication of regulations and policies that restrict competition; (x) development of property rights. For a reassessment of this framework of reform by John Williamson himself see Williamson, "The Strange History of the Washington Consensus."
12 Mallaby, "Globalization Resets."
13 Kennedy, *The Rise and Fall of the Great Powers*, 611.
14 Davutoğlu, *Stratejik Derinlik*, 129–51, 323–455 (English edition is forthcoming).
15 As Philip Mansel rightly describes in his book on Aleppo, "In the twenty-first century, Aleppo has entered its dark ages." See Mansel, *Aleppo*, 65.
16 Falk, *Power Shift*, 14.

3 Systemic Earthquake: Fragile National, Regional, and Global Structures

1 For an analysis of this transformation of nationhood and nationalism in Europe in the 1990s, see Brubaker, *Nationalism Reframed*.
2 This change, which emerged in conjunction with the global economic crisis, clearly exposed a trend that deviated from the principles of the *Washington Consensus* adopted after the Cold War.
3 According to Human Rights Watch, "since late August 2017, more than 671.000 Rohingya Muslims have fled Burma's Rakhine State to escape from the military's large-scale campaign of ethnic cleansing. The atrocities committed by Burmese security forces, including mass killings, sexual violence, and widespread arson, amount to crimes against humanity." Human Rights Watch, "Rohingya Crisis."
4 This imagined phantom of White/Christian Europe is, in fact, an attempt to create a new "imagined political community" as has been described by Benedict Anderson in the definition of the nation. For this conceptualization, see Anderson, *Imagined Communities*, 6.
5 In fact, the mental, intellectual, cultural, and sociopolitical background of American debate about identity is based on a historical past. However, this debate escalated in the wake of the 9/11 trauma and turned into a sociocultural and sociopolitical challenge. Samuel P. Huntington's work on this challenge as it relates to American identity provides clues to identity tensions that intensified subsequently. See Huntington, *Who Are We?*, 365.
6 For the role of religion in the formation of nationhood in Europe see Hastings, *The Construction of the Nationhood*.
7 For the interdependency between strategic and economic perspectives in NATO and EU 1990s expansion processes and their impact on NATO, see Sandler and Hartley, *The Political Economy of NATO*.
8 For an analysis of the geopolitical environment brought about by this geopolitical earthquake in Central Asia and the surrounding region, see Banuazizi and Weiner, ed., *The New Geopolitics of Central Asia and Its Borderlands*.

9 For the twenty-five-yearly periods of transformation in the Islamic world, especially the Middle East, in the twentieth century and their impacts on the most recent period, see Davutoğlu, "Rewriting Contemporary Muslim Politics."

10 Fromkin, *A Peace to End All Peace*, 17.

11 For issues relating to the property left behind by the Palestinians and their impact on the Arab–Israel conflict, see Fischbach, *Records of Dispossessions*.

12 For details see United Nations Relief and Works Agency, "Palestine Refugees."

13 "8. To support and empower the Palestinian people to exercise their right to self-determination and establish their sovereign State with al-Quds al-Sharif as its capital, while safeguarding its historic and Islamic character as well as the Holy places therein." See OIC, "Charter of the Organisation of Islamic Cooperation (OIC)."

14 "21. The Headquarters of the General Secretariat shall be in the city of Jeddah until the liberation of the city of al-Quds so that it will become the permanent Headquarters of the Organization." See ibid.

15 Although its contents have not been fully revealed, Trump's "Deal of the Century" Middle East peace plan is highly unlikely to succeed in achieving a basis for legitimacy and a sustainable peace on account of de facto steps such as the moving of the US Embassy to Jerusalem as well as the corrosion of the main lines of a possible solution from the Oslo Process to the present.

16 See Shlaim, *The Iron Wall*, 568–95.

17 Davutoğlu, "The Crisis of Regional Order in the Gulf."

18 For a report on the flow of refugees and migration in the region from the UN High Commissioner for Refugees see The UN Refugee Agency, "Middle East and North Africa."

19 For a comprehensive approach to international legitimacy "as an attribute of international society, while at the same time suggesting that its normative content may be derived, in part, from alternative sources, including world society," see Clark, *International Legitimacy and World Society*, 1.

4 Systemic Earthquake: Global Powers and the "Multiple Balances of Power" System

1 Immanuel Wallerstein strongly opposed this mainstream assumption in the early days of the post-Cold War era: "Although many commentators have been hailing 1989 as the beginning of Pax Americana the thesis of this book is that, quite the contrary, it marks the end of the Pax Americana. The Cold War was the Pax Americana! The Cold War is over; thus the Pax Americana has now ended." Wallerstein, *Geopolitics and Geoculture*, 2.

2 This approach, put forward by Fukuyama in the early 1990s and linking US-dominated liberalism with the world order, was still trending in the late 1990s: "A remarkable aspect of world politics at the century's end is the utter dominance of the United States. Fifty years after it emerged hegemonic, the United States is still the dominant world power at the center of a relatively stable and expanding democratic capitalist order ... Fundamentally, American hegemony is reluctant, penetrated, and highly institutionalized – or in a word, liberal." Ikenberry, "Liberal Hegemony and the Future of American Postwar Order," 123, 139.

3 See President George H. W. Bush's "Address to the General Assembly of the UN" on 1 October 1990: "It is in our hands to leave these dark machines behind, in the Dark Ages where they belong, and to press forward to cap a historic movement towards a new world order and a long era of peace ... I see a world of open borders, open trade and, most importantly, open minds; a world that celebrates the common heritage

that belongs to all the world's people, taking pride not just in hometown or home-land but in humanity itself."

4 "The Strategic Concept reaffirms the enduring purpose of the Alliance and sets out its fundamental security tasks. It enables a transformed NATO to contribute to the evolving security environment, supporting security and stability with the strength of its shared commitment to democracy and the peaceful resolution of disputes." See concluding paragraph of "The Alliance's Strategic Concept" approved by the heads of State and Governments participating in the meeting of the North Atlantic Council in Washington DC issued on 24 April 1999.

5 An analysis of the conceptual framework and content between the above-quoted address of George H. W. Bush to the first UN General Assembly (1 October 1990) after the end of the Cold War and Iraq's invasion of Kuwait and George W. Bush's address to the same body in the wake of the 9/11 attacks clearly exposes this psychological change. Bush *père*'s conceptualization and vision of a new world order was replaced by Bush *fils*'s threat-focused defensive and reactive psychology: "We meet in a hall devoted to peace, in a city scarred by violence, in a nation awakened to danger, in a world uniting for a long struggle. Every civilized nation here today is resolved to keep the most basic commitment of civilization: We will defend ourselves and our future against terror and lawless violence." George W. Bush first address to the UN General Assembly delivered 10 November 2001, "Address by President George W. Bush."

6 Tony Blair expressed sorrow and regret for the consequences of the Iraqi war on 6 July 2016 following publication of the Chilcot Report. See "Tony Blair Expressed Sorrow, Regret and Apology."

7 Robert D. Kaplan strikingly sees this dilemma as a feature of the American approach that contains elements of continuity: "Americans will fight and kill if they feel themselves directly threatened or insulted, but preserving democratic orders across oceans might eventually become too much of an abstract and costly enterprise for them." Kaplan, "America's Darwinian Nationalism," 3.

8 For a collection of articles on the failure of the nation-building efforts in Afghanistan and Iraq, see Fukuyama, ed., *Nation-Building*.

9 Brent Scowcroft justifiably describes the Guantanamo process as an act against human dignity: "Simply to talk about dignity, to assert that one human being ought to be considered as valuable as another, is important, but it also has to be reflected in the way one behaves. I think Barack Obama represents those values, so does Hillary Clinton – and so does John McCain in his crusading about immigration, about Guantanamo, and against mistreatment of detainees. These issues are at heart about dignity, about how you treat other human beings." Brzezinski and Scowcroft, *America and the World*.

10 See Huntington, *Who Are We?*

11 See Obama, "Remarks of President Barack Obama at Student Roundtable."

12 These words of Barack Obama in the Turkish parliament were seen as a commitment to a multilateral foreign policy: "This much is certain: no one nation can confront these challenges alone, and all nations have a stake in overcoming them. That is why we must listen to one another, and seek common ground. That is why we must build on our mutual interests, and rise above our differences. We are stronger when we act together. That is the message that I have carried with me throughout this trip to Europe. That will be the approach of the United States of America going forward." Obama, "Remarks by President Obama to the Turkish Parliament."

13 With its messages on closing the gap that had opened between the United States and the Islamic world during the George W. Bush presidency, Barack Obama's Cairo

speech signaled a period of restoration: "I've come here to Cairo to seek a new beginning between the United States and Muslims around the world, one based on mutual interest and mutual respect, and one based upon the truth that America and Islam are not exclusive and need not be in competition. Instead, they overlap, and share common principles – principles of justice and progress; tolerance and the dignity of all human beings." Obama, "Remarks by the President at Cairo University 6-04-09."

14 Huntington, *Who Are We?*, 364.

15 For the challenges and dilemmas of US Middle East policy in the Obama period, see Gerges, *Obama and the Middle East.*

16 Samuel P. Huntington's Anglo-Protestant based definition of the difference and uniqueness of American identity is a noteworthy example: "America cannot become the world and still be America. Other peoples cannot become American and still be themselves. America is different and that difference is still defined in large part by its Anglo-Protestant culture and its religiosity." See Huntington, *Who Are We?*, 365.

17 The policy adopted by Trump also marks the end of Obama's efforts to overcome tensions between the United States and the Islamic World and to see the Islamic identity as being included within the elements of American identity: "I also want to be clear that America's relationship with the Muslim community, the Muslim world, cannot, and will not, just be based upon opposition to terrorism. We seek broader engagement based on mutual interest and mutual respect. We will listen carefully, we will bridge misunderstandings, and we will seek common ground. We will be respectful, even when we do not agree. We will convey our deep appreciation for the Islamic faith, which has done so much over the centuries to shape the world – including in my own country. The United States has been enriched by Muslim Americans. Many other Americans have Muslims in their families or have lived in a Muslim-majority country – I know, because I am one of them." Obama, "Remarks by President Obama to the Turkish Parliament."

18 For the whole article see Fischer, "Goodbye to the West."

19 Kissinger, *The Troubled Partnership*, 251.

20 See "General Assembly Overwhelmingly Adopts Resolution Asking Nations Not to Locate Diplomatic Missions in Jerusalem."

21 C. V. Wedgwood's conclusion on the Thirty Years War is a striking analysis in this sense: "The war solved no problem. Its effects both immediate and indirect, were either negative or disastrous. Morally subversive, economically destructive, socially degrading, confused in its causes, devious in its course, futile in its result, it is the outstanding example in European history of meaningless conflict ... They (the overwhelming majority in Europe) wanted peace and they fought for thirty years to be sure of it. They did not learn then, and have not since, that war breeds only war." Wedgwood, *The Thirty Years War*, 526.

22 "In a letter written to a friend on the day before the battle (the Battle of Jena in autumn 1806) ... he spoke of seeing Napoleon 'I saw the Emperor – that world-soul – ride through to town to reconnoitre. It is a strange feeling to see such a person, who here, from a single point, sitting on his horse, reaches over and masters the World!" See Adler, "Biographical Note."

23 For the geopolitical imagination of Hitler's idea of establishing a world hegemony through a united Europe under a single Germany-centered authority immediately before the Second World War, see Pahl, *Das politische Antlitz der Erde.*

24 These words of Heinrich von Treitschke, whose ideas had a profound influence on German nationalism and Hitler, written in a period when the unification of Germany had been achieved and German armies were closing in on Paris, show that the legacy

of the Holy Roman Germanic Empire that was thought to have been consigned to history in the Thirty Years War carried on in an intellectual continuum and under a new ideological guise: "Thus had the higher nobility of the once great German nation been already shaken in its moral forces, when the Elector of Bavaria, in the Thirty Years War, abandoned Alsace to the French, upon which the instrument of the Peace of Westphalia ..." See Treitschke, *Germany, France, Russia and Islam*, 131.

25 The 1974 Paris Summit was a significant milestone in the process that would subsequently turn into the EU: "3. The Heads of Government have therefore decided to meet, accompanied by the Ministers of Foreign Affairs, three times a year and, whenever necessary, in the Council of the Communities and in the context of political co-operation ... 4. With a view to progress towards European unity, the Heads of Government reaffirm their determination gradually to adopt common positions and co-ordinate their diplomatic action in all areas of international affairs which affect the interests of the European Community. The President-in-Office will be the spokesman for the Nine and will set out their views in international diplomacy. He will ensure that the necessary Concentration Always Takes Place in Good Time." See CVCE, "Final Communiqué of the Meeting of Heads of Government of the Community (Paris, 9 and 10 December 1974)."

26 These elections were based on Clause 12 of the 1974 Paris Summit final communiqué: "12. The Heads of Government note that the election of the European Assembly by universal suffrage, one of the objectives laid down in the Treaty, should be achieved as soon as possible. In this connection, they await with interest the proposals of the European Assembly, on which they wish the Council to act in 1976. On this assumption, elections by direct universal suffrage could take place at any time in or after 1978. Since the European Assembly is composed of representatives of the peoples of the States united within the Community, each people must be represented in an appropriate manner. The European Assembly will be associated with the achievement of European unity. The Heads of Government will not fail to take into consideration the points of view which, in October 1972, they asked it to express on this subject. The competence of the European Assembly will be expanded in particular by granting it certain powers in the Communities legislative process." See CVCE, "Final Communiqué of the Meeting of Heads of Government of the Community."

27 "Treaty on European Union (TEU) commonly known as the Maastricht Treaty ... was signed in February 1992, and came into force on 1st November 1993. It was this Treaty that marked the changeover from the European Economic Community (EEC) to the European Union. It introduced a number of significant changes including: a) it established economic and monetary union, b) it established the implementation of a common foreign and security policy, c) it started to give the European Parliament teeth, by introducing the co decision procedure, d) it enshrined the principle of proportionality and subsidiarity, e) It provided a mechanism for developing cooperation between Member States on justice and home affairs issues, f) It introduced the concept of being a 'citizen of the Union'." See European Law Monitor, "A Brief History of the EU Treaties."

28 See Organization for Security and Co-Operation in Europe, "Charter of Paris for a New Europe."

29 For an analysis of this issue of trust see Cohen-Tanugi, *An Alliance at Risk*.

30 Some commentaries went as far as conceptualizing this gap of trust as a betrayal: "As the United States and France faced off in the United Nations in late 2002 and early 2003, France's betrayal of America seemingly had no end." See Timmermann, *The French Betrayal of America*, 1.

31 For example, it has been stated that "the Bush administration punished Germany for its opposition to the US invasion of Iraq by refusing to support Germany's bid for a permanent seat on the UN Security Council," the idea being that Germany's opposition to the Bush administration's Iraq intervention was punishment for the rejection of Germany's request to become a Permanent Member of the UNSC. See Lind, *The American Way of Strategy*, 135.

32 US Secretary of Defense Donald Rumsfeld's statement on 22 January 2003 represents the most striking example of this differentiation: "Now, you're thinking of Europe as Germany and France. I don't. I think that's *old Europe*. If you look at the entire NATO Europe today, the center of gravity is shifting to the east. And there are a lot of new members. And if you just take the list of all the members of NATO and all of those who have been invited in recently – what is it? Twenty-six, something like that? – you're right. Germany has been a problem, and France has been a problem." Baker, "US: Rumsfeld's 'Old' And 'New' Europe Touches on Uneasy Divide."

33 Schmidt, *Grand Strategy for the West*, 5.

34 For an example see Orbán, "Wer überrannt wird, kann niemanden aufnehmen."

35 Churchill, "Winston Churchill, Universität Zürich, 19 September 1946."

36 Even in the early 1990s there were signs that the immigration issue would have an impact on intra-European political culture, especially with respect to right-wing voters and the need to draw the required lessons on this matter was emphasized: "Thus employers will have access to cheap foreign labor at minimum risk; aliens can enter the community, at least for a time; and European governments can assure their right-wing voters that they are doing something about immigration issue. Surrounded as it is by complex questions of economics, culture and ethics, the immigration of foreign workers can never be simple, and the Community still has much to learn." See King, "Migration and the Single Market for Labour," 241.

37 For the significance of this line on German strategy before the Second World War, see Pahl, *Das politische Antlitz der Erde*, 160.

38 Russia assumed control over all former Soviet embassies abroad on 3 January 1992.

39 For the changes and processes experienced in relations between Russia and the states that emerged in the wake of this geopolitical earthquake, see Dawisha and Parrott, *Russia and the New States of Eurasia.*

40 "What is a unipolar World? ... It is a world in which there is one master, one sovereign. And at the end of the day this is pernicious not only for all those within this system, but also for the sovereign itself because it destroys itself from within. And this certainly has nothing in common with democracy ... Unilateral and frequently illegitimate actions have not resolved any problems. Moreover, they have caused new human tragedies and created new centres of tension ... And independent legal norms are, as a matter of fact, coming increasingly closer to one state's legal system. One state and, of course, first and foremost the United States, has overstepped its national borders in every way." See Putin, "Speech and the Following Discussion at the Munich Conference on Security Policy."

41 "I am convinced that we have reached that decisive moment when we must seriously think about the architecture of global security. And we must proceed by searching for a reasonable balance between the interests of all participants in the international dialogue." See Putin, "Speech and the Following Discussion at the Munich Conference on Security Policy."

42 "The combined GDP measured in purchasing power parity of countries such as India and China is already greater than that of the United States. And a similar calculation with the GDP of the BRIC countries – Brazil, Russia, India and China – surpasses the cumulative GDP of the EU. And according to experts this gap will only increase in

the future. There is no reason to doubt that the economic potential of the new centres of global economic growth will inevitably be converted into political influence and will strengthen multipolarity. In connection with this the role of multilateral diplomacy is significantly increasing. The need for principles such as openness, transparency and predictability in politics is uncontested and the use of force should be a really exceptional measure, comparable to using the death penalty in the judicial systems of certain states." See Putin, "Speech and the Following Discussion at the Munich Conference on Security Policy."

43 See Putin, "The President signed Executive Order on National Goals and Strategic Objectives of the Russian Federation through to 2024."

44 For an example, see Rosecrane and Guoliang, *Power and Restraint*.

45 In this framework, see Shambaugh, *China Goes Global*.

46 Kissinger, *On China*, 530.

47 Yew, *One Man's View of the World*, 13.

48 A content analysis of the speeches of Chinese leaders in the early years of post-Cold War era "indicates that they did not fundamentally alter their conceptions of China's international role even though they did recognize and fully appreciate the significance of systemic changes; rather they choose to adapt to the new international conditions by keeping their existing role conceptions and elaborating new ones, thus noticeably redesigning the structure of the existing role-set." See Beylerian and Canivet, "Role Conceptions after the Cold War," 187–88.

49 See World Bank, "China."

50 See ibid.

51 See ibid.

52 "The theme of the Congress is: Remain true to our original aspiration and keep our mission firmly in mind, hold high the banner of socialism with Chinese characteristics, secure a decisive victory in building a moderately prosperous society in all respects, strive for the great success of socialism with Chinese characteristics for a new era, and work tirelessly to realize the Chinese Dream of national rejuvenation." See Xi, "Secure a Decisive Victory."

53 For an analysis of the risk of transformation of power competition in South China Sea from tension to confrontation, see Haytop, *The South China Sea*.

54 Xi, "Work Together to Build the Silk Road Economic Belt."

5 Future Projections and Basic Principles of a New Order of Inclusive Governance: The Five I's

1 For the concept of *asabiyyah* (group feeling) see Ibn Khaldūn, *The Muqaddimah*, 1:264.

2 See Ibn Khaldūn, *The Muqaddimah*, 1:57.

3 "The Ottomans derived great benefits from their strategic tolerance. First, it bought them the cooperation, or at least the acquiescence, of conquered populations from Transylvania to Yemen to the Iranian plateau. As with every empire, there were sporadic rebellions, put down viciously by the Ottoman war machine. But by and large, the fundamental ethnic and racial tolerance of Islam proved a stunning strategic asset for the Ottomans. Large numbers of Christians converted to Islam shortly after being conquered." Chua, *Day of Empire*, 174.

4 For a striking analysis of the origins and consequences of the geopolitics of exclusion in the post-Cold War era, see Falk, "False Universalism and the Geopolitics of Exclusion."

5 "In transmitting simultaneously to the Security Council and the General Assembly the report on the incident which took place on 21 August 2013 in the Ghouta area of Damascus, the Secretary-General expresses his profound shock and regret at the conclusion that chemical weapons were used on a relatively large scale, resulting in numerous casualties, particularly among civilians and including many children. The Secretary-General condemns in the strongest possible terms the use of chemical weapons and believes that this act is a war crime and grave violation of the 1925 Protocol for the Prohibition of the Use in War of Asphyxiating, Poisonous or Other Gases, and of Bacteriological Methods of Warfare and other relevant rules of customary international law. The international community has a moral responsibility to hold accountable those responsible and for ensuring that chemical weapons can never re-emerge as an instrument of warfare." See United Nations, "United Nations Mission to Investigate Allegations of the Use of Chemical Weapons in the Syrian Arab Republic."

6 See International Court of Justice, "Legality of the Threat or Use of Nuclear Weapons," 5.

7 See Israel Ministry of Foreign Affairs, "Declaration of Principles."

8 UN Secretary-General, "Report of the Secretary-General on his good offices mission in Cyprus."

9 For a historical analysis on the link between climate change and worldwide catastrophe leading to disorder and wars in the seventeenth century see Parker, *Global Crisis*.

10 This Resolution was accompanied by a call for a very wide-ranging participation: "2. Authorizes Member States co-operating with the Government of Kuwait, unless Iraq on or before 15 January 1991 fully implements, as set forth in paragraph 1 above, the above-mentioned resolutions, to use all necessary means to uphold and implement resolution 660 (1990) and all subsequent relevant resolutions and to restore international peace and security in the area; 3. Requests all States to provide appropriate support for the actions undertaken in pursuance of paragraph 2 above." See UNSC, "Resolution 678: Iraq-Kuwait (29 November)."

11 For this principle and the LDC report prepared for 2015 G20 Summit in Antalya, see G20, "The G20 and Low Income Developing Countries Framework."

6 Inclusive National Governance: From Survival to Sustainability

1 Kohn, *World Order in Historical Perspective*, 93.

2 For the experiences of countries in various cultural basins of the process of importing and changing over to this state model, see Badie, *The Imported State*.

3 Warsi, *The Enemy Within*, xxvi.

4 For instance, "as pharaoh, Alexander publicly sacrificed to Apis the sacred bull, amidst his other celebrations. His sacrifice to a divinity for whom there was no counterpart in the Hellenic world was a masterful diplomatic stroke. It offered a vivid illustration of his respect for this distinctly Egyptian god, and served notice that he intended to meet his priestly obligations as pharaoh." See O'Brien, *Alexander the Great*, 86.

5 "Bureaucracy has increased and the imperial power was sliding towards 'the practices of oriental despotism' ... Septimius Severus, of African and possibly Carthaginian origin, carried this transformation even further." Braudel, *Memory and the Mediterranean*, 310.

6 This act, also widely regarded as the first written constitution, "specifies very clearly that everyone was to be not only free in respect of the dogma and practice of the

religion but also free to comply with the laws of the community to which he belonged: Jews were to be judged by Jewish law, Christians by Christian law, and so on; f.i. 25. The Jews of Banu Awf are a community along with his believers. To the Jews their religion and to the Muslim their religion. (This applies) both to their clients and to themselves ..." For the impact of this act on Muslim political history, see Davutoğlu, *Alternative Paradigms*, 159–63; for the original Arabic text, see Hamidullah, *Majmū'at al-wathā'iq al-siyāsiyah*, 59–64; for an English translation, see Watt, *Islamic Political Thought*, 130–34.

7 For a collection of papers on the *millet* system submitted at a conference held at Princeton in 1978 entitled "The *Millet* System: History and Legacy," see Braude and Lewis, eds., *Christians and Jews in the Ottoman Empire*.

8 Watson, *The German Genius*, 44–45.

9 See Holborn, *A History of Modern Germany*, 30–31.

10   We fired for a day or two
          Then we thought
          We will clean the old man's clock
          That is what!
          Reversing one's jacket,
          That is not enough, comrades'
          Go on, turn yourselves inside!

See Sinyavski, *Soviet Civilization*, 114–15.

11 "Identity might be seen as a way of social recognition which need two parties, while self-perception is a purely consciousness of individuality. An identity might be given or imposed by some authorities and therefore, may be arbitrary or artificially dependent on the existing political structures; f.i. the Yugoslav state gave an identity to its citizens which was dependent on the existing political structure, but when this structure has been dissolved, the real identities as a reflection of self-perceptions have been revived." For a comparative analysis of self-perception and identity, see Davutoğlu, *Civilizational Transformation and the Muslim World*, 82.

12 I used this phrase first in an interview in November 2002 before the American intervention in Iraq to underline the possible negative consequences of the division of Iraq. See Davutoğlu, "Türkiye köprü değil, merkez ülkedir," 7. Also see the Council on Foreign Relations, "Turkey's Top Foreign Policy Advisor Worries about False Optimism in Iraq, Interview by Ahmet Davutoglu": "Iraq became another Lebanon because of ethnic and sectarian definitions ... the most alarming indication of this is in Kirkuk. Iraq is a small [microcosm of the] Middle East. You have all the ethnicities of the Middle East in Iraq. And Kirkuk is a small Iraq. In Kirkuk ... all ethnicities of Iraq are living side by side: Arabs, Kurds, Turkomen, Christians, Shiites, Sunnis."

13 For example, Christian families who migrated from the Middle East to Latin America at the beginning of the twentieth century were called "el-Turco." One of the most famous scions of these families was Carlos Menem, President of Argentina from 1989 to 1999.

14 For the perception of the hierarchy of race as the foundation of the exclusivist approach in American history and its impact on foreign policy, see Hunt, *Ideology and U.S. Foreign Policy*, 47–91.

15 The formation of Muslim perceptions in American society has a history stretching back to the sixteenth century. For the change from early American perceptions of the Islamic world as an anti-Christian and despotic threat to the present day, see Marr, *The Cultural Roots of American Islamicism*.

16 For a general analysis of the Evangelical influence on American foreign policy see Amstutz, *Evangelicals and American Foreign Policy*.

17 Reid, *The United States of Europe*, 199.
18 See "Negotiating Framework (Luxembourg, 3 October 2005)," Article 3.
19 "Therefore the European Council will, at its meeting in December 2006, have a debate on all aspects of further enlargements, including the Union's capacity to absorb new members ... It recalls in this connection that the pace of enlargement must take the Union's absorption capacity into account." Council of the European Union, Presidency Conclusions, 18.
20 For an analysis of Catalanism and the rise of Catalan Independence, see Dowling, *The Rise of Catalan Independence*.
21 For the historical origins and sources of the Cold War geopolitical theories, see Glassner and de Blij, *Systematic Political Geography*.
22 For the perception of Cold War geopolitics immediately before the end of the Cold War, see Faringdon, *Strategic Geography*.
23 For a comparative analysis see Johnston, "The Rise and Decline of the Global Corporate-Welfare State."
24 For the geopolitical consequences of this process see Corbridge, "Colonialism, Post-Colonialism and the Political Geography of the Third World."
25 See Shaban, "Senegal – Gambia Prefer to Build Bridges not Walls."
26 For an analysis of geopolitical change in the post-Cold War era and its impact on geopolitical units, see Cohen, *Geopolitics of the World System*.
27 For example, Tell Abyad/Akça Kale, Ra's al-Ayn/Ceylanpınar, etc.
28 See interview with Davutoğlu, "Türk Dış Politikasına Bakış (2002–2003)," 112–13.
29 President Obama's observations during a visit to Baghdad as a Senator three years after the invasion provides a good depiction of the shift from authoritarian order to chaos in Iraq: "Even from the air the city (Baghdad) looked worn and battered, the traffic on the street intermittent ... Such violence wasn't unusual in Baghdad these days, they said, although Iraqis overwhelmingly bore the brunt of it. Fighting between Shi'ites and Sunnis had become widespread." See Obama, *The Audacity of Hope*, 296, 298.
30 "In Syria ... the Ba'thist regime which had held power since the 1960's had been dominated since 1970 by a group of officers and politicians, with Assad at their head, drawn largely from the Alawi community, a dissident branch of the Shi'is; opposition to the government therefore tended to take the form of a strong assertion of Sunni Islam by the Muslim Brothers and similar bodies." See Hourani, *A History of the Arab Peoples*, 436.
31 Middle-income status is defined as *per capita* gross national income from US$1,006 to US$3,955 (lower middle income) and US$3,956 to $12,235 (upper middle income) see World Bank, "New Country Classifications by Income Level: 2017–2018."
32 Eichengreen, Park, and Shin, "Growth Slowdown Redux."
33 Acemoglu and Robinson, *Why Nations Fail*, 70–79.
34 Held, "The Decline of Nation State," 408.
35 For a critical analysis of this approach see Weiss, *The Myth of the Powerless State*.
36 For a striking example of this assumption see Ohmae, *The End of the Nation State*.
37 Gellner, *Nationalism*, 5.
38 "The solution to the economic and political failure of nations today is to transform their extractive institutions toward inclusive ones. The vicious circle means that this is not easy. But it is not impossible, and the iron law of oligarchy is not inevitable." For a comprehensive study of the role of institutions in the destiny of nations, see Acemoglu and Robinson, *Why Nations Fail*, 402.
39 Bush, "Read James Mattis' Full Resignation Letter."

40 For a study of democracy's governance bases in the post-Cold War period, see Marsh and Olsen, *Democratic Governance.*
41 For a collection of articles on this subject see Diamond and Plattner, *The Global Resurgence of Democracy.*
42 See Held, *Models of Democracy.*
43 Ibid., 352.

7 Inclusive Regional Governance: From Regional Cold Wars to Regional Orders

1 For a collection of articles on the rise of regionalism in the 1990s, see Gamble and Payne, eds., *Regionalism and World Order.*
2 See African Union, "AU in a Nutshell."
3 See ASEAN, "ASEAN Charter."
4 For an analysis of this crisis and its impact on the regional order, see Davutoğlu, "The Crisis of the Regional Order in the Gulf."
5 These meetings were: (1) Istanbul, 23 January 2003; (2) Riyadh, 18 April 2003; (3) Tehran, 28 May 2003; (4) Damascus, 2 November 2003; (5) Kuwait, 14–15 February 2004; (6) Cairo, 21 July 2004; (7) Amman, 6 January 2005; (8) Istanbul, 29–30 April 2005; (9) Tehran, 8–9 July 2006. Expanded format meetings: (10) Sharm el Sheikh, 4–5 May 2007; (11) Istanbul, 2–3 November 2007; (12) Kuwait, 21–22 April 2008.
6 Republic of Turkey Ministry of Foreign Affairs, "NO:136 – 30 July 2008, Press Release Regarding the Fourth Round of the Indirect Peace Talks Between Syria and Israel Under the Auspices of Turkey"; Israel Ministry of Foreign Affairs, "Syria and Israel Start Peace Talks."
7 For a copy of this letter see Obama, "Letter by Barack Obama to Lula da Silva."
8 Article 1 of the agreement reiterated the commitment of the parties to the NPT, while Articles 6, 7, and 8 focused on the framework of the implementation of the agreement. For the full text of the agreement, see Republic of Turkey Ministry of Foreign Affairs, "Joint Declaration of the Ministers of Foreign Affairs of Turkey, Iran and Brazil."
9 "The Turks felt like they had been stabbed in the back. They bristled at the way Russia, China, and the United States had looked past their own differences and banded together to elbow out the rising powers. The powers of yesterday behaved like they still ran the planet, the Turks thought, it was so Cold War." Ghattas, *The Secretary,* 152.
10 Government of Turkey, "Regional Initiative on Iraq: Joint Declaration."
11 For this speech see Republic of Turkey Ministry of Foreign Affairs, "Sayın Bakanımızın 132. Arap Ligi Olağan Dışişleri Bakanları Konseyi Toplantısının Açılış Oturumunda Yaptığı Konuşma."
12 For an analysis of this policy see Davutoğlu, "Turkey's Foreign Policy Vision: The Assessment of 2007," 80–81; also see Davutoğlu, *Teoriden Pratiğe,* 113–14.
13 For an assessment of these negotiations from a third perspective, see Clinton, *Hard Choices,* 218–20.
14 For an analysis of the causes, types, and consequences of proxy wars see Mumford, *Proxy Warfare.*
15 For a testimony of this process, see Kamel, *The Camp David Accords.*
16 High Level Strategic Cooperation Council Mechanisms have been established between Turkey and Iraq on 10 July 2008 (48 agreements); between Turkey and Syria on 22 July 2009 (50 agreements); between Turkey and Egypt on 14 September 2011 (40 agreements); between Turkey and Azerbaijan on 15 October 2010

(30 agreements); see Republic of Turkey Prime Ministry Public Diplomacy Coordination Office, "Yüksek Düzeyli İşbirliği Mekanizmaları."

17 High Level Cooperation Council Mechanisms have been established between Turkey and Russia on 12 May 2010 (41 agreements and visa liberalization started in 2011); between Turkey and Greece on 12 May 2010 (47 agreements); between Turkey and Iran on 22 January 2014 (8 agreements); between Turkey and Bulgaria on 22 March 2012 (21 agreements); see Republic of Turkey Prime Ministry Public Diplomacy Coordination Office, "Yüksek Düzeyli İşbirliği Mekanizmaları."

18 See Republic of Turkey Permanent Mission-OSCE, "Joint Statement on The Third Meeting of The Trilateral Summit among Turkey, Bosnia and Herzegovina and Serbia."

19 See Republic of Turkey Ministry of Foreign Affairs, "Istanbul Statement on Friendship and Cooperation in the 'Heart of Asia'."

20 Beckwith, *Empires of the Silk*, 328.

21 See Barr, *A Line in the Sand*.

22 Republic of Turkey Prime Ministry Public Diplomacy Coordination Office, "Yüksek Düzeyli İşbirliği Mekanizmaları."

23 For the multicultural character along the Silk Road as a transport-commerce corridor in the eighth century, see Whitheld, *Life along the Silk Road*.

24 The formation of the Visegrad Group between Czechoslovakia, Hungary, and Poland on 15 February 1991 referring to the Congress of Visegrad in 1335 between John I of Bohemia, Charles I of Hungary, and Casimir III of Poland to form an anti-Habsburg alliance, is a good example of such a sense of cultural/historical belonging for a base of subregional cooperation along this belt. In the wake of the disintegration of Czechoslovakia, the Visegrad group has been called the V4. See Visegrad Group, "History of the Visegrad Group."

8 Inclusive Global Governance: A New Paradigm of Global Order

1 As Richard Falk rightly underlines, "The problematic character of world order premised on the interplay of territorial sovereignty and hegemonic geopolitics (that is, its horizontal juridical aspect of the equality of the states, and its vertical political aspect of control exerted by the leading state actors) is unable to address in satisfactory fashion any of humanity's most urgent challenges: climate change, nuclear weaponry, global poverty, unregulated world economy, pandemics, genetic engineering, preserving biodiversity." Falk, *(Re)Imagining Humane Global Governance*, 87.

2 For a critical analysis of the role of international civil society in global affairs, see Colas, *International Civil Society*.

3 For an analysis of the impact of the information and communication revolution on world politics, see Hanson, *The Information Revolution and World Politics*.

4 For a collection of articles on digital diplomacy as "the use of social media for diplomatic purposes," see Bjola and Holmes, *Digital Diplomacy*, 4.

5 Luck, "American Exceptionalism and International Organization."

6 For a collection of articles on a comparative analysis of imperial traditions and American power, see Calhoun, Cooper, and Moore, eds., *Lessons of Empire*.

7 Luck, "American Exceptionalism and International Organization," 27.

8 See United Nations, "UN Charter."

9 The leaders of the G4 launched a joint effort for permanent seats on the UNSC and made a declaration stating that "based on the firmly shared recognition that they are legitimate candidates for permanent membership in an expanded Security Council,

[they] support each other's candidature." See "G4 Nations Bid for Permanent Security Council Seat."

10 See United Nations, "Universal Declaration of Human Rights."

11 See United Nations, "General Assembly Overwhelmingly Adopts Resolution Asking Nations Not to Locate Diplomatic Missions in Jerusalem."

12 "*Resolves* that if the Security Council, because of lack of unanimity of the permanent members, fails to exercise its primary responsibility for the maintenance of international peace and security in any case where there appears to be a threat to the peace, breach of the peace, or act of aggression, the General Assembly shall consider the matter immediately with a view to making appropriate recommendations to Members for collective measures, including in the case of a breach of the peace or act of aggression the use of armed force when necessary, to maintain or restore international peace and security. If not in session at the time, the General Assembly may meet in emergency special session within twenty-four hours of the request therefor. Such emergency special session shall be called if requested by the Security Council on the vote of any seven members, or by a majority of the Members of the United Nations;" see United Nations, "Resolution adopted by the General Assembly 377 (V). Uniting for Peace."

13 "Despite Britain's long history of tackling racism and anti-Semitism, on Islamophobia policy-making is still playing catch-up. These are not simply statistics, these are children bullied in playgrounds, women assaulted in the street, graduates not invited for job interviews, the media misreporting events and destroying reputations. Real people, real lives. So let's not fall for 'there is no Islamophobia'." Warsi, *The Enemy Within*, 139.

14 See United Nations, "The Alliance of Civilizations: draft resolution: addendum."

15 See United Nations, "Resolution adopted by the General Assembly on 6 July 2015."

16 See United Nations Peacemaker, "Group of Friends of Mediation."

17 See Republic of Turkey Ministry of Foreign Affairs, "Statement Delivered by H. E. Ahmet Davutoğlu Minister of Foreign Affairs of The Republic of Turkey at the Press Conference of the Fourth United Nations Conference on The Least Developed Countries (13 May 2011, Istanbul)."

18 United Nations, "Program of Action for the Least Developed Countries for the Decade 2011–2020," 8.

19 G20, "G20 and Low Income Developing Countries Framework."

20 See G20, "Antalya Action Plan."

21 See United Nations, "Report of the Fourth United Nations Conference on the Least Developed Countries," 117.

22 Sachs, *The End of Poverty*, 258–59.

23 Davutoğlu, "The Clash of Interests."

24 Davutoğlu, "The Formative Parameters of Civilizations," 73.

25 "Today, all the countries and peoples in the world stand under a universal mandate or directive: to 'develop' or modernize and hence catch up with the civilizational standards established and exemplified by the West (and some of its non-western proxies). 'Globalization' involves to a large extent the spreading or dissemination of modern western forms of life around the globe." Dallmayr, *Alternative Visions*, 1.

26 That textbook was Sabine and Thorson, *A History of Political Theory*.

27 "This brings us to the twin-concepts of homogenization and hegemonization … While 'homogenization' is the process of expanding homogeneity, 'hegemonization' is the emergence and consolidation of the hegemonic centre. With globalization there have been increasing similarities between and among the societies of the World.

However, this trend has been accompanied by the disproportionate global power among a few countries." Mazrui, "Pretender to Universalism," 12–13.

28 "The objective of a textbook is to provide the reader, in the most economical and easily assimilable form, with a statement of what the contemporary scientific community believes it knows and of the principal uses to which that knowledge can be put." Kuhn, *The Essential Tension*, 186.

BIBLIOGRAPHY

Acemoglu, Daron, and James A. Robinson. *Why Nations Fail: The Origins of Power, Prosperity and Poverty*. London: Profile Books, 2013.

Adler, Mortimer Jerome. "Biographical Note." In *Great Books of the Western World: Hegel, Kierkegaard, Nietzsche*, edited by Mortimer Jerome Adler, 43: ix–x. 2nd ed. Chicago: University of Chicago, Encyclopedia Britannica Inc., 1990.

African Union. "AU in a Nutshell." https://au.int/en/history/oau-and-au.

Agoston, Gabor. "A Flexible Empire: Authority and Its Limits on the Ottoman Frontiers." *International Journal of Turkish Studies* 9, 1–2 (1993): 15–31.

Akarlı, Engin. *The Long Peace: Ottoman Lebanon, 1861–1920*. Berkeley: University of California Press, 1993.

Aksakal, Mustafa. *The Ottoman Road to War in 1914: The Ottoman Empire and the First World War*. Cambridge: Cambridge University Press, 2008.

Amstutz, Mark R. *Evangelicals and American Foreign Policy*. Oxford: Oxford University Press, 2014.

Anderson, Benedict. *Imagined Communities: Reflections on the Origin and Spread of Nationalism*. London: Verso, 2006.

Armstrong, Karen. *The Great Transformation: The World in the Time of Buddha, Socrates, Confucius and Jeremiah*. London: Atlantic Books, 2016.

ASEAN, "ASEAN Charter." https://asean.org/asean/asean-charter/.

Badie, Bertrand. *The Imported State: The Westernization of the Political Order*. Stanford: Stanford University Press, 2000.

Baker, Mark. "US: Rumsfeld's 'Old' and 'New' Europe Touches on Uneasy Divide." *Radio Free Europe Radio Liberty*. 24 January 2003. www.rferl.org/a/1102012.html.

Banuazizi, Ali, and Myron Weiner, eds. *The New Geopolitics of Central Asia and Its Borderlands*. Indianapolis: Indiana University Press, 1994.

Barkey, Karen. *Empire of Difference: The Ottomans in Comparative Perspective*. Cambridge University Press, 2008.

Barnet, Richard J. *Global Imperial Corporations and the World Order Dreams*. New York: Touchstone/Simon & Schuster, 1994.

Barr, James. *A Line in the Sand: Britain, France and the Struggle for the Mastery of the Middle East*. London: Simon & Schuster, 2011.

Beckwith, Christopher I. *Empires of the Silk: A History of Central Asia from the Bronze Age to the Present*. Princeton: Princeton University Press, 2009.

Beer, George Louis. *The Origins of the British Colonial System 1578–1660*. New York: Peter Smith, 1933.

Bellah, Robert N., and Hans Joas, eds. *The Axial Age and Its Consequences*. Cambridge: The Belknap Press of Harvard University Press, 2012.

Bennison, Amira K. *The Great Caliphs: The Golden Age of the Abbasid Empire*. New Haven: Yale University Press, 2009.

Bennison, Amira K. "Muslim Universalism and Western Globalization." In *Globalization in World History*, edited by A. G. Hopkins, 73–98. New York: W. W. Norton, & Company, 2002.

Beylerian, Onnig, and Christophe Canivet. "Role Conceptions after the Cold War." In *Role Quest in the Post-Cold War Era: Foreign Policies in Transition*, edited by Philippe G. Le Prestre, 187–224. Montreal: McGill-Queen's University Press. 1997.

Bjola, Corneliu, and Marcus Holmes. *Digital Diplomacy: Theory and Practice*. Oxford: Routledge, 2015.

Braude, Benjamin, and Bernard Lewis, eds. *Christians and Jews in the Ottoman Empire: The Functioning of a Plural Society*. 2 vols. New York: Holmes and Meier, 1982.

Braudel, Fernand. *Memory and the Mediterranean*. New York: Vintage, 2001.

Brubaker, Rogers. *Nationalism Reframed: Nationhood and the National Question in the New Europe*. New York: Cambridge University Press, 1996.

Bryce, James. *The Holy Roman Empire*. New York: A. L. Burt, 1886.

Brzezinski, Zbigniew, and Brent Scowcroft. Moderated by David Ignatius. *America and the World: Conversations on the Future of American Foreign Policy*. New York: Basic Books, 2008.

Bush, Daniel. "Read James Mattis' Full Resignation Letter." Public Broadcasting Service. *December 20, 2018*. www.pbs.org/newshour/politics/read-james-mattis-full-resignation-letter.

Bush, George [H. W.] "Address to the General Assembly of the UN (1990)." Oxford University Press. global.oup.com/us/companion.websites/fdscontent/uscompanion/us/static/companion.websites/9780199338863/Whittington-Readings/chapter-11/VI.-America-and-the-World/Bush-Address-to-the-General-Assembly-of-the-United-Nations.docx.

Bush, George W. "Address by President George W. Bush." First Address to the UN General Assembly delivered 10 November 2001. www.state.gov/documents/organization/18967.pdf.

Carr, E. H. *The Twenty Years Crisis*. London: Palgrave Macmillan, 2016.

Chang, Chun-shu. *The Rise of the Chinese Empire*, vol. 1, *Nation, State, and Imperialism in early China, ca. 1600 B.C.–A.D. 8*. Ann Arbor: The University of Michigan Press, 2010.

Chua, Amy. *Day of Empire: How Hyperpowers Rise to Global Dominance and Why They Fall*. New York: Anchor, 2007.

Churchill, Winston. "Winston Churchill, Universität Zürich, 19 September 1946." www.churchill-in-zurich.ch/site/assets/files/1807/rede_winston_churchill_englisch.pdf.

Clark, Ian. *International Legitimacy and World Society*. Oxford: Oxford University Press, 2007.

Clinton, Hillary Rodham. *Hard Choices*. New York: Simon & Schuster, 2014.

Cohen, Saul B. "Geopolitics in the New World Era: A New Perspective on an Old Discipline." In *Reordering the World: Geopolitical Perspective on the 21st Century*, edited by George J. Demko and William B. Wood, 15–48. Boulder: Westview, 1994.

Cohen, Saul Bernard. *Geopolitics of the World System*. Rowman & Littlefield, 2003.

Cohen-Tanugi, Laurent. *An Alliance at Risk: The United States and Europe since September 11*. Baltimore: Johns Hopkins University Press, 2003.

Colas, Alejandro. *International Civil Society: Social Movements in World Politics*. Cambridge: Polity, 2002.

Collins, John M. *America's Small Wars: Lessons for the Future*. Washington: Brasseys (US), 1991.

Corbridge, Stuart. "Colonialism, Post-Colonialism and the Political Geography of the Third World." In *Political Geography of the Twentieth Century*, edited by Peter Taylor, 171–201. London: Belhaven Press, 1993.

Council of the European Union. "Presidency Conclusions, 15–16 June 2006 Brussels." www.consilium.europa.eu/uedocs/cms_data/docs/pressdata/en/ec/90111.pdf.

Council on Foreign Relations. "Turkey's Top Foreign Policy Advisor Worries about False Optimism in Iraq, Interview by Ahmet Davutoglu." 22 September 2008. www.cfr.org/interview/turkeys-top-foreign-policy-aide-worries-about-false-optimism-iraq.

Cox, Robert. "Towards a Post Hegemonic Conceptualization of World Order: Reflections on the Relevancy of Ibn Khaldūn." In *Governance without Government: Order and Change in World Politics*, edited by James N. Rosenau, 132–59. Cambridge: Cambridge University Press, 1992.

CVCE, "Final communiqué of the meeting of heads of Government of the Community (Paris, 9 and 10 December 1974)." www.cvce.eu/content/ publication/1999/1/1/2acd8532-b271-49ed-bf63-bd8131180d6b/ publishable_en.pdf.

Dallmayr, Fred. *Alternative Visions: Paths in the Global Village.* Lanham: Rowman & Littlefield, 1998.

Dann, Uriel, ed. *The Great Powers in the Middle East 1919–1939.* New York/ London: Holmes & Meier, 1988.

Davutoğlu, Ahmet. *Alternative Paradigms: The Impact of Islamic and Western Weltanschauungs on Political Theory.* Lanham: University Press of America, 1994.

Davutoğlu, Ahmet. *Civilizational Transformation and the Muslim World.* Kuala Lumpur: Quill, 1994.

Davutoğlu, Ahmet. "Civilizational Transformation and Political Consequences." Paper presented at the Annual Convention of the International Studies Association on New Dimensions in International Relations, Vancouver, Canada, 20–23 March 1991.

Davutoğlu, Ahmet. "The Clash of Interests: An Alternative Explanation of the World (Dis)Order." *Intellectual Discourse* 2, 2 (1994): 107–31 [reprinted in *Perceptions: Journal of International Affairs* 2, 4 (December 1997–February 1998): 92–122].

Davutoğlu, Ahmet. "The Crisis of Regional Order in the Gulf." 27 July 2017. www.aljazeera.com/indepth/opinion/2017/07/crisis-regional-order-gulf-170727173842629.html.

Davutoğlu, Ahmet. "The Formative Parameters of Civilizations: A Theoretical and Historical Framework." In *Civilizations and World Order: Geopolitics and Cultural Difference*, edited by Fred Dallmayr, M. Akif Kayapınar, and İsmail Yaylacı, 73–98. Lanham: Lexington, 2014.

Davutoğlu, Ahmet. "Globalization and the Crisis of Individual and Civilizational Consciousness." In *Globality versus Democracy?: The Changing Nature of International Relations in the Era of Globalization*, edited by Hans Köchler, 185–203. Vienna: International Progress Organization, 2000.

Davutoğlu, Ahmet. *Medeniyetler ve Şehirler [Civilizations and Cities].* Istanbul: Küre, 2016.

Davutoğlu, Ahmet. "Rewriting Contemporary Muslim Politics: A Twentieth-Century Periodization." In *Border Crossings: Toward a Comparative Political Theory*, edited by Fred Dallmayr, 89–119. Lanham: Lexington, 1999.

Davutoğlu, Ahmet. *Stratejik Derinlik: Türkiye'nin Uluslararası Konumu [Strategic Depth: Turkey's International Position]*, Istanbul: Küre, 2001.

Davutoğlu, Ahmet. "Tarih İdraki Oluşumunda Metodolojinin Rolü: Medeniyetlerarası Etkileşim Açısından Dünya Tarihi ve Osmanlı [The Role of Methodology in the Formation of the Historical Consciousness: Ottoman

State and the World History from the Perspective of the Civilizational Interaction]." *Dîvân: İlmî Araştırmalar* 4, 7 (1999): 1–63.

Davutoğlu, Ahmet. *Teoriden Pratiğe: Türk Dış Politikası Üzerine Konuşmalar [From Theory to Practice: Interviews on Turkish Foreign Policy]*, Istanbul: Küre, 2013.

Davutoğlu, Ahmet. "Türk Dış Politikasına Bakış (2002–2003) [View on Turkish Foreign Policy (2002–2003)]. Moderated by Gurkan Zengin. CNN Turk, 17 February 2004." In *Teoriden Pratiğe: Türk Dış Politikası Üzerine Konuşmalar [From Theory to Practice: Interviews on Turkish Foreign Policy]*, 97–120. Istanbul: Küre, 2011.

Davutoğlu, Ahmet. "Turkey's Foreign Policy Vision: The Assessment of 2007." *Insight Turkey* 10, 1 (January 2008): 77–96.

Davutoğlu, Ahmet. "Türkiye köprü değil, merkez ülkedir [Turkey is not a bridge, but a center]." *Yarın* 1, 7 (November 2002): 12–13 (reprinted in *Teoriden Pratiğe: Türk Dış Politikası Üzerine Konuşmalar [From Theory to Practice: Interviews on Turkish Foreign Policy]*, 77–86. Istanbul: Küre, 2011).

Dawisha, Karen, and Bruce Parrott. *Russia and the New States of Eurasia: The Politics of Upheaval*. Cambridge: Cambridge University Press, 1994.

Diamond, Larry, and Marc F. Plattner. *The Global Resurgence of Democracy*. Baltimore: The Johns Hopkins University Press, 1996.

Dowling, Andrew. *The Rise of Catalan Independence: Spain's Territorial Crisis*. New York: Routledge, 2018.

Eichengreen, Barry, Donghyun Park, and Kwanho Shin. "Growth Slowdown Redux." *Japan and the World Economy*, 32 (November 2014): 65–84.

Emmerson, Charles. *1913: The World before the Great War*. London: Vintage, 2013.

European Law Monitor, "A Brief History of the EU Treaties." www .europeanlawmonitor.org/treaties/eu-treaties-treaty-on-european-union-maastricht-treaty-of-nice-lisbon-treaty.html.

Falk, Richard. "False Universalism and the Geopolitics of Exclusion: The Case of Islam." *Third World Quarterly* 18, 1 (1997): 7–23.

Falk, Richard. *(Re)Imagining Humane Global Governance*. London: Routledge, 2014.

Falk, Richard. *Power Shift: On the New Global Order*. London: Zed Books, 2016.

al-Farabi, Abu Nasr. *Al-Farabi on the Perfect State: Abū Naṣr Al-Fārābī's Mabādi' ārā' Ahl Al-madīna Al-fāḍila: A Revised Text with Introduction, Translation, and Commentary*. Translated by Richard Walzer. Oxford: Clarendon Press, 1985.

Faringdon, Hugh. *Strategic Geography: NATO, the Warsaw Pact and the Superpowers*. New York: Routledge, 1989.

Figes, Orlando. *Crimea: The Last Crusade*. London: Allen Lane/Penguin, 2010.

Fischbach, Michael R. *Records of Dispossessions, Palestinian Refugee Property and the Arab–Israeli Conflict.* New York: Columbia University Press, 2003.

Fischer, Joschka. "Goodbye to the West." *Project Syndicate.* December 5, 2016. www.project-syndicate.org/commentary/goodbye-to-american-global-leadership-by-joschka-fischer-2016-12.

Fraser, P. M. *Cities of Alexander the Great.* Oxford: Clarendon Press Oxford, 1996.

Fromkin, David. *A Peace to End All Peace: The Fall of the Ottoman Empire and the Creation of the Modern Middle East.* 1st American ed. New York: Henry Holt, 1989.

Fukuyama, Francis. *After the Neo-Cons: America at the Crossroads.* London: Profile, 2006.

Fukuyama, Francis. "The End of History?" *National Interest,* 16 (Summer 1989): 3–18.

Fukuyama, Francis. *The End of History and the Last Man.* New York: Free Press, 1992.

Fukuyama, Francis. *Identity: The Demand for Dignity and the Politics of Resentment.* New York: Farrar, Straus and Giroux, 2018.

Fukuyama, Francis, ed. *Nation-Building: Beyond Afghanistan and Iraq.* Baltimore: Johns Hopkins University Press, 2006.

"G4 Nations Bid for Permanent Security Council Seat." Deutsche Welle. 22 September 2004. www.dw.com/en/g4-nations-bid-for-permanent-security-council-seat/a-1335522.

G20. "Antalya Action Plan." 2015. www.oecd.org/g20/summits/antalya/Antalya-Action-Plan.pdf.

G20. "The G20 and Low Income Developing Countries Framework." www.oecd.org/g20/topics/development/G20-Low-Income-Developing-Countries-Framework.pdf.

Gamble, Andrew, and Anthony Payne, eds. *Regionalism and World Order.* London: Macmillan Press, 1996.

Gargola, Daniel J. *The Shape of the Roman Order: The Republic and Its Spaces.* Chapel Hill: The University of North Carolina, 2017.

Gellner, Ernest. *Nationalism.* London: Weidenfeld & Nicolson, 1997.

Gerges, Fawaz A. *Obama and the Middle East: The End of America's Moment.* New York: Palgrave St. Martin Press, 2012.

Ghattas, Kim. *The Secretary: A Journey with Hillary Clinton from Beirut to the Heart of American Power.* New York: Times Books, 2013.

Glassner, Martin Ira, and Harm J. de Blij. *Systematic Political Geography.* New York: Wiley, 1967.

Goodwin, Jason. *Lords of Horizons: A History of the Ottoman Empire.* New York: Henry Holt and Company, 1998.

Gorbachev, Mikhail. *Perestroika: New Thinking for our Country and the World*. New York: Harper & Row, 1987.

Government of Turkey. "Regional Initiative on Iraq: Joint Declaration." *Regional Initiative Meeting*, Istanbul, 23 January 2003. https://reliefweb.int/report/iraq/regional-initiative-iraq-joint-declaration.

Hamidullah, Muhammad. *Majmū'at al-wathā'iq al-siyāsiyah*. Beirut: Dâr al-nafāis, 1987.

Hanson, Elizabeth. *The Information Revolution and World Politics*. Lanham: Rowman & Littlefield, 2008.

Hastings, Adrian. *The Construction of the Nationhood: Ethnicity, Religion, and Nationalism*. New York: Cambridge University Press, 1997.

Haytop, Bill. *The South China Sea: The Struggle for Power in Asia*. New Haven: Yale University Press, 2014.

Held, David. "The Decline of Nation State." In *Becoming National: A Reader*, edited by Geoff Eley and Ronald Grigor Suny, 407–16. New York: Oxford University Press.

Held, David. *Models of Democracy*. Cambridge: Polity Press, 1996.

Hobsbawm, Eric. *The Age of Extremes: A History of the World 1914–1991*. New York: Pantheon, 1994.

Hodgson, Marshall G. S. *Rewriting World History: Essays on Europe, Islam and World History*. Cambridge: Cambridge University Press, 1993.

Hofstadter, Richard. *The American Political Tradition and the Men Who Made It*. New York: Vintage, 1973.

Holborn, Hajo. *A History of Modern Germany: 1840–1945*. Princeton: Princeton University Press, 1982.

Hourani, Albert. *A History of the Arab Peoples*. Cambridge: The Belknap Press of Harvard University Press, 1991.

Human Rights Watch. "Rohingya Crisis." www.hrw.org/tag/rohingya-crisis.

Hunt, Michael H. *Ideology and U.S. Foreign Policy*. New Haven: Yale University Press, 1987.

Huntington, Samuel P. "The Clash of Civilizations?" *Foreign Affairs* 72, 3 (1993): 22–49.

Huntington, Samuel P. *The Clash of Civilizations and the Remaking of World Order*. New York: Simon and Schuster, 1996.

Huntington, Samuel P. *Who Are We?: The Challenges to America's National Identity*. New York: Simon & Schuster, 2004.

Huxley, Julian. *Man in the Modern World*. London: Chatto and Windus, 1947.

Ibn Khaldun. *The Muqaddimah: An Introduction to History*. 3 vols. Translated by Franz Rosenthal. London: Routledge & Kegan Paul, 1986.

Ikenberry, G. John. "Liberal Hegemony and the Future of American Postwar Order." In *International Order and the Future of World Politics*, edited by T. V. Paul and John A. Hall, 123–46. Cambridge: Cambridge University Press, 1999.

İnalcık, Halil. *Essays in Ottoman History*. Istanbul: Eren, 1998.

İnalcık, Halil. *The Ottoman Empire: The Classical Age 1300–1600*. Translated by Norman Itzkowitz and Colin Imber. London: Weidenfeld and Nicolson, 1973.

İnalcık, Halil, and Donald Quataert, eds. *An Economic and Social History of the Ottoman Empire*. Cambridge: Cambridge University Press, 1994.

International Court of Justice. "Legality of the Threat or Use of Nuclear Weapons." 8 July 1996. www.icj-cij.org/files/case-related/95/095-19960708-ADV-01-00-EN.pdf.

Israel Ministry of Foreign Affairs. "Declaration of Principles on Interim Self-Government Arrangements." 13 September 1993. https://mfa.gov.il/mfa/foreignpolicy/peace/guide/pages/declaration%20of%20principles.aspx.

Israel Ministry of Foreign Affairs. "Syria and Israel Start Peace Talks." 21 May 2018. https://mfa.gov.il/mfa/pressroom/2008/pages/syria%20and%20israel%20start%20peace%20talks%2021-may-2008.aspx.

Jaspers, Karl. *The Origin and Goal of History*. Translated by Michael Bullock. London: Routledge & Kegan Paul; New Haven: Yale University Press, 1953.

Jaspers, Karl. *Vom Ursprung und Ziel der Geschichte*. Zurich: Artemis, 1949.

Johnston, R. J. "The Rise and Decline of the Global Corporate-Welfare State: A Comparative Analysis in Global Context." In *Political Geography of the Twentieth Century*, edited by Peter Taylor, 115–70. London: Belhaven Press, 1993.

Kafadar, Cemal. *Between Two Worlds: The Construction of the Ottoman State*. Berkeley: University of California Press, 1995.

Kamel, Mohamed Ibrahim. *The Camp David Accords: A Testimony by Sadat's Foreign Minister*. Oxford: Routledge, 2011.

Kant, Immanuel. "To Perpetual Peace: A Philosophical Sketch." In *Perpetual Peace and Other Essays on Politics, History and Morals*. Translated by Ted Humphrey. Indianapolis/Cambridge: Hackett Publishing Company, 1992.

Kaplan, Robert D. "America's Darwinian Nationalism." *National Interests*, (August 13, 2017): 1–11. http://nationalinterest.org/print/feature/americas-darwinian-nationalism-21889.

Kaufmann, Stuart, Richard Little, and William C. Wohlforth, eds. *Balance of Power in World History*. New York: Palgrave Macmillan, 2007.

King, Russell. "Migration and the Single Market for Labour: An Issue in Regional Development." In *The European Challenge: Geography and Development in the European Community*, edited by Mark Blacksell and Allan M. Williams, 218–41. Oxford: Oxford University Press, 1994.

Kissinger, Henry. *On China*. New York: Penguin, 2011.

Kissinger, Henry. *The Troubled Partnership: A Re-Appraisal of the Atlantic Alliance*. New York: McGraw Hill, 1965.

Kissinger, Henry. *World Order*. New York: Penguin, 2014.

Kjellén, Rudolf. *Der Staat als Lebensform*. Leipzig, 1917.

Kohn, Hans. *World Order in Historical Perspective*. Cambridge: Harvard University Press, 1942.

Kuhn, Thomas S. *The Essential Tension: Selected Studies in Scientific Tradition and Change*. Chicago: University of Chicago Press, 1977.

Kuhrt, Amelie. *The Persian Empire: A Corpus of Sources from the Achaemenid Period*. Oxford: Routledge, 2007.

Lind, Michael. *The American Way of Strategy: US Foreign Policy and the American Way of Life*. Oxford: Oxford University Press, 2006.

Lowry, Heath W. *The Nature of the Early Ottoman State*. New York: State University of New York Press, 2003.

Luck, Edward C. "American Exceptionalism and International Organization." In *US Hegemony and International Organizations: The United States and Multilateral Institutions*, edited by Rosemary Foot, S. Neil MacFarlane, and Michael Mastanduno, 25–48. Oxford: Oxford University Press, 2003.

Machiavelli, Nicolò. *The Prince*. In *Great Books of the Western World*, edited by Mortimer Jerome Adler, 21: 1–37. 2nd ed. Chicago: Encyclopedia Britannica, 1990.

Mackinder, Halford J. *Britain and British Seas*. London: Heinemann, 1902.

Mackinder, Halford J. "The Geographical Pivot of History." *Geographical Journal* 23, 4 (April 1904): 421–37.

Mackinder, H. J. "The Round World and the Winning of the Peace." *Foreign Affairs* 21, 4 (July 1943): 595–605.

MacMillan, Margaret. *The War That Ended Peace: How Europe Abandoned Peace for the First World War*. London: Profile, 2013.

McNeill, William H. *The Rise of the West: A History of the Human Community*. Chicago and London: The University of Chicago Press, 1963.

Mahan, Alfred Thayer. *The Influence of Sea Power upon the French Revolution and Empire: 1793–1812*. 2 vols. Boston: Little Brown, 1892.

Mahan, Alfred Thayer. *The Influence of Sea Power upon History: 1660–1783*, Boston: Little Brown, 1890.

Mahan, Alfred Thayer. *The Interest of America in Sea Power: Present and Future*. London: Sampson Low & Company, 1897.

Mahan, Alfred Thayer. *Letters and Papers of Alfred Thayer Mahan*. 3 vols. Annapolis, MD: Naval Institute Press, 1975.

Mahan, Alfred Thayer. *The Problem of Asia and Its Effect upon International Politics*. Boston: Little Brown, 1900.

Mallaby. Sebastian. "Globalization Resets: The Retrenchment in Cross-Border Capital Flows and Trade May Be Less Dire than It Seems." *Finance & Development* 53, 4 (December 2016): 7–10.

Mander, Jerry, and Edward Goldsmith, eds. *The Case against the Global Economy and for a Turn toward the Local.* San Francisco: Sierra Club Books, 1996.

Mansel, Philip. *Aleppo: The Rise and Fall of Syria's Great Merchant City.* London: Tauris, 2016.

Marr, Timothy. *The Cultural Roots of American Islamicism.* Cambridge: Cambridge University Press, 2006.

Marsh, James G., and Johan P. Olsen. *Democratic Governance.* New York: The Free Press, 1995.

Mazrui, Ali A. "Pretender to Universalism: Western Culture in a Globalizing Age." In *Globalization and Civilization: Are They Forces in Conflict,* edited by Ali A. Mazrui, Patrick M. Dikirr, and Shalahudin Kafrawi, 9–34. New York: Global Scholarly Publications, 2008.

Moore, John Bassett. *The Principles of American Diplomacy.* New York: Harper and Brothers, 1918.

Mumford, Andrew. *Proxy Warfare.* Cambridge: Polity, 2013.

"The National Security Strategy of the United States of America." September 2002. https://georgewbush-whitehouse.archives.gov/nsc/nss/2002/.

NATO. "The Alliance's Strategic Concept." Approved by the heads of State and Governments participating in the meeting of the North Atlantic Council in Washington D.C. issued on 24 April 1999, www.nato.int/cps/ie/natohq/official_texts_27433.htm.

"Negotiating Framework (Luxembourg, 3 October 2005)." https://ec.europa.eu/neighbourhood-enlargement/sites/near/files/pdf/turkey/st20002_05_tr_framedoc_en.pdf.

Nye, Joseph S. *The Paradox of American Power: Why the World's Only Superpower Can't Go it Alone.* New York: Oxford University, 2002.

Obama, Barack. *The Audacity of Hope: Thoughts on Reclaiming the American Dream.* New York: Three Rivers Press, 2006.

Obama, Barack. "Letter by Barack Obama to Lula da Silva." Voltairenet.org. 20 April 2010. www.voltairenet.org/article165719.html.

Obama, Barack. "Remarks by the President at Cairo University 6-04-09." https://obamawhitehouse.archives.gov/issues/foreign-policy/presidents-speech-cairo-a-new-beginning.

Obama, Barack. "Remarks of President Barack Obama at Student Roundtable." In Tophane Cultural Center, Istanbul, 7 April 2009. https://obamawhitehouse.archives.gov/realitycheck/the-press-office/remarks-president-barack-obama-student-roundtable-istanbul.

Obama, Barack. "Remarks by President Obama to the Turkish Parliament." 6 April 2009. https://obamawhitehouse.archives.gov/the-press-office/remarks-president-obama-turkish-parliament.

O'Brien, John Maxwell. *Alexander the Great: The Invisible Enemy.* London: Routledge, 1999.

Ohmae, Kenichi. *The End of the Nation State: The Rise of Regional Economies.* New York: The Free Press, 1995.

OIC. "Charter of the Organisation of Islamic Cooperation (OIC)." www.oic-oci .org/upload/documents/charter/en/oic_charter_2018_en.pdf.

Orbán, Viktor. "Wer überrannt wird, kann niemanden aufnehmen." 01.09.2015. www.faz.net/aktuell/politik/fluechtlingskrise/viktor-orban-wer-ueberrannt-wird-kann-niemanden-aufnehmen-13782061.html.

Organization for Security and Co-operation in Europe. "Charter of Paris for a New Europe." 21 November 1990. www.osce.org/mc/39516.

Pagden, Anthony. *Lords of All the World: Ideologies of Empires in Spain, Britain and France (1500–1800).* New Haven: Yale University Press, 1995.

Pahl, Walther. *Das politische Antlitz der Erde: Ein Weltpolitischer Atlas.* Leipzig: Wilhelm Goldmann Verlag, 1938.

Pamuk, Şevket. "Institutional Change and the Longevity of the Ottoman Empire, 1500–1800." *Journal of Interdisciplinary History* 35, 2 (Autumn 2004): 225–47.

Parker, Geoffrey. *Global Crisis: War, Climate Change and Catastrophe in the Seventeenth Century.* New Haven: Yale University Press, 2013.

Parsons, Timothy H. *The Rule of Empires: Those Who Built Them, Those Who Endured Them and Why They Always Fall.* Oxford: Oxford University Press, 2010.

Putin, Vladimir. "The President signed Executive Order on National Goals and Strategic Objectives of the Russian Federation through to 2024." 7 May 2018. en.kremlin.ru/events/president/news/57425.

Putin, Vladimir. "Speech and the Following Discussion at the Munich Conference on Security Policy." 10 February 2007. en.kremlin.ru/events/president/ transcripts/24034.

Ratzel, Friedrich. "Studien über politische Räume." *Geographische Zeitschrift* 1, 3–4 (1894): 163–82; 5–6 (1894): 286–302.

Ratzel, Friedrich. "The Territorial Growth of States." *Scottish Geographical Magazine* 12, 7 (July 1896): 351–61.

Reid, Thomas Roy. *The United States of Europe: The New Superpower and the End of American Supremacy.* New York: Penguin, 2004.

"The Report of the Iraq Inquiry." 6 July 2016. https://webarchive .nationalarchives.gov.uk/20171123122743/http://www.iraqinquiry.org.uk/ the-report/.

Republic of Turkey Ministry of Foreign Affairs. "NO:136 – 30 July 2008, Press Release Regarding the Fourth Round of the Indirect Peace Talks Between Syria and Israel Under the Auspices of Turkey." www.mfa.gov.tr/no_136—30-july-2008_-press-release-regarding-the-fourth-round-of-the-indirect-peace-talks-between-syria-and-israel-under-the-auspices-of-turkey.en.mfa.

Republic of Turkey Ministry of Foreign Affairs. "Istanbul Statement on Friendship and Cooperation in the 'Heart of Asia.'" www.mfa.gov.tr/istanbul-statement-on-friendship-and-cooperation-in-the-_heart-of-asia_.en.mfa.

Republic of Turkey Ministry of Foreign Affairs. "Joint Declaration of the Ministers of Foreign Affairs of Turkey, Iran and Brazil." 17 May 2010. www.mfa.gov.tr/17_05_2010-joint-declaration-of-the-ministers-of-foreign-affairs-of-turkey_-iran-and-brazil_.en.mfa.

Republic of Turkey Ministry of Foreign Affairs. "Sayın Bakanımızın 132. Arap Ligi Olağan Dışişleri Bakanları Konseyi Toplantısının Açılış Oturumunda Yaptığı Konuşma, 09 Eylül 2009, Kahire [Statement Delivered by H. E. Ahmet Davutoğlu at the Opening Session of the 132nd Ordinary Meeting of the Foreign Ministers Council of the Arab League on 9th September 2009]." www.mfa.gov.tr/sayin-bakanimizin-132_-arap-ligi-olagan-disisleri-bakanlari-konseyi-toplantisinin-acilis-oturumunda-yaptigi-konusma.tr.mfa.

Republic of Turkey Ministry of Foreign Affairs. "Statement Delivered by H. E. Ahmet Davutoğlu Minister of Foreign Affairs of The Republic of Turkey at The Press Conference of The Fourth United Nations Conference on The Least Developed Countries (13 May 2011, Istanbul)." www.mfa.gov.tr/statement-delivered-by-h_e_-ahmet-davutoglu-minister-of-foreign-affairs-of-the-republic-of-turkey-at-the-press-conference-of-the-fourth-united-nations-conference-on-the-least-devoloped-countries-_13-may-2011_-istanbul__.en.mfa.

Republic of Turkey Permanent Mission-OSCE. "Joint Statement on The Third Meeting of the Trilateral Summit among Turkey, Bosnia and Herzegovina and Serbia." www.osce.org/pc/101689?download=true.

Republic of Turkey Prime Ministry Public Diplomacy Coordination Office. "Yüksek Düzeyli İşbirliği Mekanizmaları [High Level Cooperation Mechanisms]." 15 June 2016. https://kdk.gov.tr/haber/yuksek-duzeyli-isbirligi-mekanizmalari/452.

Reston, James. *Defenders of Faith: Charles V, Suleyman the Magnificent, and the Battle for Europe, 1520–1536.* New York: Penguin, 2009.

Rosecrane, Richard, and Gu Guoliang. *Power and Restraint: A Shared Vision for U.S.-China Relationship*, New York: Public Affairs, 2009.

Sabine, George H., and Thomas L. Thorson. *A History of Political Theory.* Hinsdale: Dryden Press, 1973.

Said, Edward W. "The Clash of Definitions." In *The New Crusades, Constructing the Muslim Enemy*, edited by Emran Qureshi and Michael A. Sells, 68–87. New York: Columbia University Press, 2003.

Sandler, Todd, and Keith Hartley. *The Political Economy of NATO: Past, Present, and into the 21st Century.* New York: Cambridge University Press, 1999.

Schmidt, Helmut. *Grand Strategy for the West: The Anachronism of National Strategies in an Interdependent World.* New Haven: Yale University Press, 1985.

Schonfeld, Reese. *Me and Ted against the World: The Unauthorized Story of the Founding of CNN.* New York: Cliff Street/Harper Collins, 2001.

Shaban, Abdur Rahman Alfa. "Senegal – Gambia Prefer to Build Bridges not Walls – Macky Sall 'Jabs' Trump." 14 March 2018. www.africanews.com/2018/03/14/senegal-gambia-building-bridges-whiles-others-building-walls-macky-sall/.

Shambaugh, David. *China Goes Global: The Partial Power.* Oxford: Oxford University Press, 2013.

Shlaim, Avi. *The Iron Wall: Israel and the Arab World.* London: Penguin, 2000.

Sinyavski, Andrei. *Soviet Civilization: A Cultural History.* New York: Arcade, 1990.

Smith, Tony. *A Pact with the Devil: Washington's Bid for World Supremacy and the Betrayal of the American Promise.* New York: Routledge, 2007.

Spykman, Nicholas John. *America's Strategy in World Politics.* Hamden: Shoe String Press, Anchor Books, 1970.

Spykman, Nicholas John. *The Geography of the Peace.* New York: Harcourt, Brace, 1944.

Starr, S. Frederick. *Lost Enlightenment: Central Asia's Golden Age from the Arab Conquest to Tamerlane.* Princeton: Princeton University Press, 2013.

Stevens, William Oliver, and Allan Westcott. *A History of Sea Power.* New York: Doubleday & Company, 1948.

Teschke, Benno. *The Myth of 1648: Class, Geopolitics and Making of Modern International Relations.* London: Verso, 2009.

Thapar, Romila. *Asoka and the Decline of the Mauryas.* New Delhi: Oxford University Press, 1997.

Timmermann, Kenneth R. *The French Betrayal of America.* New York: Three Rivers Press, 2004.

"Tony Blair Expressed Sorrow, Regret and Apology." 6 July 2016. www.bbc.com/news/av/world-36727331/tony-blair-expressed-sorrow-regret-and-apology.

Toynbee, Arnold J. *A Study of History.* 2 vols. New York: Oxford University Press, 1965.

Toynbee, Arnold. "The Ottoman Empire's Place in World History." In *The Ottoman State and Its Place in World History*, edited by Kemal Karpat, 15–27. Leiden: E. J. Brill, 1974.

Treitschke, Heinrich von. *Germany, France, Russia and Islam.* London: Jarrold & Sons, Allen & Unwin, 1915.

The UN Refugee Agency. "Middle East and North Africa." www.unhcr.org/middle-east-and-north-africa.html.

UN. Secretary-General. "Report of the Secretary-General on his Good Offices Mission in Cyprus." UN Security Council. 28 May 2004. https://digitallibrary.un.org/record/522514?ln=en.

United Nations. "The Alliance of Civilizations: Draft Resolution: Addendum/ Afghanistan, Albania, Algeria, Andorra, Angola, Argentina, Australia, Austria, Azerbaijan, Bahrain, Bangladesh, Belarus, Bosnia and Herzegovina, Brazil, Canada, Cape Verde, Chile, China, Costa Rica, Croatia, Ecuador, Egypt, El Salvador, Estonia, Ethiopia, Finland, Greece, Guatemala, India, Indonesia, Italy, Jordan, Kazakhstan, Kuwait, Latvia, Lebanon, Lithuania, Luxembourg, Malta, Mexico, Montenegro, Morocco, New Zealand, Pakistan, Paraguay, Peru, Philippines, Poland, Portugal, Qatar, Republic of Korea, Romania, Saudi Arabia, Senegal, Serbia, Slovenia, Somalia, Spain, Sweden, Switzerland, the former Yugoslav Republic of Macedonia, Timor-Leste, Tunisia, Turkey, United Republic of Tanzania, Uruguay and Yemen." 10 November 2009. https://digitallibrary.un.org/record/671233?ln=en.

United Nations. "General Assembly Overwhelmingly Adopts Resolution Asking Nations Not to Locate Diplomatic Missions in Jerusalem." 21 December 2017. www.un.org/press/en/2017/ga11995.doc.htm.

United Nations. "Program of Action for the Least Developed Countries for the Decade 2011–2020." Fourth UN Conference on the Least Developed Countries, Istanbul, Turkey, 9–13 May 2011. http://unohrlls.org/UserFiles/File/IPoA.pdf.

United Nations. "Report of the Fourth United Nations Conference on the Least Developed Countries, Istanbul, Turkey, 9–13 May 2011." http://unohrlls.org/UserFiles/File/A-CONF_219-7%20report%20of%20the%20conference.pdf.

United Nations. "Resolution Adopted by the General Assembly 377 (V). Uniting for Peace." www.un-documents.net/a5r377.htm.

United Nations. "Resolution adopted by the General Assembly on 6 July 2015." 31 July 2015. https://undocs.org/A/RES/69/312.

United Nations. "UN Charter." 26 June 1945. www.un.org/en/sections/un-charter/index.html.

United Nations. "United Nations Mission to Investigate Allegations of the Use of Chemical Weapons in the Syrian Arab Republic." Report on the Alleged Use of Chemical Weapons in the Ghouta Area of Damascus on 21 August 2013. Note by the Secretary-General. www.un.org/zh/focus/northafrica/cwinvestigation.pdf.

United Nations. "Universal Declaration of Human Rights." 10 December 1948. www.un.org/en/universal-declaration-human-rights/.

United Nations Peacemaker. "Group of Friends of Mediation." https://peacemaker.un.org/friendsofmediation.

United Nations Relief and Works Agency for Palestine Refugees in the Near East. "Palestine Refugees." www.unrwa.org/palestine-refugees.

United Nations Security Council. "Resolution 678 Iraq-Kuwait (29 November)." 29 November 1990. www.unscr.com/en/resolutions/678.

Vick, Brian E. *The Congress of Vienna: Power and Politics after Napoleon.* Cambridge MA: Harvard University Press, 2014.

Visegrad Group, "History of the Visegrad Group." www.visegradgroup.eu/.

Wallerstein, Immanuel. *Geopolitics and Geoculture: Essays on the Changing World-System.* Cambridge University Press, 1991.

Warsi, Sayeeda. *The Enemy Within: A Tale of Muslim Britain.* London: Allen Lane/Penguin, 2017.

Watson, Peter. *The German Genius: Europe's Third Renaissance, the Second Scientific Revolution and the Twentieth Century.* New York: Harper Perennial, 2011.

Watt, William Montgomery. *Islamic Political Thought.* Edinburgh: Edinburgh University Press, 1968.

Wedgwood, C. Veronica. *The Thirty Years War.* London: Pimlico, 1992.

Weigley, Russell F. *The Age of Battles: The Quest for Decisive Warfare from Britenfeld to Waterloo.* Bloomington & Indianapolis: Indiana University Press, 1991.

Weiss, Linda. *The Myth of the Powerless State: Governing the Economy in a Global Era.* Cambridge: Polity Press, 1998.

Whitheld, Susan. *Life along the Silk Road.* Berkeley: University of California Press, 1999.

Williams, Andrew. *Failed Imagination? New World Orders of the Twentieth Century.* Manchester: Manchester University Press, 1998.

Williamson, John. "The Strange History of the Washington Consensus." *Journal of Post Keynesian Economics* 27, 2 (Winter 2004–2005): 195–206.

Wilson, Woodrow. "President Wilson's Message to Congress, January 8, 1918." Records of the United States Senate; Record Group 46; Records of the United States Senate; National Archives. www.ourdocuments.gov/doc.php?flash=false&doc=62#.

World Bank, "China." https://data.worldbank.org/country/china.

World Bank, "New Country Classifications by Income Level: 2017–2018." The Data Blog. 7 January 2017. https://blogs.worldbank.org/opendata/new-country-classifications-income-level-2017-2018.

Xi Jinping. "Secure a Decisive Victory in Building a Moderately Prosperous Society in All Respects and Strive for the Great Success of Socialism with Chinese Characteristics for a New Era." 8 October 2017. www.chinadaily.com.cn/china/19thcpcnationalcongress/2017–11/04/content_34115212.htm. Updated 4 November 2017.

Xi Jinping. "Work Together to Build the Silk Road Economic Belt and the 21st Century Maritime Silk Road." 14 May 2017. www.xinhuanet.com/english/2017-05/14/c_136282982.htm.

Yew, Lee Kuan. *One Man's View of the World.* Singapore: Straits Times Press, 2013.

INDEX